Psychologist Rob Yeung, PhD, is a researcher and educator in the areas of human communication, influence and persuasion, and high achievement. He is the author of over a dozen international bestsellers, including *Confidence: The power to take control and live the life you want* and *The Extra One Per Cent: How small changes make exceptional people*. As well as teaching at universities and business schools, he is an in-demand expert on television, providing expert comment on programmes ranging from CNN and BBC news to *Big Brother*. He has written for the *Financial Times*, the *Daily Telegraph* and the *Guardian* and has been quoted in publications ranging from *Men's Health* and *Glamour* to the *Wall Street Journal*.

www.robyeung.com
www.twitter.com/robyeung

i IS FOR INFLUENCE

THE NEW SCIENCE OF PERSUASION

ROB YEUNG

MACMILLAN

First published 2011 by Macmillan
an imprint of Pan Macmillan, a division of Macmillan Publishers Limited
Pan Macmillan, 20 New Wharf Road, London N1 9RR
Basingstoke and Oxford
Associated companies throughout the world
www.panmacmillan.com

ISBN 978-1-9057-4465-7

The author and publisher would like to thank for the following for their kind
permission to reproduce copyrighted material: The 99 per cent poster and graphics
courtesy of the London Serious Youth Violence Board; Patrick the Incurable Optimist
campaign poster courtesy of the Motor Neurone Disease (MND) Association.

9 8 7 6 5 4 3 2 1

A CIP catalogue record for this book is available from the British Library.

Designed and set by seagulls.net
Printed by CPI Mackays, Chatham ME5 8TD

Visit **www.panmacmillan.com** to read more about all our books and to buy them.
You will also find features, author interviews and news of any author events, and you
can sign up for e-newsletters so that you're always first to hear about our new releases.

CONTENTS

Acknowledgements

Thanks to Bonnie Chiang for her insightful comments as always and Becky Mallery for her diligent research. Thanks also to the Talentspace team for giving me the time and space to write uninterrupted! Dedicated to my parents, and Steve and Byron as always.

INTRODUCTION

'If you would persuade, you must appeal to
interest rather than intellect.'
Benjamin Franklin

In 1957, a middle-aged American market researcher announced a discovery that so outraged and frightened the general public that the CIA was ordered to investigate its potentially terrifying implications. *Newsday* magazine called it the most alarming invention since the atomic bomb.

The man responsible for the uproar was James Vicary, a heavyset man with the oversized features and perpetual scowl of a security guard. Vicary was a self-proclaimed expert at 'depth-probing', or the alleged science of delving into the psyche of consumers. Earlier in the 1950s, he had spent time researching the behaviour of customers in shops, using hidden cameras to investigate the relationship between women shoppers' patterns of eye blinks and their purchasing intentions. The goal was to predict women's shopping preferences from their eyes alone, but his research findings were disappointing and he quietly dropped the topic.

But it was his innovation in a movie theatre in suburban New Jersey for which he shall forever be remembered. During showings of the movie *Picnic* over a period of six weeks, he repeatedly projected the words 'Drink Coca-Cola' and 'Hungry? Eat popcorn' on screen at five-second intervals. Each phrase appeared on screen for only a three-thousandth of a second, too briefly for the audience to be aware that they had seen advertising messages at all. Rather amazingly though, Vicary reported that he managed to boost sales of Coca-Cola by 18 per cent and popcorn by a startling 58 per cent. He had invented subliminal advertising.

The public was appalled. Average Americans worried that they could be made to buy just about anything against their will while the *New Yorker* magazine condemned Vicary's machinations because, in its view, minds were being 'broken and entered'. Legislators in Washington, D. C., launched campaigns against what they saw as a clearly unethical technique, asking the government's Federal Communications Commission to ban the use of subliminal advertising.

There were other concerns too. This was the 1950s, the height of the Cold War against the communist regime of the Soviet Union. The Soviets had just beaten the United States in the space race by successfully launching their Sputnik 1 craft into orbit around the Earth. The fact that the Soviets had succeeded in launching the world's first ever man-made object into space was a serious blow to the American public's belief in capitalism. To compound the problem, communism was establishing a stronghold in China too. The American public felt under siege from all sides and paranoia about the threat from communist countries was high. What if a foreign government used this terrifying new subliminal technology for the purpose of political indoctrination, slipping the propaganda message 'convert to communism' into American movies? Whole swathes of the American public might be coerced into altering their political beliefs or committing other heinous acts *without even realising they had been influenced to do so.*

The CIA moved swiftly to investigate Vicary's claims. Assembling a task force of psychologists, behaviour experts, and intelligence operatives to examine the dangers of subliminal advertising, they produced a secret report within the space of a year. 'The Operational Potential of Subliminal Perception' was thankfully declassified in 1994, so we now know the document's findings.[1]*

The CIA concluded that the power of subliminal advertising had been greatly exaggerated. Despite the furore in the popular press, the effects were short-lived and too unpredictable to manipulate people's behaviour in any meaningful fashion. Certainly, there was no threat that it could be deployed to coerce people to behave dangerously or against their will. Perhaps certain members of the CIA were even disappointed that the practice couldn't be used to compel foreign agents to act in ways that might benefit the United States.

Reputable researchers from universities around the world were also unable to replicate Vicary's findings. In identical tests, they reported over and over again that subliminal messages either had no effects or only tiny effects that were nearly inconsequential. How could Vicary have boosted popcorn sales by 58 per cent?

Answer: he hadn't. A few years later, in 1962, Vicary finally admitted in a magazine interview that he had made the whole story up. He had *not* collected data about the effects of subliminal advertising even once, let alone over the course of six weeks. He had *not* succeeded in boosting Coke and popcorn sales. In fact, he confessed that 'we hadn't done any research'. It had all been a hoax, a lie, a patent untruth. He had dreamed up the idea in a desperate attempt to 'stir things up', to generate publicity for the floundering agency that he ran.[2]

---

* You'll find numbered notes throughout the book. Most readers can enjoy the book without turning to the notes at the back of the book at all. Notes are provided principally for the more academically minded readers who may wish to read the original scientific papers, perhaps to further their own research.

To repeat then: subliminal advertising doesn't work. Yet if you ask most people today, they still think it does. It persists as a legend. It lives on as an urban myth, because we all remain fascinated by the psychological methods that can be used to influence us.

The psychology of influence and persuasion

I was about 10 years old the first time I can remember really wanting to influence someone, to change someone's mind. We'd learned in school one week that smoking cigarettes was bad for us. *Really* bad. In a biology lesson, there was a hush amongst the class as our teacher Mrs Beard told us of the poisons contained within cigarette smoke. She told us that cigarettes contained a gooey black substance called tar that could clog our lungs. She reminded us that when we went swimming and got water in our mouths by accident, we choked and coughed when it got into our lungs. And she asked us to imagine how it might feel if we got tar – which was 10 times thicker, more syrupy, and poisonous too – into our lungs.

I was horrified. Not because I had ever smoked a cigarette or even planned on trying one, but because my dad smoked. I went home and told him how dangerous smoking was for him. I told him how cigarettes led to lung diseases, how he could end up having breathing difficulties, how he could even end up with lung cancer.

Dad listened stoically to the arguments. He nodded and said he'd think about quitting. Except he carried on smoking.

I didn't understand why. He had definitely grasped the arguments against smoking. He even seemed to agree with the points I'd made. I felt confused, frustrated, even a little scared. Why wouldn't he stop?

Thankfully, the tale has a happy ending. Dad did stop smoking. But it took nearly *three years* of constant nagging and pleading, encouraging and cajoling from myself and the rest of the family before he quit. Surely there had to be a better, less frustrating way of changing someone's mind than that?

Fast-forward 10 years and I was looking for my answers, to uncover the methods and manoeuvres that could change people's attitudes and alter their behaviour. Studying for an undergraduate degree in psychology at the University of Bristol, I came across one particular research report that resonated deeply with me.

In 1964, the Surgeon General in the United States published a definitive report linking cigarette smoking to lung cancer. The connection between the two is widely accepted nowadays, but at the time it was sensational news and a shock to many people. Shortly after the announcement, two academics at UCLA in California conducted a survey of several hundred people in nearby Santa Monica, gathering their views on the Surgeon General's conclusions.[3]

They found that the vast majority of non-smokers acknowledged there was enough evidence to prove that smoking could cause cancer. Perhaps rather predictably though, smokers were far more sceptical of the link between the two and tended to play down the health risks; they dismissed the overwhelming medical evidence by making arguments such as 'Smoking is better than excessive eating or drinking,' and 'Many smokers live a long time.' My favourite retort was when smokers claimed, 'Lots of things are a hazard.' Yes, lots of things are dangerous, but doctors don't recommend swimming with sharks or jumping off tall buildings without a parachute either.

The study confirms what most of us have long suspected. People are rarely convinced by facts alone. Even when faced with a well-crafted argument and irrefutable evidence about why they should stop doing something or start doing something else, they can still choose to ignore it.

Think about your own experiences of trying to influence and persuade the people in your life. I'm willing to bet that you've been frustrated on plenty of occasions that your words and arguments weren't enough to change people's minds. Maybe you have tried to get a member of your family to do a couple more household chores, perhaps to take the rubbish out or not to leave wet towels on the bathroom floor, only to find yourself being the one to have to do it time and time again. Perhaps you've explained to colleagues why they should do a project your way only to discover it all went wrong because they chose to ignore your good advice. Or you've tried to coax a child to eat her greens, but still saw her feeding her broccoli to the dog when she thought you weren't looking.

People can be irrational, fiercely obstinate, self-indulgent, capricious, and even childish. Telling them how they *should* behave rarely gets them to change their ways. No matter how logical and sensible our advice or recommendations, they can decide to continue regardless. Worse than that, by telling people what they should or shouldn't do, we may actually make them feel like doing *exactly the opposite*.

I decided to write this book because I felt frustrated. There are a fair few books that claim to reveal the secrets of influence or hidden techniques for persuasion. You're probably familiar with the genre. Do their techniques work? Maybe some of the time. But because they are based only on their own personal experiences rather than the proven science of persuasion, they may not work for everyone.

Well, this book isn't about *my* theories or the ideas of any single person, no matter how well meaning but perhaps misguided they may be. It's based on proven studies published by eminent researchers, lauded professors, and even the occasional Nobel Prize-winning academic; these studies come with *proof* that certain tactics and techniques can work for completely ordinary people. You're in the right place if you wish to understand the psychology of influence and persuasion without all of the hype and outlandish claims that are sometimes made about the field.

Over the last few decades, a stellar cast of researchers including psychologists and anthropologists, neuroscientists and economists all over the world have been quietly amassing evidence about the forces and methods that genuinely change minds and alter behaviour. In field studies and laboratory experiments covering situations ranging from dating and children's education to business negotiations and the promotion of environmentally friendly behaviour, pioneering scientists have gathered a remarkable body of evidence about the approaches that encourage or even compel people to change their attitudes and actions.

How can we make requests that others won't want to refuse? How can we use our body language to change how people see us? How can we motivate people to work harder? How can we encourage people to behave more honestly? How can we encourage friends and family, customers and colleagues to heed our advice and do as we say? These are the sorts of questions we'll explore. In attempting to answer such questions, I've structured the book into nine chapters and a conclusion, each of which covers a major theme as follows:

- **Chapter One: The Wisdom of Crowds.** Anxious parents worry that peer pressure could push their children into dangerous behaviours such as trying drugs or having underage sex. But it turns out that people of *all* ages are swayed by social pressures. No matter how independent we might think we are, it turns out that we're actually pack animals, following the crowd and going along with what everyone else is doing. The good news is that this revelation can help us to influence others in situations ranging from winning over intransigent family members and customers to conquering unruly children in the classroom.

- **Chapter Two: Secret Signals.** Scientists have made remarkable discoveries about how our body language sends secret messages directly into the minds of other people, somehow bypassing their conscious awareness yet still boosting our chances of success when we ask people out on a date or want to make a great impact during a job interview. Really, there's a lot of nonsense on television and in popular magazines about body language, but in this chapter I'll share with you lessons that are proven by science.

- **Chapter Three: The Power of Words and Labels.** We're so used to communicating with language that we don't always appreciate the power of the words we choose. In fact, psychologists know that changing even a *single* seemingly insignificant word in a sentence can have astonishing effects on our ability to convince and persuade others. Want to know how? In this chapter, I'll reveal how a little more care with language and the labels we use to describe others can help us to shape both people's expectations and their behaviour.

- **Chapter Four: From Small Steps to Big Effects**. How do you eat an elephant? One bite at a time, of course. The old riddle tells us that we should break down large, daunting goals into smaller steps, which seems eminently sensible advice. Along similar lines, when we want someone to agree to a huge request, we might be better off getting them to agree to a smaller one first. Because when people invest even a seemingly insignificant amount of time or effort in an activity, it can create a snowball of momentum that can lead to powerful changes in behaviour.

- **Chapter Five: Invoking the Imagination and Telling Tales.** Human beings are the only species on the planet with the ability to conceive things we've never seen. We're also the only species that tells stories. We tend to think of conjuring up imaginary scenes and telling stories as the provenance of children, but it turns out that both tap into the way the brain is wired, giving us further hooks for influencing and persuading others.

Chapter Six: Friendship and Favours. It's hardly news that people are more likely to be wooed and won over by folks they know and like. While lasting friendships can take months or even years to develop though, psychologists have isolated the social forces that accelerate how people bond and connect with each other. So if you'd like to win friends and influence people, this chapter will show you not only how but also why it works.

Chapter Seven: The Perils of Prizes. Of course we can change people's behaviour by rewarding them with gifts and bonuses for doing something. But research tells us that incentives – not only in the workplace but also in the home and even classroom – can often have unintended, disastrous consequences too. Thankfully, researchers do not leave us in the lurch and tell us exactly how we can use the right kinds of rewards to motivate and guide people in ways that benefit us all.

Chapter Eight: The Peculiar Power of Circumstantial Persuasion. In the world of fine art, the curators of galleries go to great pains to find the right frame to display portraits. The right frame can help a work of art to become breathtaking; the wrong one can make it seem humdrum or even amateurish. It turns out the same is true in human decision-making too. People are swayed by so-called framing effects. We don't simply listen to offers or requests and calculate in a cool-headed fashion the one that suits us best. Instead, we're highly sensitive to the circumstances in which we find ourselves and the contexts in which information is presented. Even when those circumstances should be irrelevant, they often are not, which causes at times both miraculous and frightening results.

- **Chapter Nine: Instant Influence: Speedy Techniques for Persuasion in a Hurry.** Most of us get into habits, routines, and customary ways of thinking. We get used to saying 'no' to certain requests because that's what we're used to doing, for example when an unwanted caller tries to sell us something over the phone or when a stranger on the street asks us to sign a petition. In this chapter, we'll discover how the art of surprise and breaking people out of their reverie can encourage other people to take our requests more seriously.

- **Conclusions: Practising Principled Persuasion.** At the risk of sounding a little melodramatic, the techniques contained within this book are so powerful that they could equally be used for good or evil. We could choose to influence people in mutually beneficial ways or manoeuvre people into doing what they might not really want to do. So this concluding chapter talks about the psychology of manipulation – and why it might not ultimately be such a great idea.

As we delve into the psychology of influence and persuasion, we'll cover all sorts of territory. We shall look at studies in which hapless research assistants asked women out on dates or even begged for money from strangers on the street – all in the interests of science, of course. We will expose the inner workings of the human mind with the aid of modern brain-scanning technologies as used by the world's leading neuroscientists. We shall even look at observations of monkeys by animal behaviourists to understand not only the psychology of changing minds, but also the very evolutionary origins of humanity.

The research on influence and persuasion is endlessly varied and I promise it's going to be a fascinating journey with occasionally unexpected insights and conclusions. Shall we start in Chapter One by exploring what Nazism, people's likes and dislikes in pop music, and meal choices in Chinese restaurants can teach us about the science of changing minds?

'So what?'

After finishing my studies (I spent three years as an undergraduate psychologist, one year working as a research assistant, and a further three years researching my PhD in psychology), I decided to leave the world of research. I'd had enough of the gentle pace of academic life and wanted something a little more dynamic. My first job was as a junior consultant at The Boston Consulting Group, an international management consultancy.

As a junior consultant, my job for the two years I spent at the firm was to gather and analyse data about organisations and the markets in which they operated. Once I'd 'crunched' the data for a client organisation, I typed up my conclusions and recommendations as a set of PowerPoint slides. Before sending them to the client, I'd show them to my manager, who would frequently ask me, 'So what?'

Time and again, he'd go through my slide presentation with a pen, scribbling the phrase 'So what?' when I wasn't clear enough with my line of thinking. He explained that clients weren't interested in the data or even really the analyses that I'd performed; what they most wanted to know were the conclusions, what the data meant, the implications, and actions they should take.

In that spirit, I've included a number of boxes to capture the 'So what?'. If you're reading this book because you want to become more influential and persuasive, I'll pop key recommendations about the actions you might take into these boxes.

If you get to the end of the nine chapters and conclusions but find that you're still hungry for even more practical advice, the book doesn't stop there. I've also included a separate collection of resources at the very end of the book, which I've called The Influence Toolkit. It starts on page 271 and includes not only brief summaries of the key findings from each chapter, but also exercises and activities that will help you to incorporate the tools of influence and persuasion into both your professional and personal life.

CHAPTER ONE
the wisdom of crowds

'When people are free to do as they please,
they usually imitate each other.'
Eric Hoffer

At around the same time as James Vicary was conning the world with his subliminal advertising, a respectable professor of psychology named Solomon Asch was also deceiving people in his own way. In a series of landmark experiments in the 1950s, Asch demonstrated that individuals' actions were unduly swayed by the behaviour of the people around them. For over half a century, his studies have been interpreted as evidence that we smother our intentions and conform to peer pressure in order to be accepted. However, the advent of brain imaging technology in the last handful of years has uncovered that the truth may be even more startling: social pressures may change not only how we behave, but how we see the world itself.

Born in 1907, Solomon Asch grew up in Warsaw in Poland but moved to the United States in 1920, where he was drawn to the study of human behaviour and became a professor at the prestigious Swarthmore College in Pennsylvania. When the rise of Nazism in Germany ignited the Second World War and led to the occupation of Poland, he took a very personal interest in understanding how such hateful ideologies had managed to sweep across not only his homeland but so much of Europe. He felt driven to ask: was there something fundamentally *wrong* with the German people or could Nazism have happened even in the heart of the US?

In his most famous experiment, he invited college students to participate in a psychological experiment on visual judgement.

Imagine for a moment that you're one of these student volunteers. You arrive at a classroom to find six other students there with you. The researcher, a pipe-smoking gentleman with receding white hair and quizzical eyebrows, allows you all to sit down before he begins. With the merest hint of an Eastern European accent, he asks you and the rest of the group to settle in a row of chairs facing him.

The researcher explains that he will hold up two large white cards. One card will have a single black line on it; the second card will have three lines on it. Your task is simple enough: you must pick which of the three lines (marked 1, 2 or 3) is identical to the single line in length.

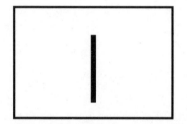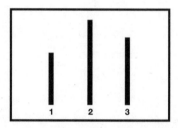

During each round, the researcher says that he will show the group different pairs of cards and, without conferring, everyone must call out their answers in turn, starting with the person on his right and ending with the person on his left. Finding yourself sat on his far left, you will be the last person in the group to speak.

The researcher turns over the first pair of cards. Looking at the two cards, you're certain it's line 3 that matches the single line. Indeed, the other subjects in the experiment call out, 'Three,' unanimously. When it gets to your turn, you confidently say, 'Three,' as well.

On the second round, everyone agrees this time that the match is with line number 2. Despite some initial apprehension about taking part in a psychological experiment, you relax a little.

On the third round, you think the matching line is number 1. However, the first person in the group says, 'Two.' You turn to look at him but the next person also says, 'Two,' and so does the third person. You look back at the lines and scrutinise them carefully to make sure that you didn't make a mistake. Squinting at the lines and flicking your eyes back and forth, you're not quite so certain now. Maybe it is one of the other lines after all?

By the time it's your turn to speak, you're feeling distinctly uncomfortable. Sure, you initially thought it was line number 1, but all six of the other people in the room have said they think it's line 2. All eyes are on you. Will you trust what you thought was the right answer and say, 'One' or go with the crowd and say, 'Two'?

In Asch's rather devious original study, what subjects didn't know was that there was only one real participant every time: the one who was last to answer. All of the other members of the group were accomplices who had been instructed beforehand to give unanimously incorrect answers during specified rounds of the experiment.

Nowadays it's common knowledge that research investigators – especially pesky psychologists like me – often deceive experimental subjects in the interests of science. Being savvy citizens of the twenty-first century, you and I would probably suspect that we're being hoodwinked under similar circumstances. But back in the 1950s, only a handful of subjects suspected that the rest of the group was colluding together.

Removing those few subjects from his data, Asch found that 75 per cent of the remaining, unsuspecting participants bowed to majority rule and, in seeming defiance of their senses, called out the incorrect line at least once. By comparison, when subjects were allowed to match the lines without the presence of the other alleged subjects, they made mistakes less than 1 per cent of the time.[4]

Many commentators have interpreted Asch's findings as evidence that people are weak-willed and unable to speak the truth in the face of unanimous peer pressure. In the context of the Second World War, some observers opined that maybe the people of Germany were not remarkable for having let Nazism spread. Faced with such strong social forces, even the most questioning and morally observant individuals – in any nation – may perhaps have found it almost impossible to resist the majority view.

In our own lives, most of us have at times found it easier to conform and go along with the group's judgement than to stand out as a lone dissenter. When five of your friends all want to dine at the new Italian restaurant in town, it seems churlish to declare that you ate Italian two days ago and that you're craving Mexican. Instead you smile and agree that Italian would be great too. Or when your boss and seven colleagues stridently agree that the company should open an office on the other side of the city, you may decide to keep your reservations to yourself rather than risk being labelled a naysayer.

Asked individually, we may state one preference. But when everyone else seems to be heading in a particular direction, it doesn't always pay to speak up. We sometimes go along with the crowd to avoid their scorn or gain their favour.

Even when we believe that a behaviour or practice is wrong, we're more likely to go along with it simply because others do. But other recent studies suggest that there's more to the tale. Something else more complex is going on. It's not just that we suppress what we want to say in order to avoid kicking up a fuss. No, it seems that social pressures can affect not only our public behaviour, but our attitudes and private beliefs too.

Social sways in private tastes

What kind of music do you like? Perhaps you love The Beatles, Elvis Presley, U2, or Madonna. Or maybe you prefer The Black Eyed Peas, Coldplay, or Lady Gaga? Whatever you think of such artists, you can't deny that they've sold a lot of records. But were they talented and their songs so sublime that success was inevitable or were they … lucky?

The search for an answer tells us something about the risks of working in the music industry, of trying to turn new artists into superstars. More importantly for us though, it also tells us something rather fundamental about how people make decisions about what they like or dislike.

Matthew Salganik, a young sociologist with round features and round, wire-rimmed glasses who lists New York-based rapper Jay-Z amongst his favourite artists, is something of an authority in the field of online social research. Early on in his career, while a graduate student at Columbia University, he conducted an ingenious experiment, recruiting over 14,000 participants from a teen-interest social networking website to listen to up to 48 new songs from previously unheard-of artists.[5] Visitors arriving at his website were invited to rate the songs from 1 star ('I hate it') to 5 stars ('I love it'), with the ratings published to help other users decide what to listen to. In return, the visitors were allowed to download the songs for free.

However, participants weren't told that they were being directed not to the same website, but to one of eight nearly identical portals. Each of the websites operated in its own self-contained bubble, with its visitors listening to songs, rating and downloading them, and producing unique league tables, charts of what was hot or not.

Within the space of a couple of months, the researchers found that entirely different songs became hits in each of the eight online worlds. Hits and misses couldn't be predicted. For example, the rock/Motown song 'Out of the Woods' by the band Shipwreck Union could be the most downloaded track on one website, but come 37th out of 48 on another. The track 'Miseries and Miracles' by the guitar collective A Blinding Silence could be top of the pops in one online world, but placed 43rd out of 48 elsewhere, and so on.

Witnessing these results, Salganik and his collaborators concluded that visitors to each website were heavily influenced by what earlier visitors had enjoyed and rated. New visitors didn't tend to make their own independent assessments of what was good or not; they simply went with the crowd, choosing to download and rate what was already popular.

The implications for the musical landscape as we know it are startling. Artists such as The Beatles and Lady Gaga should be deliriously grateful for their success. Salganik's research suggests that their remarkable triumphs involved more than a smattering of luck. When such acts accrued some initial popularity, other people probably followed the crowd, creating a self-perpetuating cycle of success begetting further success, which exploded into the musical phenomena that we know. At the other end of the spectrum, struggling artists and their record labels can take solace from the fact it's not lack of talent or the quality of their music that may be holding them back, but simply not being in front of the right numbers of people at the right time.

What does the experiment say about the exercise of influence in the real world? Salganik's work suggests that even our personal tastes are formed much more through social influence than we generally believe. While Solomon Asch forced his participants to call out their answers in front of other people, Matthew Salganik allowed his participants to visit his websites with complete anonymity. Even though website visitors were free to rate songs however they wished, the reality was that they didn't. They were influenced more by popularity than any perceptions of inherent song quality.

Of course most of us believe that we're independent-minded consumers; we all think that we like the songs and artists we listen to because they're good. We can defend our song and band choices, citing perhaps clever lyrics, the arrangement of melodies and harmonies, or the ways they've been choreographed and produced. Whether we're talking about our musical tastes or other consumer decisions – such as the dishes we order at a restaurant, the films we choose to watch, or even the cars we buy – most of us would disagree strongly with the suggestion that we simply follow the crowd. However, research by people like Salganik suggests that we're wrong.

Halfway across the world in China, for example, applied economist Hongbin Cai persuaded the owners of a restaurant chain in Beijing to participate in an experiment looking at the effects of information about popularity on diners' orders. Across the chain of 13 restaurants, some patrons were seated at a table with a plastic plaque listing the five best-selling dishes at that particular location. Other patrons were given a plastic plaque listing five randomly chosen dishes, on the pretext that these were the restaurant's recommendations. In a third, control condition, patrons were given no further information when placing their orders. All customers were also given the restaurant's full menu, listing dozens and dozens of dishes.

Analysing the bills for a rather impressive 12,895 tables, Cai and a fellow researcher found that the information that a particular dish was amongst the top five dishes ordered by others boosted sales of the dish by an average of between 13 and 20 per cent. However, giving customers information about the restaurant's alleged recommendations didn't increase sales of those dishes as compared with the third, control condition.

As patrons ignored the restaurant's recommendations, it clearly wasn't just the plaque that led to the uplift in sales of certain dishes. Customers were only swayed by the knowledge that other people in the same restaurant had also eaten certain dishes. The patrons were free to choose whatever they liked from the main menu, but it seems that their individual dining choices – their personal tastes – were influenced by their awareness of what was popular.

Additionally, customers seated at the tables with the additional list of best-sellers were statistically more likely to say that they were 'very satisfied' with their dining experience than customers in the other two groups. In other words, the mere knowledge about the most popular dishes *eaten by total strangers* seemed to enhance customers' enjoyment.[6]

In study after study, we see repeatedly that people are swayed by knowledge of what's popular. Individuals tend to follow the people around them even when making private decisions about their health and wealth; they tag along in a herd-like fashion in everything from choosing health insurance[7] and pension plans[8] to stock-market investments.[9] Surveying the mass of research, we can only reach one conclusion: the somewhat unpalatable truth is that both our public tastes and private choices are in fact quietly shaped by social forces, by the reviews and recommendations of the people around us, by mere popularity.

Adopting persuasive language

Whatever the ways in which you're trying to modify people's behaviour, you might be shrewd to tap into the power of collective influence. Perhaps you're trying to get people to behave in a more environmentally conscious manner. You may be trying to get a group of people – or maybe just one specific person – to drink less alcohol, eat less saturated fat, or slap on more sunscreen. Or maybe you're simply trying to get customers to buy your goods and services. If you have genuine facts that something is already popular with other people, make sure you convey that message to your target audience.

Think about the kind of language that advertisers use. They tell us that a product is the 'top seller', or the 'fastest-growing'.

Even simply reporting that 'most people' or 'countless others' either do something or don't do something else can be a motivator. I saw a recent advert saying that 'the majority of people who expressed a preference said they preferred our [product]'. Ker-ching! I'm sure their sales went up.

But you don't have to be a major advertiser to harness the might of collective influence. Say you work as a physiotherapist treating people for knee pain. There's research showing that the majority of patients who expressed a preference said they preferred physiotherapy over surgery.[10] If you're a physiotherapist looking to boost the number of patients you treat, simply telling people that honest fact may be enough to convince more patients to seek your services rather than those of a surgeon.

I heard a story about a teacher who fortuitously learned how to pacify trouble-makers in his class. Rather than simply pointing out the undesirable behaviour, he pointed out the fact that everyone else in the class was *not* participating: 'Peter, you'll notice that there are 19 other students in the class all sitting quietly and waiting to learn. Are you going to disrupt the lesson for your 19 classmates or are you going to stop playing silly games and join in with the rest of the class?'

In trying to coax elderly relatives to take their medication, some people may say, 'You should take your medication.' However, a more effective approach may be to argue, '*Most* people with the same condition take this medication. Perhaps you should too.'

Crowd pressure in the real world

Here's a poster campaign that caught my eye many times in recent months. This was an unavoidable campaign supported both by the office of the Mayor of London as well as Transport for London, the organisation that oversees all of the capital's buses, trains, trams, and even river boats as well as the London Underground.

Can you see why the poster works? By saying that 99 per cent of young Londoners *do not* commit serious violence, the poster is saying that the vast, vast majority of youths in the capital get along with each other and are responsible members of society. Without having to spell it out, the implicit message is that if you're one of the tiny minority who considers violence acceptable, you must be a loser, a freak, a strange outlier to be shunned – certainly not one of the in-crowd no matter how cool and tough you might have thought you were.

By tapping into people's unsuspecting inclinations to follow the herd, it's an inordinately powerful social message. I think it's going to be a startlingly effective campaign.

Of course savvy marketing executives have long appreciated that we tend to follow the lead of others, even total strangers. The fashion retailer Topshop recently summoned news crews to report on the dozens of customers thronging outside their flagship London store. The customers had been lining up for hours, waiting for the doors to open so they could get to the new clothing range designed by Kate Moss. The moment the news broadcasts went out, the crowds got larger and larger.

Every Christmas, toy retailers warn parents that demand for the latest must-have toys and gadgets is likely to outstrip supply. For years, I used to wonder how manufacturers could fail to keep up with demand in producing enough Nintendo Wiis, Sony PlayStations or whatever else was hot that December. But nowadays, I strongly suspect that these are simply marketing tactics: telling us that everyone else is buying one is designed to make us covet one too.

Even highly sophisticated customers fall into the trap. In 1995, business consultants Michael Treacy and Fred Wiersema published a business strategy book, *The Discipline of Market Leaders*, which received unflattering reviews. However, the wealthy authors organised a secret campaign to buy 50,000 copies of their book from stores across the US. The authors orchestrated it so that they bought the books from stores whose sales were monitored by the *New York Times* best-seller list, ensuring that the book leapt into the chart.

Once on the prestigious list, the book gained its own momentum, riding high in the chart for 15 weeks. Seeing it on the best-seller list, new customers assumed that the book was a good one and bought it, ensuring that the book stayed on the best-seller list, which brought it to the attention of yet more book-buying customers.[11]

When it comes to the way our brains work, it seems we can't help it. When we see other people behaving in a certain way, we really are more likely to follow their lead – even when they're doing something stupid or even illegal. We think: 'If lots of people are doing it, then I probably should do too.' If we were equivocal about something beforehand, the mere knowledge that other people are doing it may be enough to change our minds and behaviour.

The invisibility of social influence

You probably accept the argument that *many* people are guided in their decisions and behaviour by the deeds of other people. But perhaps you feel that you're different, stronger. You may not believe that *you* are so impressionable or vulnerable as to be affected by what other people are saying or doing. Thing is: scarcely anyone believes that they are influenced by information about what other people are doing.

One of the most exciting areas in which the psychology of collective influence is being used is the promotion of environmentally responsible behaviour. In an intriguing study published in 2008, University of Arkansas social scientist Jessica Nolan and her colleagues decided to look at the relationships between people's stated attitudes towards energy conservation and their actual behaviour. She began by asking residents in California four questions about their motivations for cutting their energy consumption:

(a) In deciding to conserve energy, how important is it to you that using less energy saves money?

(b) In deciding to conserve energy, how important is it to you that it protects the environment?

(c) In deciding to conserve energy, how important is it to you that it benefits society?

(d) In deciding to conserve energy, how important is it to you that a lot of other people are trying to conserve energy?

Indicating the strength of their preferences on a series of rating scales, the survey respondents said that the protection of the environment was the most crucial factor (b), followed by the benefits to society (c), and then the fact that it saves money (a). The awareness that other people are doing it (d) was rated the least significant reason for trying to conserve energy.

Now that's what residents *said* was important. However, would people change their behaviour, their actual energy consumption, when presented with such arguments? Nolan and the team decided to find out by sending one of four different messages about energy conservation to several hundred households in San Marcos, a perpetually sunny district of southern California.

Remember that respondents said that the protection of the environment was the most essential reason they might cut their energy use (as in question (b) above). So some of the households received messages highlighting that energy conservation protected the environment:

Protect the Environment by Conserving Energy. Summer is here and the time is right for reducing greenhouse gases. How can you protect the environment this summer? By using fans instead of air conditioning! Why? According to researchers at Cal State San Marcos, you can prevent the release of up to 262 lbs of greenhouse gases per month by using fans instead of air conditioning to keep cool this summer! Using fans instead of air conditioning – The Environmental Choice.

Two further notes explained either that people should reduce their energy usage because it benefited society (question (c) above) or because it saved them money personally (question (a)). A fourth message encouraged people to conserve energy simply because other people were doing it (question (d)):

Join Your Neighbours in Conserving Energy. Summer is here and most people in your community are finding ways to conserve energy at home. How are San Marcos residents like you conserving this summer? By using fans instead of air conditioning! Why? In a recent survey of households in your community, researchers at Cal State San Marcos found that 77% of San Marcos residents often use fans instead of air conditioning to keep cool in the summer. Using fans instead of air conditioning – Your Community's Popular Choice!

In order to monitor which of the four messages was the most effective at actually reducing energy usage, the investigators asked for permission to read homeowners' electricity meters. You'll recall from the initial survey that people said that they didn't care whether others conserved energy. They said that the fact other people were reducing their energy usage was the least important reason for trying to do the same. However, the results proved them wrong. The message encouraging energy conservation simply because most people in the area were doing it turned out to be the *most* effective.[12]

Again, as we've seen in study after study, the news that other people were doing something was enough to modify people's private habits. More than that though, it also showed that people are remarkably unaware of the power of social information. People simply don't believe that their attitudes and behaviour are affected by knowledge about what other people are doing.

Danger, danger!

The knowledge about what other people are doing can steer people's behaviour in undesirable directions too. Consider the predicament faced by Arizona's Petrified Forest National Park. Visitors were warned that taking pieces of the irreplaceable petrified wood was an act of theft. All over the park, prominent signs announced:

> Your heritage is being vandalized every day by theft losses of
> petrified wood of 14 tons a year, mostly a small piece at a time.

Can you see how the signs were failing to prevent further theft? The park administrators estimated that around 3 per cent of visitors were taking pieces of the precious wood home with them. With many tens of thousands of visitors every month, the seemingly insignificant acts were adding up to the tune of over a ton of wood a month.

Step forward Robert Cialdini, a seasoned researcher from the nearby Arizona State University, who offered to bring the psychology of social persuasion into play. The wily social scientist first gained permission from park officials to place surreptitiously marked pieces of petrified wood along certain popular visitor paths to see how many of them disappeared into visitors' bags and pockets. Then, on consecutive weekends, he put up two entirely different versions of the sign.

The first sign had a picture of three visitors stealing chunks of wood along with the words:

Many visitors have removed petrified wood from the Park, changing the natural state of the Petrified Forest.

The second sign had a picture of a single visitor purloining a piece of wood, with a red circle-and-bar symbol superimposed over his hand. The picture was accompanied by the message:

Please don't remove the petrified wood from the Park, in order to preserve the natural state of the Petrified Forest.

Which do you think was the more effective message in reducing theft?

The first version of the sign mentioning that 'many visitors have removed petrified wood' *increased* theft to 7.92 per cent. The wording and the picture of multiple visitors stealing wood seemed to trigger people's herding instincts, making the undesirable behaviour even more popular. Thankfully, the second message simply pleading with visitors not to remove wood from the park – and the picture of the lone and lonely visitor being reprimanded for his heinous behaviour – reduced theft to 1.67 per cent.[13]

The park custodians had made a mistake with their original warning signs. By telling people that 'many' visitors had removed petrified wood from the park, they had inadvertently been encouraging the activity. Visitors seemed to interpret the original sign as condoning the act of walking off with mementos from the park.

Understanding that social influence can work in *either* direction

When lots of people are engaging in an undesirable behaviour, it's definitely not a good idea to point it out. If a significant chunk of the people at work are handing their expense claims in late, don't send out an indignant email telling people the fact: it'll only encourage the ones who are currently handing them in on time to follow the crowd and slack off! Or if you find that most of the kids at your child's school have cheated on their homework, you might be better off staying quiet about it.

The warning that worked in the Petrified Forest National Park deliberately included a picture of a lone visitor stealing wood. The implication was: 'Most of our visitors don't steal wood. You'd be in a tiny, lonely minority if you do.'

So if you're trying to persuade people not to do something that they're thinking of doing, you may wish to imply that they would be the exception, that they would be shunned for joining in with such reprehensible behaviour.

The neuroscience of social influence

Why are we so heavily influenced by the behaviour of our fellows? Why do we so unwittingly rely on others rather than making our own assessments, coming up with our own judgements about what we should be doing?

For the answers we turn our attention to the work done by Emory University professor Gregory Berns and his colleagues. With his halo of curly brown hair and an unlined face that breaks easily into a broad smile, Berns looks barely older than the undergraduate students that he teaches. Yet he holds three degrees in medicine, physics, and biomedical engineering and is at the forefront of a wave of researchers using the hot young science of functional magnetic resonance imaging (fMRI) procedures to peer into the way the brain works when confronted with social pressure.

Updating Solomon Asch's 1951 study with twenty-first-century technology, Berns and his team invited experimental volunteers to respond to a series of mental tasks on a computer while their brains were scanned. Here's an example. Imagine you're presented on a computer screen with a pair of three-dimensional shapes. Your challenge: to decide whether the two are exactly the same object rotated through three-dimensional space, or different.

Try it for yourself. Same or different?

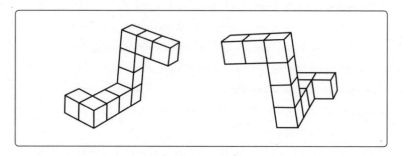

And here's another example. Again, the question is the same: are the two the same object or subtly different?

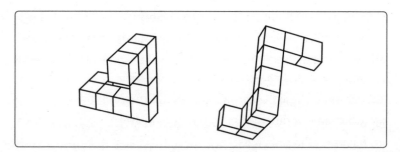

You can flick to the notes at the end of the book if you'd like to check your answers.[14] Straightaway though, you'll notice that the task is considerably more challenging than the test that Asch used in his experiment. Add in to the mix the fact that volunteers were only given 12 seconds in which to respond and you can understand that they got the answers wrong about 14 per cent of the time.

As in Asch's experiment though, the participants were told that they were taking part in a study looking at group decision-making. Each participant was told that he or she was part of a group of five participants, who would each be able to see the judgements that everyone else had made. However, the truth was that these other ostensible participants were in fact – you guessed it – actors, hired to play the role of innocent experimental subjects.

Each real participant was briefed alongside the four fake participants. Corralled together in one room, the entire group was informed about the nature of the experiment. They then signed consent forms for taking part in the experiment and were given 20 practice trials of the mental rotation task on a network of five laptop computers. Only then was the sole real participant escorted into the imaging room and seated within the fMRI machine in front of a computer.

As the fMRI whirred into life, the experiment began properly. During initial rounds of the mental rotation task, the participant was asked to judge whether the pair of objects was the same or different, just as in the earlier practice rounds. On a handful of later rounds though, the participant's computer flashed up with additional information, telling them what the other four members of the alleged group had chosen. In half of these social influence rounds, the actors all chose the correct answer as to whether the two objects were the same or different; in the other half, they unanimously made an incorrect choice.

You probably won't be surprised to hear that participants made nearly three times as many errors when they were given wrong information by the other members of the group. The mere knowledge that other people had chosen a particular answer was enough to steer participants into making the incorrect choice 41 per cent of the time. Remember that they only made mistakes a mere 14 per cent of the time when they weren't given any further information. But recording their error rate wasn't the main point of the study.

By looking at the brain scans taken during the experiment, Berns and his investigative team were able to observe the brain regions that buzzed with activity during different rounds. Previous research had shown that the prefrontal cortex tends to fire up when we make deliberate judgements about the world around us. So if we see that a colour is black but decide to claim that we see 'white', a brain scan would show a spike of activity in the prefrontal cortex. Similarly, if we believed that we were seeing two objects that were the same, but felt we had to go along with the rest of the group who were claiming they were different, we'd see commotion there too.

But the prefrontal cortex remained cool and quiet when participants were given information about what the rest of the group was doing. Participants weren't making a conscious decision to follow the crowd. Instead, the area that lit up was the visual cortex, the part of the brain responsible for sight. Translating that from geek-speak to plain English: when given wrong information about whether two objects were either the same or different, *participants genuinely believed that they were seeing the same answer as the rest of the group.*[15] The participants weren't making a conscious decision to play along and say that they saw something or not. A deep-seated part of their brain was choosing to *interpret* reality differently, purely on the basis of what the rest of the group was saying.

The research team also made a second, significant observation. When participants struck out on their own to make a choice that went against the group, a part of their brains called the amygdala pulsated with activity. This brain centre usually fires up when we're experiencing negative emotional states such as pain or anxiety. So the researchers' finding suggests that choosing to disregard the recommendation of others causes the brain something akin to discomfort or even distress. Our brains are literally wired to follow the lead of those around us and we suffer when we don't.

Abhijit Banerjee, a notable economist at the Massachusetts Institute of Technology, has observed – in the typically dry language that we might expect of his profession – that our tendency to be swayed by the words and deeds of others is 'inefficient'.[16] He's right. From the cold, analytical stance of an economist, human beings are definitely inefficient. But the reality is that we don't have the time, energy, or brain capacity to be more efficient.

Our brains are marvels of biological engineering, testament to hundreds of thousands of years of evolution. Yet to weigh up all of the options we face on a daily basis would cause our brains to stall. We simply don't have the processing power to compute everything in depth all the time or we'd end up paralysed by indecision.

The brain is a very special organ. Even when resting, it's permanently in an extraordinarily high-powered state. Despite representing only 2 per cent of the body's overall weight, it's a disproportionately hungry organ, greedily consuming between 20 to 25 per cent of the fuel – i.e. oxygen and glucose – needed to sustain the body on a daily basis.[17]

In ancient times when food was scarce and every calorie mattered, evolution decided that the power-hungry brain should reduce its energy consumption as much as possible. The brain was designed to cruise along, switching as many of its functions into standby mode as it could to ward off the risk of starving to death. Putting it another way, the brain was intentionally created to be as lazy a lump of meat as possible. To avoid squandering energy on mental calculations or having to come to its own judgements, evolution engineered it to take advantage of shortcuts whenever it could.

One of these shortcuts was to be guided by what everyone else is doing. Humans are a social species; we continue to cluster together in communities in the same way that our ancestors lived in tribes. When our forebears saw dozens of people running in a particular direction, it was a safer bet to start running than to stand around asking questions. Or when they saw neighbours from another tribe tying sharpened stones to tree branches to make spears, they were wise to do the same too. For most of history, copying the behaviour of those around us was a matter of survival. When someone else's brain had evaluated the options and crunched the data, we couldn't go too far awry by following their lead.

It's an evolutionary vestige that stays with us today. Consider how babies learn about the world. Babies don't question every-thing they observe and try to derive rules and patterns from first principles. No, they simply copy what they see and hear. When they hear their mothers saying the word 'mama', they don't wonder why they should do the same. When they see adults walking on two feet, they don't weigh up the possible benefits of trying to walk on their hands. They just mimic the behaviours, because that's the quickest way to learn.[18]

Humans are fundamentally social creatures. We tend to trust the judgements of others. Our brains are influenced not only by what we see, but also *who* is around us and what they are saying or doing.

Social effects in mating and dating

Our behaviour is so heavily directed by social influence that even our notions of sexual attractiveness are affected by collective influence – and all without exchanging a single word. In one study, researchers at the University of Texas at Austin asked heterosexual female participants to judge the desirability of men in different photographs and heterosexual male participants to judge the desirability of women in different photographs.

Let's start with the female participants. They were shown three types of image. A third of the photos showed a man on his own. Another third of the photos showed a man surrounded by a group of women. The final third showed men surrounded by other men.

The investigative team found that female participants rated men as being more desirable when they were surrounded by other women than when shown either alone or with other men. The mere presence of other women seemed to transmit some kind of social message: 'Hey, those women seem to like this guy, I should probably find him attractive too!'

In a similar fashion, the male participants were shown photographs of women in three types of setting: individually, or posing with either other women or a group of men. Things were markedly different for the male participants though. Men found women to be less desirable when shown with men than when shown either alone or with other women. The presence of other men in the photographs also seemed to be transmitting a social message, but of an absolutely different kind: 'Hmm, that woman is surrounded by guys so I'm going to have less of a chance with her – I should move on to someone more available.'[19]

In another study, psychologist Benedict Jones at the University of Aberdeen asked female participants to make judgements about the attractiveness of different men in photos. In half of the photos, the men were shown with a smiling woman. In the other half of the photos, they were shown with a woman wearing a neutral expression.

Perhaps unsurprisingly, the female participants in the study rated the men as more attractive when they were seen with a smiling woman. In other words, when women see a man with a cheerful woman, they see it as further validation that he's attractive.[20]

Digital dating dos and don'ts

More than a few of my friends are now playing the online dating game and this is the advice I'd have for them. If you're a guy looking to attract more interest from women, then by all means include photos of yourself with other women on your dating profile. Even better if they're all smiling and looking as if they're having a great time. Women perusing your profile will be swayed into thinking you're more attractive and desirable.

On the other hand, if you're a woman looking to attract more interest from men, you might be better off choosing photos of yourself either alone or with women friends. Men find the presence of other men in a photograph threatening, making you look less attractive, less desirable in their eyes.

Perhaps the effect isn't confined to photographs either. A buddy of mine tells me that he seems to get more interest from women since getting married than when he was single. And now it all makes sense. Perhaps women take the mere presence of a wedding ring as proof that at least one other woman finds a man attractive.

So if you're a single guy looking to snare a date, ask an obliging woman friend to hang out with you. She'll make you look really good. But if you're a single woman looking to win over a man, head out onto the town either on your own or with your women friends.

Tributes and testimonials

Were you swayed in your decision to buy this book by the testimonial on the cover? At least I *hope* you bought – or maybe borrowed – the book as opposed to stealing it!

Anyway, I digress.

Journalist and bestselling author Venetia Thompson said, 'How to influence people without getting them drunk or flirting: brilliant.' Now if *I* had said that the book was 'brilliant', that would have made me sound incredibly arrogant. But, coming from someone else, it somehow seems more valid, doesn't it?

Stanford University's Jeffrey Pfeffer and his team set out to examine precisely this question. An academic who has taught at institutions around the world including Harvard Business School, Singapore Management University, and London Business School, Pfeffer yearned to know: would third-party endorsements on behalf of an individual be seen as more persuasive than the same comment made by the individual?

Pfeffer invited university students to pretend that they had taken on the role of a book publisher. He told them that an academic called Michael Green, who had previously written a highly technical book about his specialist field, now wanted to write a book for the popular market. In the role of book publisher, they had to decide how much they liked Michael and to what extent they wished to assist him.

The students were randomly selected to watch one of four video clips:

(a) The author was pictured alone on screen giving a speech about his own credibility and qualifications and asking for not only help but also a big advance for a book deal.

(b) A different actor was introduced as Michael Green's agent. The author was not present on screen, and the agent delivered more or less the same speech about the author as the author did about himself in version (a).

(c) Both the author and agent were pictured on screen, but only the author spoke, again delivering the same speech about himself.

(d) Both the author and agent were pictured on screen, but this time only the agent spoke to promote the taciturn author's talent.

Participants in the study rated the author much more highly when the agent spoke on his behalf than when the author spoke about himself. Even when both the agent and author were visible on screen at the same time (as a reminder that the agent had a financial interest in promoting the author and therefore wasn't exactly an impartial observer), participants still reported that they liked the author significantly more and were more willing to help him.[21]

Getting other people to say nice things about you

People who talk about themselves in glowing terms are usually seen in a very negative light. However, having someone else talk about you in an equally complimentary fashion will work wonders for how you're perceived. Say you need to give a speech to an audience of sceptical managers, investors, or customers. Rather than introducing yourself, get someone else to present your biography. The study by Pfeffer and colleagues demonstrates that even when an audience realises that the third party isn't entirely objective, they'll still respond more warmly to you than if you speak about yourself.

Or say you're putting together your profile for a dating website. If you can, ask a friend to write something positive about you that you can quote. Having a named friend say that you're 'kind, funny, sexy, and intelligent' might clinch the deal.

If you can't get someone to speak up for you in person, do it in print. When writing a brochure, ask for testimonials from happy customers and clients. Get them to rave about the quality of your product or service rather than risk people's indignation at your shameless self-promotion.

Solomon Asch's investigations into the effects of peer pressure on people's judgements of line length even suggest the optimal number of testimonials to have. In a series of studies, he varied the number of accomplices in his group from one person (admittedly, not much of a group) up to 15 people.

When experimental subjects were confronted with opposition from only a single individual, they were hardly ever swayed: they continued to answer independently and correctly almost

100 per cent of the time. When two people acted in unanimous opposition, experimental subjects went along with the wrong answer 13.6 per cent of the time. When the group consisted of three unanimous challengers, experimental subjects submitted to the peer pressure in giving the wrong answer in a massive 31.8 per cent of rounds. However, even when the group size grew to between six and eight people, experimental subjects still only gave the incorrect answers 36.8 per cent of the time.

So Asch's study suggests that one or two testimonials isn't enough. Two isn't a group or a crowd. On the other hand, six or eight people might be overkill. Three testimonials should be plenty.

CHAPTER TWO
secret signals

'You can go a long way with a smile.'
Al Capone

Suppose you've got a big business meeting next week. It's huge, in fact. You and dozens of other people have been invited to pitch ideas for a new business to a panel of judges. Win the pitch and you could secure the investment you need to start your own business, become a mogul, and hopefully watch the millions roll in. So you want to win. *Really, really* want to win.

But that's still a whole five days away and in the meantime you have a business event: a cocktail party to attend tonight. It's a mixed crowd with perhaps future customers, suppliers, or even investors present, so you're on your best behaviour. Dressed in your favourite smart-casual outfit, you turn on the charm and mingle amongst the partygoers, showing your interest by asking sensible questions and nodding appropriately to the answers. You talk about yourself when asked but at the same time show you've got a sense of humour by cracking jokes and having a laugh when the opportunity arises too.

As you're about to leave, a man stops you at the door. Nudging his glasses back up his nose, he explains that he's a psychologist. He says that he was observing your body language – your gestures, posture, and how closely you stood next to people. He also listened to the sound of your voice. He couldn't hear what you were saying, just the rhythm and tone of your words. And he has made a decision: you will not be given the chance to give your business pitch next week. Based purely on how he saw you moving and on your tone of voice, he has decided that you will *not* be getting your investment.

You'd be angry, right? Incensed that you haven't been given the opportunity to deliver your presentation. Furious that the judges won't get to hear the words you had carefully chosen to sell your idea. And all because this alleged expert says he's been watching your body language!

Alex Pentland, a heavyset man with a leonine mane of white hair and a thick beard whose hands flutter constantly in front of him when he speaks, is one of a new vanguard of researchers interested in body language. But he's not a psychologist, sociologist, or even anthropologist. He's a computer scientist and professor at the Human Dynamics Lab at the Massachusetts Institute of Technology. In one research investigation, he attached digital recording devices to dozens of business executives to monitor their body language and speech characteristics at a social event over the course of an evening. Nearly a week later, Pentland was able to predict with 87 per cent accuracy how the executives' business pitches would be rated by the judges – and all without listening to a single word of what the executives actually said in their presentations.[22]

Think about that for a moment. Nearly 90 per cent of the impact that these executives had on the judges had nothing to do with the actual words they used.

How did this happen?

The executives thought that their presentations were being evaluated on rational criteria. How innovative was the idea? Did the numbers stack up? Did the business plan make sense? But quite without the judges' conscious awareness, the executives were instead being assessed on entirely different dimensions. They were being weighed up in terms of how they held themselves, how they moved and spoke. How confident did they seem? Did they come across as passionate, determined, and committed? Did they seem professional and trustworthy?

Perhaps even more shockingly, people make these judgements about us with worrying speed. While conducting research for her doctoral dissertation at Harvard University, psychologist Nalini Ambady asked a group of student volunteers to watch short video clips of over a dozen university lecturers taken at the start of an academic term. The students' task: to judge the professors along various personality dimensions, such as the extent to which they came across as attentive, honest, enthusiastic, and warm. The twist: each of the video clips lasted only 30 seconds *and* had the sound turned off.

Far from complaining about the difficulty of their assignment, the students plunged into the task and quickly came up with ratings of the professors. Ambady set these initial ratings aside and waited until after a full academic semester before asking the professors' real students to rate their professors on the same criteria. Comparing the two sets of ratings, she found a huge degree of overlap. Professors who *looked* competent, confident, and eager in the initial video clips invariably received better evaluations from their actual students too. In other words, being observed for a mere 30 seconds was enough for the professors to be evaluated with uncanny accuracy. In tune with Alex Pentland's research on his business executives, it didn't seem to matter *what* the lecturers were saying, only how they appeared when they said it.[23]

Ambady was frankly stunned by her discovery. Shocked, but also intrigued. She began to wonder: how long does it take for people to arrive at judgements about others? She shortened the length of the video clips at first to 15 seconds in length, then a mere six seconds. The results remained unchanged. Six seconds – not even double digits! – was plenty for the students to form almost ridiculously accurate judgements about their professors.

For me, the implications are almost a little scary. People take only seconds to form judgements about us – judgements that may be as accurate as those of people who spend many months with us. And remember this isn't even from paying attention to the words we use or the sound of our voices. This is just from observing our body language, the signals that we constantly and unwittingly broadcast to anyone who cares to pay attention.

It's how you say it, not what you say

Looking back on our lives, most of us have at least a few regrets. Some people have major misgivings while others can count themselves lucky that they have only minor ones. For certain people though, their regrets may be over tiny actions, seemingly trivial deeds that unfortunately had enormous consequences.

In 1960, one such gentleman probably wished that he had smiled a little more often and made a few more gestures with his hands. If he had, he might have changed the course of history in the Western world as we know it.

His name? Richard Nixon, then vice-president of the world's reigning superpower, the United States of America.

A little context first: from 1953 to 1960, Nixon had served two terms as Vice-President under President Dwight D. Eisenhower. Historians consistently rank Eisenhower amongst the top 10 US presidents of all time. And the late 1950s were remarkable for having been a period of relative peace and prosperity. Nixon had everything going for him and it wasn't an immense surprise when he won the nomination of the Republican Party to vie for the biggest job in the world.

For the first time in American history, the presidential campaign included a series of live debates between the two presidential candidates broadcast on national television. But this was September in 1960 and not every household had one of the newfangled television sets yet, so while some people watched the grainy black-and-white moving pictures, many others had to huddle around their radios to listen to the debate instead.

The audience's reactions to the debate were a shock to everyone. For people who had *listened* to the debate on radio, the majority declared either that Nixon was the winner or that it had been a draw between the two candidates. However, members of the public who had *watched* the debate on television declared the young upstart candidate John F. Kennedy to be the overwhelming victor.

Journalists, political commentators, and even the general public were enthralled by the discrepancy. While Nixon had spoken eloquently and made a compelling case with his words, his demeanour had let him down. For most of the debate, he gripped the lectern tightly, looking visibly tense and uncomfortable. In contrast, Kennedy looked serene and confident.[24]

After this first, pivotal debate, Kennedy's election campaign gained momentum, with nationwide polls mostly putting him ahead of Nixon. When it came to the election itself on Tuesday, 8 November, Kennedy defeated Nixon by a mere two-tenths of 1 per cent of the vote (with Kennedy polling 49.7 per cent and Nixon 49.5 per cent), one of the closest presidential elections of the twentieth century.

Nixon came to rue his performance in front of the camera. With perhaps more than a hint of bitterness, he remarked: 'I believe that I spent too much time in the last campaign on substance and too little on appearance.'

Nixon and his cadre of advisers were smart enough to learn from the incident. When he ran for the presidency again in 1968, he was a noticeably different person when speaking both on conference platforms and in front of the camera. He smiled more for a start. Commentators remarked that he seemed more charismatic, more likeable. And this time he clinched the biggest job in the world.

Of course, politicians since then have become much savvier about managing their body language, the secret signals they broadcast. They receive intensive instruction, performing in front of cameras for hours on end and being drilled in the art of not just sounding, but also looking the part.

The increasing focus on body language and demeanour perhaps came to its natural conclusion a decade later when the American public elected Ronald Reagan into the White House. Reagan is regularly described as one of the most sincere and affable presidents of the twentieth century. The fact he was a Hollywood actor schooled in the art of *portraying* sincerity and affability in dozens of films before he turned to politics is perhaps no mere coincidence.

In the UK, Prime Minister David Cameron himself worked as a public relations guru at a TV company for seven years before entering politics. Now, I don't want to get political here, but the point is simply this: back in 1960, when television was still a relatively novel contraption, the disconnect between what listeners heard and what viewers saw during the Nixon–Kennedy debate was revelatory.

That single presidential debate more than 50 years ago fuelled a wave of interest in body language. Even today, if there is one branch of psychology that continues to fascinate people, it's probably the study of body language.

Psychologists prefer the term 'non-verbal communication' to describe the field although, somewhat confusingly, it's a misnomer. Non-verbal communication isn't just the study of posture, movement, and gestures; it also encompasses scrutiny of the human voice and characteristics such as vocal pitch, pacing, and intonation. So really it's the study of everything apart from the words themselves.*

---

* Some researchers prefer to be much more precise by referring to the study of the human voice as paralinguistics (or vocalics), but that's more technical than we need to be.

Yes, it's an absorbing area of psychology that gets a lot of attention in the popular media. A magazine may print a photograph of two celebrities and imply that they're falling in love with each other because their arms are crossed in mirror image of each other. The TV news may broadcast footage of two heads of state glancing in opposite directions, the newsreader declaring it's a sign of a growing rift between their countries. Or a self-styled authority on body language may quote a since-discredited finding that 55 per cent of our impact comes down to our body language, 38 per cent to our tone of voice and inflection and only 7 per cent from the words we use.[25]

There are a lot of misconceptions about non-verbal communication, but the truths are perhaps even more compelling. And when it comes to influencing the people around us, we can harness the power of secret signals to become considerably more persuasive.

Influencing interviewers

I don't know about you, but most people I know seem to either hate job interviews or, seeing them as an opportunity to talk about themselves, quite enjoy them. A job interview is, if you think about it, a great example of a situation requiring the skills of influence and persuasion. From the moment we greet the interviewer, we must choose the right combination of winning words and appropriate body language to make the right impression, to get across that we are right for the role.

Jennifer Burnett, a doctoral research student, and her supervisor Stephan Motowidlo at the University of Florida set out to investigate the impact of different non-verbal cues on interview performance. Their line of enquiry: to what extent are interviewers' judgements of competence swayed by body language?

The researchers began by recording mock interview footage of 60 real managers enrolled from four different companies. They told the manager-candidates to imagine they were applying for their present positions as they answered a series of fairly tough interview questions. Here's one of the questions: 'I'd like you to think of a time when you were working with other people, either on a special project or on an everyday task, when there was some type of crisis, and it was necessary for someone to take charge. What was your role in this situation?'

Here's another of the questions: 'I'd like you to tell me about a time when you were working on an important task, but a major obstacle or disruption got in the way, and forced you to think about whether or not to continue as you had originally planned.'

How would you respond if you were asked these questions? Not easy questions, are they? Most people have to take more than a few seconds to think of appropriate answers. But then these questions were deliberately chosen to separate the great manager-candidates from the not-so-good ones.

Next, the researchers enlisted the support of volunteers to evaluate the performance of the manager-candidates, dividing the volunteers into three groups. The first group of volunteers read written transcripts of the managers' answers. They weren't given the luxury of seeing how the manager-candidates moved or even hearing the intonation and pacing of their voices. This group was asked to come up with ratings based purely on the words that the manager-candidates had chosen in response to the interview questions.

Using methods similar to those adopted by the psychologist Nalini Ambady, a second group of participants watched the video performances of the managers with the sound turned off. This group obviously judged just the visual appearance, posture, and movement of the manager-candidates.

The final group of volunteers watched the full videos with the sound turned on, giving them the fullest possible information about the manager-candidates.

In an echo of the Nixon–Kennedy debate, you won't be surprised to learn that the volunteers produced different ratings depending on whether they had either read transcripts or seen the videos. The manager-candidates who were rated highly based purely on their transcripts weren't necessarily the same ones who performed well when judged on video.

The researchers wanted to know more though: which behaviours in particular were related to interview success? They asked six experts to analyse the 60 interviews in meticulous detail, taking notes on the different non-verbal cues that the manager-candidates displayed. These experts sat with stopwatches in hand noting the amount of time the manager-candidates spent smiling, moving their hands, turning their bodies to face the interviewer, and making eye contact with the interviewer.

Two of these four non-verbal cues predicted interview performance. Go on, take a guess. Can you guess which ones?

Most of us think of smiling as something that helps us to come across as warm, but does it help us to come across as professional too? No. The results showed that smiling made no difference to observers' judgements of the manager-candidates.

Neither did body posture. Whether the manager-candidates oriented their bodies away from the interviewer or turned their bodies towards the interviewer again made no difference.

Burnett and Motowidlo did, however, observe that hand movements had a minor bearing on interview ratings. Manager-candidates who were more expressive with their hands and who gestured more received marginally stronger ratings. You may have heard well-meaning friends tell you it's a bad idea to sit with your arms crossed during an interview as you may 'look defensive'. Their reasoning as to why we shouldn't sit with crossed, unmoving arms may be a little shaky, but the observation itself does seem to have merit. Remember too that Richard Nixon was slated during that decisive presidential debate for having leaned too much on his lectern, for gripping it rather than using his hands to emphasise his points. So this finding makes sense.

But by far the most crucial of the four behaviours in predicting interview success was eye contact. Manager-candidates who spent more time looking directly at the interviewer got significantly better ratings.[26]

Eye contact matters. In fact, people can't seem to help themselves when it comes to making judgements about us based on our eye contact alone. Take another example: researchers at the University of Toronto recruited members of the general public to imagine they were jurors in a criminal court trial. The participants were asked to watch the testimony of an alleged witness (played by an actor), who was providing an alibi for a defendant charged with robbery. The evidence in the case was deliberately constructed so that the defendant's guilt or innocence was unclear: the believability of the witness's testimony would either convict or clear the defendant.

Unbeknownst to the participants, they had been randomly designated to watch one of two nearly identical versions of the same testimony. Half watched a witness who held the gaze of a lawyer during questioning; the other half observed a witness who spent some of the time looking away.

As the researchers expected, the witness who dodged eye contact was rated as significantly less credible than the one who held the lawyer's gaze. As a result, the participants who watched the witness with the evasive eyes were much more likely to reject his testimony and find the defendant guilty.[27]

Eye contact stimulates parts of the brain that are responsible for signalling attraction. Eye contact is magnetic. It creates a brain-to-brain link that pulls people together irrespective of their gender. Even babies as young as a few days of age can tell when people around them are trying to make eye contact with them, suggesting that the desire for eye contact is programmed into us rather than something that we have to learn.[28] So findings that eye contact has a huge degree of influence over how people perceive each other is hardly a revelation. In fact, you may think that it's downright obvious: ask most people whether they think eye contact is important during a conversation and of course they'd say yes. It's a message we've all heard before. So why am I talking about it at all?

Let's return briefly to the mock job interview study conducted by Burnett and Motowidlo. Remember that the manager-candidates who made eye contact got better ratings than those who didn't. Yet if the advice to make eye contact in order to improve how we come across really is so blatantly obvious, why didn't *all* of the managers do it?

Reading the detail contained within the research duo's paper, we learn that these were all managers in charge of other people. They had presumably worked their way up into management by demonstrating their intelligence and competence at the job. These were clever people. So you'd think they would know something as straightforward as the importance of making eye contact during an interview. But this illustrates a common finding in the study of non-verbal communication: what people *know* they should do isn't always the same as what people actually *do*. We often simply forget to apply some of the common sense that we think we have.

So yes, on one level we can say that the importance of making eye contact is a – pardon the choice of word – *blindingly* apparent observation. However, even in important situations in which we want to be at our best, such as the job interview, we also know that not everyone does it all of the time.

Magnetic attraction

In their study of manager-candidates in job interviews, Burnett and Motowidlo measured four non-verbal behaviours and found that both eye contact and, to a lesser extent, hand movements predicted who gained the best interview ratings. However, both of these factors were trumped by one other characteristic of the manager-candidates.

It wasn't how they moved their feet, nodded their heads, or fidgeted with their fingers. In fact it wasn't anything to do with what they said or did at all. To explain, let's pause for a moment and consider another study that was conducted several decades earlier.

Picture in your mind's eye the following scene. One day you're walking along the street when a slender young woman sidles up to you. She's pretty, with a friendly, open face and high cheekbones. Flashing you a broad smile, she explains that the nearby university's cafeterias currently serve meat and that she's trying to rally support for the cafeterias to serve only vegetarian fare at least for breakfasts and lunches. It would be better for the environment and for people's health too, she adds.

A stray lock of hair falls across her face. As she tucks it back behind her ears, you notice that she's got long lashes fringing her big brown eyes too. Finally, she asks: 'Would you be willing to sign my petition, please?'

This was the set-up for an experiment conducted by Shelly Chaiken, a social psychologist at the University of Toronto. Recruiting over a hundred undergraduate students of both genders to act as her assistants, she explained to them that she needed their help to run a study to do with the spoken word and persuasion. Without their knowledge though, she asked a team of independent arbiters to sort the students into three groups based purely on the basis of their looks, their physical attractiveness. One third were categorised as physically attractive and another third were unceremoniously classified as physically unattractive. The third of the assistants who were of middling attractiveness were thanked for having volunteered, but told that their help was no longer needed and excused from the rest of the project.

The remaining attractive and unattractive assistants were given a script to learn and each was told to saunter up to four students on campus with a proposal that the university should stop serving meat at breakfast and lunch in all of their public cafeterias. After making the appeal, each assistant then asked the students they had approached to sign a petition demanding that the university stop serving meat.

Analysing the results, Chaiken found that the attractive undergraduates gathered significantly more signatures in favour of the petition. But it wasn't that men were won over by pretty female assistants or that women swooned over handsome male assistants. Female assistants were as effective with men and women; male assistants persuaded both women and men to sign the petition. So this wasn't a sexual attraction: physical attractiveness in all cases led to greater persuasion.[29] The brutal truth was that better-looking people are more persuasive irrespective of the gender of the people they're trying to win over.

I wonder if the now-retired Shelly Chaiken was a beauty herself. A 2006 analysis looked at the relationship between professors' looks and the evaluations they received from students on a popular website, www.ratemyprofessors.com. Across four separate universities, professors who were perceived to be attractive tended to receive student evaluations about 0.8 of a point higher on a 5-point scale than their less attractive counterparts.[30] That's a 16 per cent difference simply for having movie-star looks.

Going back to the study of non-verbal behaviour in job interviews, the researchers there also found that the sturdiest predictor of the interview ratings the manager-candidates got was their looks. Physically attractive manager-candidates gained better ratings than less good-looking ones.

In fact, study after study finds that physically attractive people genuinely have an advantage when it comes to influencing and persuading others. Attractive people are also seen as more competent, intelligent, and socially skilled than their less attractive counterparts.[31] As a result, economists tell us that attractive people tend to earn more too.[32]

The science doesn't tell us what's fair or right about the world; it only reports on what actually happens. But is physical attractiveness a quality that is fixed and totally immutable – something to do with our allotted genes and the accidents of our births – or can we change it?

Marc-André Reinhard, a social psychologist at the University of Mannheim in Germany, devised a cunning experiment to explore the effects of physical attractiveness on persuasion. He invited participants to watch one of four versions of a TV home-shopping infomercial in which a single presenter tried to sell the viewer a home computer. Two of the infomercials used an attractive presenter (a man in one version and a woman in the other). The other two used an unattractive presenter (again, a man in one infomercial and a woman in the other). In all four versions of the infomercial, the presenter made it clear that this wasn't a TV show that incidentally happened to be demonstrating a product, but a deliberate attempt to sell something to the viewer.

However, Reinhard manipulated the attractiveness of the presenter in a different way to Shelly Chaiken. Rather than choosing attractive versus unattractive presenters to host the programme, he used the same two actors and made them up to look either attractive or unattractive. So the female actor was made to look attractive by putting her in an elegant but not overtly sexy dress, giving her a fashionable hairstyle, and applying a subtle amount of make-up. The 'attractive' male actor wore a fashionable suit, had freshly washed and styled hair, and wore just enough make-up to give him a healthy skin tone under the TV studio lights. In the unattractive versions of the infomercial, the same actors wore ill-fitting clothes, no make-up, and had slightly messy hair.

The results showed that the attractive presenters were rated as much more persuasive than the unattractive presenters. Viewers not only had more favourable attitudes towards the home computer, but also said that they were more likely to buy it after having watched the infomercial with the well-dressed and well-groomed presenter rather than the slightly more dishevelled one. The effects were also present for both the male and female presenters, indicating that appearance matters as much for men as women.[33]

To me though, that represents good news. Attractiveness isn't something that is fixed, a quality that you've either got or haven't got. No matter what natural gifts we are born with, wearing a smart outfit and taking a couple of minutes to do our hair can pay off.

Beauty or beast?

The American retailer Abercrombie & Fitch has long recognised the sales opportunities to be had from having good-looking staff in their stores. Far from trying to hide the fact that they purposefully hire physically attractive sales associates, they even encourage 'store models' with particularly good looks and athletic bodies to parade around in skimpy outfits or even swimwear to lure gawking customers.[34]

Some people may find it outrageous and morally reprehensible, the idea of making ourselves look more physically attractive in order to improve our influence and persuasiveness. However, science doesn't make judgements about what is right or acceptable; it merely reports on what happens in the real world.

A study by Michael Lynn, an expert in consumer behaviour at the Cornell University School of Hotel Administration, found that restaurant waitresses who had bigger breasts received more generous tips from customers. The same study also found that waitresses who had blonde hair received bigger tips.[35] While the notion of physical attractiveness of course varies across cultures and countries, a financially motivated waitress in Western Europe or North America might take from this that they would benefit from investing in some padding and a bottle of peroxide.

Another study – also conducted in the US – balanced the sexism stakes by looking at characteristics associated with physical attractiveness in men. Men with facial hair were rated as less attractive than men with clean-shaven faces. In addition, men with bald heads were rated as less attractive than men with receding hairlines, who were in turn rated as less attractive than men with full heads of hair.[36] Perhaps Western European and North American men would do well to keep a plentiful supply of razors around and to consider toupees or hair loss medication when their hairlines start to migrate north.

It would be difficult to conclude with any certainty that any methods of dress or modifications to one's appearance guarantee beneficial effects to all people in all situations. For example, what is appropriate for a woman in her fifties in a major city in Japan is unlikely to be suitable for a woman in her thirties in rural Italy. What suits a 25-year-old man going on a first date may not be suitable for a 45-year-old man going for a job interview.

Before we leave the topic of our physical appearance, let me introduce you to the 'above-average effect' – a finding that most people are extremely unrealistic and overconfident when making judgements about themselves. For example, a survey of nearly a million high-school students in the US found that 70 per cent believed they had 'above average' leadership skills – a statistical impossibility. Only 2 per cent felt their leadership skills were 'below average'. Another study found that an even more deluded 94 per cent of university professors believed that they produced above-average work. Ironically, surveys also show that the vast majority of people think they are more likely to make accurate estimates about their own abilities than other people.[37] Perhaps most unnervingly of all, more than half a dozen studies have shown that doctors and surgeons who are the most confident about their abilities are often the least skilled.[38]

When it comes to judging our appearance, the likelihood is that many of us believe (wrongly) that we dress and style ourselves in above-average ways too. The vast majority of us probably think that we look good, that our hairstyles suit us and our clothes complement what we wish to say about ourselves. The same may even be true for our non-verbal communication and broader impact on others. We think we come across as enthusiastic or charming or confident or professional through the sound of our voice and our use of gestures and body language. But the research proves that *most* of us are likely to be wrong.

If you've ever encountered someone with bad breath or body odour, you can bet that they don't realise it; we never think that *we* could ever be at fault – but we could! Whatever the situations in which you want to look attractive, influential, and persuasive – whether it's in the boardroom or the bedroom – the smart bet is to get a second opinion (and maybe a third, a fourth, and even a few more after that) from someone you can trust to give you honest, no-holds-barred feedback.

Grinning and baring teeth

Dozens of other studies have used combinations of video and sound recordings, written transcripts and observations of people in the real world to investigate the relative impact that non-verbal communication has over and above the actual words we use. While most of these studies reveal findings that most of us would have guessed anyway, some studies do throw up unpredictable discoveries.

For example, people who smile are considered more attractive, sincere, sociable, and competent than those who don't smile.[39] No surprises so far. Having said that though, not all smiles are created equally.

Specifically, smiles that appear on the face too quickly (those taking around a tenth of a second to come into existence) are rated as less authentic and trustworthy than smiles that spread across the face more slowly (those taking around half a second to materialise). Usually without even consciously realising it, most people are remarkably attuned to the fact that rapid smiles are more likely to be fake than those that unfold more gradually.[40]

Size matters too. For example, a study written up in a 2006 issue of the *Academy of Management Journal* looked at the relationship between customer satisfaction and servers' smiles in a fast-food restaurant. Independent observers scrutinised interactions between customers and servers, rating the strength of the servers' smiles; a separate group of research assistants chased after customers immediately after they had been served to ask them how satisfied they had been with the encounter.

Analysis of several hundred such service encounters found that customer satisfaction was robustly related to the strength of a server's smile. Customers who received no smile were the least happy. Customers who received a minimal smile (defined as the corners of the mouth upturning but with no teeth showing) were a little happier. But the happiest customers of all tended to be those who received full smiles (defined as the corners of the mouth upturning to reveal some teeth).[41] Like I said: size of smile matters.

But social scientists Marianne LaFrance and Marvin Hecht demonstrated an additional and rather peculiar consequence of smiling that may point to the evolutionary origins and underlying purpose of smiling. In their study, they presented participants with a folder containing information about a fictional student, Christine Wilson, who was suspected of cheating on an exam.

The file included a summary of the circumstances surrounding the alleged incident: the evidence pointed strongly – but not conclusively – towards Christine's guilt. She was described as having looked over another person's shoulder, talking during an exam, and frequently changing her answers. The file also contained background information on the student including her prior academic performance and a colour photo (measuring 3 inches by 5 inches, or 7.6 centimetres by 12.7 centimetres) of her.

The participants in the study were asked to read the file and then decide not only the likelihood of Christine's guilt but also the actions that should be taken to deal with the matter. However, different participants were randomly assigned to receive one of four different photos. One photo showed Christine with a neutral, fully relaxed facial expression. The other three showed different types of smile. The first of these was a photo of a genuine, warm smile, in which the muscles of the mouth tip upwards and the eyes wrinkle with crow's feet. The second showed a miserable smile – the muscles of the mouth tip upwards but the eyes and eyebrows betray obvious signs of anxiety. The final photo showed a fake smile, in which the muscles of the mouth tip upwards but the muscles around the eyes are static. Imagine the kind of wide-eyed smile that the runners-up in a beauty pageant slap on their faces when the winner is announced.

Participants were equally likely to find Christine guilty, irrespective of the photos they had been shown. None of them were influenced by her different facial expressions in reaching an assessment about her culpability in the incident. However, participants who saw the photo with the neutral expression subjected Christine to greater punishments; participants who saw a smiling photo – irrespective of whether it was genuine, miserable, or outright insincere – tended towards greater leniency.[42]

The researchers go to pains to explain that smiles don't make people judge us as any less guilty or wrong then. However, smiles do get us off the hook. Why?

We mostly think of the smile as an expression that conveys happiness. When we gather a group of friends together for a photo, we ask them to smile. However, studies of non-human primates such as apes and chimpanzees suggest that the human smile may have evolved for utterly different reasons. When non-human primates play with each other and demonstrate what we would describe as happiness, they tend to have relaxed, open-mouthed expressions – an expression that human babies also display when playing with their mothers. In contrast, non-human primates pull back the corners of their mouths and show their teeth as a sign of appeasement rather than happiness; they seem to show their teeth to say, 'Don't attack me.'[43]

It suggests that the smile may have evolved more as a conciliatory signal, with our ancestors smiling to ingratiate themselves, showcase their submission, and pacify others. It's only in modern times that humans may have muddied the message behind a smile by wearing a grin when a full-blown laugh seems too extravagant or contrived. But the finding by LaFrance and Hecht that participants meted out less severe punishments to a smiling Christine suggests that, even today, a smile may say at some deeper, primal level: 'Please don't hurt me,' 'Please forgive me,' or 'Go easy on me, please.' Remember that participants did not find a smiling Christine any less guilty; they only treated her more leniently.

The research suggests how we might all behave the next time we're caught out for a transgression. The next time we're caught flirting with someone inappropriate, cutting corners at work, or telling a lie to get out of going to the mother-in-law's party, just *smile*. No matter how disingenuous or miserable or real, a smile may help us to get out of trouble.

The power of touch

You can probably spot market researchers on the street from a mile away. It's not only the clipboards and pens, but invariably the earnest smiles as they try to manoeuvre themselves into your line of sight in an attempt to draw you into completing their surveys.

Put yourself into the scenario that you're ambushed by one such researcher, a woman in her early twenties. She has a kind, round face and the giddy enthusiasm of a nursery-school teacher. She appears to be holding a bracelet made of polished copper in her left hand. She says: 'Sorry to disturb you. I am a student and my marketing teacher asked us to do a survey on jewellery. Will you agree to take a look at this bracelet and tell us what you think about it?'

You hesitate for a moment. You want to help but you have chores to do and people to see.

You're just about to apologise and move away. But then she reaches out with her right hand and touches your forearm for a second.

The touch is ever so light, a mere brush. And suddenly you decide you're not so busy.

That couldn't happen, could it? You wouldn't be so easily manipulated by the touch of a total stranger, would you?

Mounting evidence suggests that you wouldn't even notice the touch, at least not consciously. Just ask Nicolas Guéguen, a psychology professor at Université de Bretagne-Sud in France. An animated Frenchman with a dark crop and almost ink-black eyes, Guéguen has spent more than a decade investigating the effects of physical touch on behaviour and is widely considered a superstar in the field.

As the architect of this study ostensibly asking members of the public to evaluate a copper bracelet, he found that only 28 per cent of the people pounced upon by his market researchers noticed the fleeting physical contact when they were touched on the forearm. But the effect of the touch was astonishing. Guéguen instructed his market researchers to touch exactly half of the people they approached and to avoid all physical contact with the other half. While only 4 in 10 people agreed to take part in the survey when they weren't touched, the response rate nearly doubled, jumping to 7 in 10 people when they were touched lightly on the forearm.[44] And remember that this was merely a light touch on the forearm for the space of just a second or two.

A similar experiment by a pair of American academics presented people on the street with a lengthy survey packed with questions about deliberately provocative social issues such as politics, religion, euthanasia, abortion, and racial discrimination. Participants who were touched briefly on the arm on average completed 25 per cent more questions before quitting than participants who weren't touched on the arm.[45]

In study after study, Guéguen has uncovered the effects of brief physical touch on different types of request and in different scenarios – from cavernous shopping precincts to busy nightclubs and bars, and all with similar results. For example, he found that customers in a restaurant were more likely to order the suggested dish of the day when the waiter or waitress briefly touched them on the arm.[46] So touch would be a good way for a restaurant to boost its profits if the waiting staff suggested expensive dishes.

Perhaps most impressively though, in one of his studies Guéguen succeeded in rehabilitating customers' impressions of one of the modern world's most unloved professions by the use of momentary touch. Which profession? The fast-talking, truth-flexing second-hand car salesman.

Under Guéguen's tutelage, a second-hand car salesman made forays towards potential customers and either lightly touched them on the forearm for a second while showing them the car or spoke to them entirely without touching them. Ratings gathered immediately after each encounter confirmed that the salesman received significantly higher evaluations from customers when he brushed their forearms. Customers who were touched rated the salesman as more friendly, sincere, agreeable, and kind. They also tended to agree with the statement, 'I feel there will be little risk in negotiating with this seller.' And, in the best news for car salespeople everywhere, a brief touch also made customers more likely to agree with the rather chilling statement, 'This seller is someone that I could appreciate in my circle of friends.'[47]

Touching a person lightly on the arm – and only for the space of a couple of heartbeats – seems to be a devastatingly effective method of encouraging people to agree to many different types of request. And the gender of either the person making the request or the person being touched doesn't matter either. It's not just a case of men being manipulated by women they're attracted to or vice versa. Men are equally swayed by men and women by women too.

Why though?

Some experts have argued that touch is enjoyable and may put people in a better mood. After all, we hug people when we want to show affection for them and slap them on the backs when we congratulate them. So even the faintest, briefest physical contact may itself be pleasurable in some small way, making people more amenable to our requests.

Other social scientists suggest that touch may be another animalistic signal, in the same way that the human smile may have evolved from non-human primates' way of indicating the desire for appeasement. In this case though, touch may be a way of signalling status, of saying, 'I am more important, further up the hierarchy than you are,' or 'I am your superior; you are my underling,' with the implicit message that the person being touched should therefore do as the other person requests.[48]

Ultimately, we don't know for certain why touch helps to increase people's compliance with our requests. We just know that it works.

The humble handshake

As a corporate psychologist, I often get invited by organisations to train their managers in interviewing skills, in the art of asking probing questions to separate strong candidates from their weaker counterparts, from the candidates who may be exaggerating or outright lying about their skills and experience.[49] I remember tutoring a group of managers at a prestigious law firm. One of the managers was more than a little sceptical about the need for training and said that he could always tell how good an interviewee would be simply by shaking hands with them.

I cautioned him against making such snap decisions. Why bother to interview a candidate for close to an hour if you're going to make your mind up within mere seconds? Why not simply line up the prospective employees, shake hands with them all, and then hire the one with the best handshake?

However, his comment did make me think. Most of us – certainly those in Western cultures – are very used to shaking hands with the people we meet, whether at business meetings, social events, or even parent-teacher evenings. Clearly a firm handshake mattered to that lawyer. But what does scientific evidence tell us more generally about handshakes – how much does a good handshake really matter?

Surprisingly, the question was only properly examined a few years ago in 2008. Led by Greg Stewart, a professor of organisational behaviour at the University of Iowa, a crew of intellectually adventurous scholars asked nearly a hundred students to take part in mock interviews with real interviewers from local businesses. To motivate the students to take the interviews seriously and try their hardest to shine, Stewart and his team told the students that past participants had occasionally obtained real interviews and even actual jobs as a result of the mock interviews.

Each participant attended a one-hour interview but was introduced to six people. One main interviewer managed the whole interview, asking questions and rating the participant's overall suitability for the job. The other five people joined the interview – ostensibly other managers who were popping in to say hello – staying long enough only to be introduced and shake hands. Their role was solely to rate the participants on the characteristics of their handshake.

Stewart and his crew crunched the numbers for the many dozens of interviews and discovered that *five* separate characteristics of a handshake helped certain participants to gain better interview evaluations, irrespective of what they actually said during the interview.[50] These five handshake qualities were:

- **Completeness of the handshake.** Participants who pushed the webbed part of their hands (the piece of skin between the thumb and index finger) against the same part of the interviewer's hand got significantly better ratings than participants who merely clasped or touched the fingers of the interviewer's hand.
- **Strength of the handshake.** The stronger the squeeze during the handshake, the stronger the judgements about the participant.
- **Duration of the handshake.** Participants who shook hands for a few seconds were rated more highly than participants who held the handshake for only a brief moment.
- **Vigour of the handshake.** Participants who pumped their hands a couple of times gained higher interview evaluations than participants who shook hands less energetically.
- **Eye contact during the handshake.** Participants who held the gaze of the interviewer were rated more highly than those who glanced away.

So it *does* help to have a sturdy handshake. But a good handshake isn't simply about gripping the other person's hand in a bone-crushing fashion; Stewart's research advises that multiple, separate characteristics contribute to the perception of a good handshake. No matter what our qualifications or experience, we can exercise influence over interviewers and boost our odds of receiving a favourable evaluation simply by focusing on our handshakes and getting them right. First impressions matter. Perhaps we would all be wise to apply Stewart's recommendations the next time we meet an interviewer or a potential customer, a new colleague or even someone at a party.

It's not what you say (again)

Going into hospital for a major operation is possibly one of the most daunting experiences a person may ever have. So contemplate how you'd feel if you went under the surgeon's knife – say to fix a knee injury or replace a worn-out hip. You're lying on a hospital gurney being wheeled into an operating room. You haven't eaten anything or even been allowed a sip of water in advance of the anaesthetic so you're hungry and thirsty as well as apprehensive. Your body is shaved and scrubbed with antiseptic and you can hear the surgeon barking orders at a bevy of nurses. But that's the easy bit.

Now imagine that you wake up to be told that there were dreadful complications. The procedure went wrong. Perhaps you're left with unusually ugly scarring, difficulty breathing, pain when you move, or even permanent loss of mobility. You'd be right to feel scared and angry. You may even decide to sue the surgeon who left you this way.

The psychologist Nalini Ambady (whom we first encountered towards the start of this chapter) was interested in the link between surgeons' conversational styles and patients' evaluations of them. In particular, she wanted to know: to what extent did a doctor's bedside manner dictate their likelihood of being sued for medical malpractice?

She painstakingly collected audio recordings of over a hundred consultations between surgeons and their patients in the run-up to surgery. Half of the surgeons had been sued for medical malpractice at least twice; the other half had never been sued.

She edited out the patients' voices and cut together a 40-second clip of each surgeon speaking. Then she made the recordings unintelligible by subjecting them to a process known as 'content-filtering' – removing the high-frequency sounds that allow us to identify individual words. Imagine being in a cheap hotel and over-hearing a conversation in the adjoining room. Through the wall, you can still pick out the pitch, speed, and intonation of the speaker. You can make out if someone is shouting or gabbling quickly, or if a speaker is talking slowly and calmly, just not the words themselves.

Ambady then played each of the audio clips to a panel of judges, asking them to rate the surgeons on the extent to which they sounded warm, genuine, dominant, and other characteristics. She didn't tell her judges which surgeons had been sued and which hadn't. However, she found that the judges could predict which surgeons got sued and which ones didn't, just by listening to how the messages were delivered.[51]

Bear in mind that the judges only had this 40-second record-ing of how the surgeons sounded. They weren't given any additional information about the skill or experience of the surgeons, the awards they'd received, or even the training they'd been given. They didn't know if the person they were listening to was a highly acclaimed surgeon who had graduated in the top 5 per cent of their class at a prestigious medical school or merely a middle-of-the-road surgeon from a backwater training hospital.

Ambady's research demonstrated that a surgeon who botched an operation could still avoid being sued for malpractice if he or she had treated the patient with empathy and concern during the initial consultation. It was only surgeons who made a mess of an operation *and* who had talked to the patient in perhaps bossy or seemingly uncaring tones who tended to get sued.

Ambady's findings may be of particular interest to all manner of experts and consultants – ranging from lawyers and accountants to perhaps even plumbers and decorators. *How* a message is delivered may be as important as *what* is said.

I learned that lesson the hard way. I once had a job in telephone sales. It was in the summer between my first and second years at university and I had just turned 19. The sales trainer explained that we had to cold-call people at home to explain that we had an 'amazing' offer: in return for agreeing to attend a sales presentation about holiday homes, they could take home an electronic clock-radio! Unfortunately, I wasn't terribly good at the job. I kept calling people only to be told that they weren't interested, that my call was unwanted, or that I should stick my offer where the sun doesn't shine. The rejection was soul-destroying and I hated it. Despite the fact that everyone doing the job was given a script to work from, some people were much better than others. At the time, I didn't understand that the words I was saying weren't enough on their own to be convincing – that the misery I was feeling was probably very audible in my voice. At the end of my first day, I left the office and never went back.

A few people aren't merely good, but extraordinary at enticing people at home to give up their time. For an example, let me transport you to the Survey Research Center at the University of Michigan – it's a modern building with an unprepossessing exterior of glass and beige stone. Within its walls, a team of several hundred employees works from early in the morning until late at night, calling homeowners and businesses, gathering data for scientific surveys on topics spanning family planning, substance abuse, economic policy, and consumer attitudes. As you can imagine, the highly trained team makes a lot of calls every year. However, researcher Lois Oksenberg and her colleagues noticed that some of the outbound-calling tele-phone interviewers had success rates of up to 94 per cent while others had success rates of barely over 50 per cent.

All of the interviewers followed the same script. So success or failure was nothing to do with what they said, but how they said it. Oksenberg decided to delve into the secrets of becoming a persua-sive telephone interviewer by asking a panel of judges to rate tele-phone callers on different criteria. By comparing successful versus less successful callers, she found a pattern: successful callers had higher-pitched voices and greater ranges of variation in pitch (as opposed to more monotonous voices), which helped them to sound more enthusiastic. They also spoke more loudly, more quickly, and articulated their words more clearly.[52]

Nothing in that description is exactly staggering. If someone calls you up who speaks in a monotonous, barely audible voice, why would you want to listen to them? But the studies by Nalini Ambady of surgeons' speech and Lois Oksenberg of call-centre workers together illustrate a more important point: no one particular way of speaking is the best to appeal to people across *all* situations.

I've read some well-intentioned but ill-informed experts advising that we should speak quickly, loudly, and brightly to be persuasive. Others have recommended speaking in a more languid fashion, choos-ing our words and articulating them slowly and with great care. But the research says neither approach is right. Indeed, no single manner is likely to be uniformly effective. What works when you're a surgeon offering advice on a tricky operation isn't appropriate when you're a market researcher calling people at home to ask their opinions on some new product or service. The tone of voice that works when you're soliciting donations for charity on a street pavement or in a shopping mall probably differs from the manner you'd need to persuade a bank manager to lend you the money to start a new business.

I wish I could offer easy, one-size-fits-all advice on how to use our voice, intonation, and pacing to become a master of persuasion. But I can't. Perhaps the major lesson from the research is to be wary of gurus and advisers who tell us that we should always speak a certain way if we want to be effective; we must tailor how we use our voices to the different situations we encounter.

Monkey see, monkey do

To explore one of the most potent methods of interpersonal influence that researchers have identified, consider for a moment that you're in a fine French restaurant. It's a lovely evening and you're seated at a charming table with suitably dimmed lights and reproductions of French masterpieces on the walls. As you glance through the menu, you remember from the work of French psychologist Nicolas Guéguen and his colleagues that you would be sensible to avoid letting the waiter or waitress touch you on the arm. Even a brief touch may charm you into ordering a more expensive dish than you had intended.

Eventually you decide on the meal that you'd like. Perhaps you have a hankering for a juicy steak while your dining companion wants the coq au vin with creamy dauphinoise potatoes. Your waitress repeats the order back and departs. So far so good. You haven't been manipulated by your waitress. Or have you?

A team of social psychologists at the University of Nijmegen in the Netherlands (since renamed Radboud University Nijmegen) wanted to understand the effects of mimicry on customer behaviour. Led by Rick van Baaren, a handsome, rangy professor who looks more like a former professional athlete than a university lecturer, the team asked a waitress in a local restaurant to take customers' orders in one of two ways. For half of her customers, the waitress was instructed to repeat back exactly what the customers had ordered. If a customer said, 'I'll have the chicken with a side salad,' she responded by saying, 'Chicken with a side salad.' For the other half of her customers, she communicated that she had understood the order by saying something along the lines of 'Okay,' or 'Coming up!'

Van Baaren spotted that not every table of customers left a tip. But when he compared the proportion of customers who'd been mimicked versus those who hadn't, he observed a crucial difference. Customers were 33 per cent more likely to leave a tip when the waitress repeated customers' orders using exactly the same words that they had chosen. In addition, the tips she received were significantly more generous when she aped their orders.[53]

Why should repeating an order verbatim influence customers to tip more frequently and leave more money? Again, the answers may lie in anthropological research pointing to the evolutionary purpose of the non-verbal signals we give off.

Scholars have long noticed that people tend to adopt the postures, gestures, and mannerisms, and even accents of the people they're interacting with. In the first of two studies written up in the prestigious journal *Psychological Science*, behavioural scientists Jessica Lakin and Tanya Chartrand introduced experimental subjects one at a time to a stranger and tasked the subjects with the goal of building a rapport with the newcomer. After watching dozens of interactions, the researchers spotted a pattern: the subjects were naturally mimicking the body language of the new arrival. However, interviews with the subjects afterwards confirmed that they hadn't been conscious of their mimicry. In an attempt to engineer a bond, the subjects had instinctively gravitated towards the same bodily movements. Without realising it, they had turned themselves into mirrors, copying the gestures and postures of the other person.

In the second of their pair of studies, Lakin and Chartrand asked a different group of subjects to work with a research assistant on a task in which they took turns describing what they saw in various photographs. The research assistant mirrored the posture and mannerisms of half of the subjects and did not with the other half. Afterwards, subjects who had been subtly copied reported liking the assistant more; they also thought the task had gone more smoothly than those who had not been mimicked.[54]

Taking the two studies together, the picture seems to be that the relationship between mimicry and rapport goes both ways. We automatically copy others' body language when we want to cosy up to them. At the same time, we tend to warm to people who are imitating us.

The tendency to mimic people – some researchers call it a 'chameleon effect' – seems to be hard-wired into our neural circuitry. Even one-month-old infants smile, stick out their tongues, and open their mouths in imitation when they see someone else doing the same, which suggests that we do it naturally. We are likely to be born with the gift rather than learning it as we grow up.

The chameleon effect is so strong and deeply embedded in our behavioural repertoire that many anthropologists and social scientists believe that it evolved as a shortcut to help our ancestors to bond with each other. Back in the tooth-and-nail days of our distant prehistory, individuals who lived in groups or tribes probably benefited significantly from sharing resources. They had a much better chance of surviving and passing on their genes than those who struck out on their own. So the tendency to adopt the mannerisms and postures of others may have served the purpose of saying, 'Hey, I'm like you – I'm practically family so let's work together and support each other.'[55] In other words, the social dance that is mimicry may have provided an evolutionary advantage to those who knew its steps.

Going back to the waitress in the study conducted by Rick van Baaren, she probably gained both more frequent and bigger tips when she repeated back customers' orders because of this chameleon effect. By making a conscious effort to echo diners' orders, she triggered something almost arcane within their brains, causing them to feel more attuned to her. Without realising why, they bonded with her a little more, liked her, and couldn't help but behave more generously towards her.

The subtleties of mimicry

When it comes to becoming more persuasive, there are a lot of different non-verbal signals we could think about: how we use our hands and legs, whether we should lean forwards or back, how we should hold or tilt our heads, and so on. However, a simpler way of enhancing our influence may simply be to copy the mannerisms of other people.

In a paper published in 2008, a team led by William Maddux at the INSEAD business school in France asked pairs of MBA students to prepare for a complex negotiation exercise as part of their coursework. Half of the class were asked to take on the role of the owner of a petrol station, looking to sell it on. The other half were assigned to the role of a buyer, looking to buy the station as cheaply as possible.

The students were given a week to get ready for the negotiation by working through a file of instructions and information about the scenario; in addition, they were told to prepare a planning document, laying out their individual strategies. On the day of the negotiation itself, the students were told that they would have 30 minutes to complete their discussions.

Immediately before the negotiation began, the academics split the students who had been assigned the role of buyers into two groups, giving them five minutes to read one of two different paragraphs. One group was given instructions to mimic their opponents:

Successful negotiators recommend that you should mimic the mannerisms of your negotiation partner to get a better deal. For example, when the other person rubs his/her face, you should too. If he/she leans back or leans forward in the chair, you should too. However, they say it is very important that you mimic subtly enough that the other person does not notice what you are doing, otherwise this technique completely backfires. Also, do not direct too much of your attention to the mimicking so you don't lose focus on the outcome of the negotiation. Thus, you should find a happy medium of consistent but subtle mimicking that does not disrupt your focus.

The other student-buyers acted as a control group, receiving a message that just reiterated the importance of the planning document they had spent the week preparing:

Many successful negotiators recommend focusing on the information in your planning document, and to negotiate with this always in the back of your mind. They say that this will help get you through the negotiations and get a good deal.

The researchers had predicted that mirroring would create a greater rapport between the two parties and encourage them to reach an agreement more easily, yet the results threw up a phenomenal finding. Only 13 per cent of the control group buyers managed to reach a deal with the sellers of the petrol station. Yet a massive 67 per cent of the mimicking buyers reached a deal.

In a second study written up in the same paper, the researchers asked a different group of students to take the roles of either a boss looking to hire an employee or the employee looking to get the best pay package out of the boss. Again, the students were given a week to prepare and half of the students were given specific instructions to mirror the behaviour of their opponents. In this easier negotiation scenario, the experimenters expected that most of the students would come to a deal. However, the researchers wanted to assess the quality of the deals that they reached by scoring their performances on a number of objective criteria.

As you might expect by now, the students who had been told to mimic scored significantly more points than those who had been given the control instructions. However, the researchers were intrigued to find that the people who had been mimicked also achieved more of their objectives and scored more points. So it's not that the person doing the mimicking achieves more by taking away from the party being copied. No, the researchers concluded rather adamantly that 'chameleons bake bigger pies and take bigger pieces'.[56] Mimicry doesn't just avoid harming the party being mimicked; it actually helps *both* parties to get more out of the discussion. Putting it another way, if Christina mimics Lee, both Christina *and* Lee come away from the discussion better off than if Christina had not mimicked Lee. Everybody wins.

To put the result in context, remember that these were driven, competitive MBA students. They had spent a whole week preparing for the negotiation. Yet reading an instruction to mimic their partners – a paragraph of barely over a hundred words that took a mere five minutes to digest – helped them to derive a better outcome not just for themselves but also for their opponents.

CHAPTER THREE
the power of words and labels

*'For me, words are a form of action,
capable of influencing change.'*
Ingrid Bengis

Cast your mind back to your school or university days, those days when you sat behind a desk and listened to someone droning on and on at you. Irrespective of whether your days of learning were mere months or distant decades ago, you can probably bring to mind the best and worst teachers you had. Do it now and you may see yourself back in the class. I'm sure you can picture how those educators looked and maybe even sounded too. You probably liked some of your teachers but were ambivalent about others. Hopefully there were a few that inspired you and not too many that you actively disliked. But did you formulate those judgements based entirely on the evidence of your own eyes and ears? Or did you rely on comments and rumours, on the hearsay of others?

The students of one particular economics class at the Massachusetts Institute of Technology had just sat down when a university official burst into the room with news, breathlessly announcing that the professor who usually taught the introductory Economics 70 class would not be able to give the lecture today. Apologising, he explained that a stand-in instructor would be filling in for the day. There was a minor wrinkle though: the economics department was interested in how students reacted to new instructors so would be asking the students to complete an evaluation form on the lecturer. But first, to give the class a little background on the instructor, the students were given a brief biography about him.

Of course, this was an experiment so half of the students received one biography and the other half received a slightly different one. Can you spot the difference?

Here's the first biography:

> *Mr Long is a graduate student in the Department of Economics and Social Science here at MIT. He has had three semesters of teaching experience in psychology at another college. This is his first semester teaching Ec 70. He is 26 years old, a veteran, and married. People who know him consider him to be a very warm person, industrious, critical, practical, and determined.*

And here's the second, slightly different version:

> *Mr Long is a graduate student in the Department of Economics and Social Science here at MIT. He has had three semesters of teaching experience in psychology at another college. This is his first semester teaching Ec 70. He is 26 years old, a veteran, and married. People who know him consider him to be a rather cold person, industrious, critical, practical, and determined.*

The substitute instructor then appeared and led a 20-minute discussion on topics that the class had already covered. Now, only two words differed in the pair of biographies.* How did it affect students' evaluations of the teacher?

The differences were striking. Students in the group that had been told that the instructor was warm gave him more favourable

---

* I'm sure you spotted it, but the only difference between the two paragraphs lies in the final sentence. The first version describes the instructor as 'very warm' while the second describes him as 'rather cold'.

ratings on a variety of personality dimensions than the students who had been told he was cold. The 'warm' students also described the instructor as 'good-natured, humane, considerate of others, sociable, popular and humorous'. The students who had been led to believe the instructor was cold were damning in their criticism, saying that he was 'ruthless, unsociable, unpopular, irritable, humourless, and self-centred'. What's more, while nearly two-thirds of the 'warm' students actively participated in the class by answering questions and engaging in the class discussion, less than one-third of the 'cold' students made any contribution.[57]

Had the two groups attended the same class? Well, yes and no. Yes, they had been physically present during the same event. But no, they had experienced the class in extraordinarily different ways. Despite the fact that both groups had attended the same 20-minute discussion, the change of a mere two words was enough to alter their perceptions dramatically.

Even small differences in the words we use can matter enormously. In Chapter Two: Secret Signals, we explored the importance of the non-verbal messages we broadcast all the time. In many instances, it doesn't matter what we say: how we appear, the amount of eye contact we make, and how we sound is enough for people to make judgements about us. But in this chapter, we'll discuss how seemingly inconsequential modifications in the words we use can influence not only how other people see the world, but also whether they're likely to do as we suggest or spurn our requests.

The effects of expectations on experience

The effects of labelling the MIT professor as either 'warm' or 'cold' illustrate the importance of choosing our words precisely when we describe people. Whether chosen carefully or carelessly, our words could easily influence many of the encounters of the people we know.

Suppose you introduce your friend Jessica to a mutual acquaintance, Daniel. Warn Jessica beforehand that Daniel can be 'rather stupid' in his comments and she is likely to go into the encounter looking for evidence to confirm that view. Even if Daniel demonstrates his intelligence with a raft of smart observations, Jessica may unconsciously ignore them. If Daniel cracks a sexist joke, Jessica may latch onto it – again, quite unwittingly – and come away agreeing that he is, sadly, not the brightest person she has ever met.

On the other hand, tell Jessica that Daniel is 'articulate and intelligent' and she may interpret the same joke as knowing and ironic rather than crass and unsophisticated. The expectation that he will be clever is likely to shield her from noticing any comments he makes that may genuinely be insensitive or poorly judged.

That may sound like a hypothetical example, but I see it happening all the time. I mentioned in Chapter Two that I often train managers within organisations of all sizes in how to interview candidates more effectively. When I've had the opportunity to observe managers interviewing candidates *before* having been trained, I often see that they succumb to these same effects, which we might call self-fulfilling prophecies.

At one international investment bank, for example, I spotted that managers tended to ask easier questions of candidates who had come from top universities such as Oxford, Cambridge, Harvard, and Yale. Asking easier questions meant that candidates tended to perform better and were therefore more likely to get offered a job, confirming the expectation that those few institutions always turned out stronger graduates. When managers encountered the occasional candidate who had attended universities that they deemed inferior, they asked trickier questions, gave candidates less time to answer, and scored them more harshly. Given such punishing treatment, candidates from the less prestigious institutions hardly ever got offered jobs, which 'proved' to the managers that those candidates should never have been invited to attend an interview in the first place.

When I shared my observation with the managers, they denied it, of course. Thankfully I also recorded all of the interviews and was able to show them their unwitting behaviour. And now all interviewers work from an agreed list of questions to ensure that candidates are treated in an equally thorough yet fair fashion regardless of their education.

Experimental research has demonstrated the same effect too. Princeton University researchers John Darley and Paget Gross wanted to understand the effects that labels about kids at primary school could have on the treatment they received from their teachers. The pair of academics asked undergraduate students to take part in a research study in which they would watch video footage of a nine-year-old girl with a view to evaluating her academic performance and future prospects. First though, the students were shown a six-minute clip about little Hannah's home life. Being an experiment on the effects of different expectations on the judgements that the students would make, there were of course two versions of the six-minute clip.

Half of the students saw Hannah playing in a tree-lined playground with playing fields nearby next to a newly built and modern school building. She lived in a suburban neighbourhood of five- and six-bedroom homes set in pretty, landscaped grounds. Both of her parents had attended university: her father was a lawyer and her mother was a freelance writer. Everything about the video clip implied that Hannah was from a comfortable if not prosperous background.

The other half of the students watched a very different portrayal of Hannah's home life. They saw her playing in a bleak, fenced-in school yard next to a stark three-storey brick school. She was shown living in a modest house set on a rather grim, urban street of run-down homes. The students learned that neither of her parents had attended university: her father worked as a meat packer and her mother worked as a seamstress. This version of Hannah clearly came from the other side of the tracks.

After watching one of the videos of Hannah's life and upbringing, all of the students inspected a 12-minute video of Hannah being interviewed and answering questions testing her arithmetic, reading, and knowledge of science and social science. All of the students watched the same footage of Hannah's actual academic performance. However, they couldn't help but be influenced in their judgements about her ability. The students who thought that Hannah had come from a privileged background rated her as significantly more motivated, sociable, mature, and cognitively able than the students who thought she was poor.[58]

Despite the fact that the students had expressly been asked to judge Hannah on what they saw of her academic ability, they ended up being distracted by what they thought they knew about her home life. The implications for children in schools are frightening: if a teacher thinks a child comes from a poorer background, the teacher may inadvertently give the child less support, attention, and perhaps even less demanding homework. Ultimately, the teacher's expectations may create a self-fulfilling prophecy that could cripple the child's fortunes.

Consider the ramifications away from the classroom too. Paint the right picture for *anyone* and they may see what you wish for them to see. People in all sorts of situations have a tendency to find what they're looking for. When they have an expectation that the world will be a particular way, their brains may selectively attend to what's going on around them; they tend to stop looking for contrary evidence. The good news though is that you can use this 'cognitive confirmation effect' to exercise influence over people's expectations and behaviour in positive ways.

Helping people to perceive the world positively

Related studies show that people could be encouraged to work harder or collaborate more simply by being presented with the right words. In one investigation, subjects who completed a word-search puzzle that included words such as 'win', 'strive', and 'attain' went on to do better on a subsequent intelligence test than subjects who saw neutral words such as 'carpet' or 'shampoo'. Clearly, they didn't become more intelligent; however, they seemed to put more effort into the test when they had been primed with the achievement-oriented words. Similarly, subjects in another study who were presented with words such as 'friendly', 'support', and 'dependable' were more cooperative in a subsequent team game than subjects who were shown a list of neutral words. They didn't even have to be consciously aware of the effect for the words to influence their performance.[59]

Suppose a colleague is about to embark on a project widely acknowledged by everyone in the office to be demanding. If you say that it will be 'difficult', he may find it challenging in all sorts of unpleasant ways. But hey, tell the same colleague that the project could be 'challenging yet rewarding' and you may help him to find evidence to prove that it is indeed worthwhile.

Or imagine that one of your teenage children has to prepare for a French test. You offer to help her learn the required verbs and vocabulary. Say that it is 'important and essential' and you may turn it into a necessary chore. On the other hand, explain that it could be 'exciting and fun' to spend some time together and you may help to make it more enjoyable – or at least slightly less laborious.

Of course, people aren't stupid. Even the most carefully chosen words won't be able to convince someone that black is white or that a horrendous task will be pleasant. But the words we use may be of particular importance when the outcome of an encounter or situation may be ambiguous. How could you next influence the perceptions of someone in your life?

The persuasive power of words

At the start of the chapter, we came across the MIT economics students who thought they were being taught by either a 'warm' or 'cold' professor. The study demonstrates that the words we choose can create a self-fulfilling prophecy in the minds of other people. By choosing the right words, we can help other people to have positive experiences. Or, by changing the language we use only slightly, we can potentially wreak havoc.

That in itself is a dramatic discovery. I'm sure your mind is already spinning with the possibilities of how you can influence people's perceptions of the encounters and experiences they go on to have. But there's more to come. The words we choose may not just affect the experiences we *will* have, they may also affect our memories of the experiences we've *already* had.

When I was 20 years old, I was involved in a car accident. In the summer between my second and third years at university, I had a job as a data entry clerk at an air freight company at Birmingham airport.* I was running late one sweltering Thursday morning in late August. As temporary workers, we earned an hourly rate and, if we were late by more than five minutes, our bosses deducted a half-hour's pay from our wages, which at the time was a huge incentive to rush and try to get there on time.

Driving my mother's car, a white Mazda 323i, I found a parking space on the fourth floor of the multi-storey car park and guided the car head-first into the space. As I got out of the car though, I noticed that it was sliding backwards on the gently inclined surface. In my rush to get to the office, I'd forgotten to put on the handbrake.

Any sensible person would have unlocked the car door and put the handbrake on to stop the car's backward glide. But not me. In a panic, I jumped in the car, put the keys in the ignition, and slammed my foot on the accelerator to get it moving forward.

Unfortunately, the Mazda 323i was a sporty car that accelerated away from a standstill rather promptly, thanks to its fuel injection engine. My car lurched forward, crushing the flimsy internal barrier that separated the fourth floor from the third floor. The windscreen burst in a shower of glass and I closed my eyes as the tiny fragments of glass fell over me.

When I opened my eyes, I saw that I was suspended in mid-air. Driving off the fourth storey, my fall had been halted by a Volvo. The Volvo was crushed, totally devastated. Yet I was fine – there wasn't a scratch on me. I even reached over to the passenger seat to pick up the Tupperware box containing my sandwich lunch.

Or at any rate that's how I remember it and how I've told it to friends over the years. But is that what actually happened? If I had

---

* I really enjoyed that job and even wrote about it in one of my previous books, *The Extra One Per Cent: How small changes make exceptional people* (Macmillan).

been required to testify about the accident in court – perhaps by the understandably furious owner of the crushed Volvo – would my recollections have been correct?

Psychologist Elizabeth Loftus was named as one of the hundred most eminent psychologists of the twentieth century and was the highest-ranked woman on the list.[60] Her work on eyewitness testimony has rightly earned her accolades the world over. In a seminal study conducted with her colleague John Palmer at the University of Washington, Loftus showed short film clips of minor traffic accidents to a group of experimental subjects. Immediately after watching each film, the subjects completed a questionnaire asking them to 'give an account of the accident as you have just seen'. The questionnaire also asked the subjects to answer a series of specific questions.

The question that most interested the researchers asked the subjects to judge the speed at which the cars had been moving. While one group on average thought that the car was moving at 31.8 miles per hour, another group thought that the car was moving nearly 30 per cent faster at 40.8 miles per hour. Why?

Loftus and her colleague had actually asked subtly different questions of the different groups. The first group had been asked, 'About how fast were the cars going when they contacted each other?' The group that thought that cars had collided at the higher speed had been asked, 'About how fast were the cars going when they smashed each other?' Changing just one word had modified people's recollections of the event. Clearly, the word 'smashed' is much more suggestive of a high-speed collision than 'contacted'.

But in a second study, Loftus and Palmer discovered a perhaps more chilling effect. They invited a hundred students to watch a one-minute film of a car accident. Immediately afterwards, the subjects were again asked to describe the accident in their own words and to complete a series of questions.

Half of the students were asked, 'About how fast were the cars going when they smashed into each other?' The other half were asked, 'About how fast were the cars going when they hit each other?' Again, the students who heard the word 'smashed' said that the car seemed to be going at a higher speed than the students who heard 'hit'.

It was only later that the full effect of the change in wording was revealed though. A week after having seen the footage of the accident, the students were brought back to answer 10 further questions about the incident. One of the questions asked, 'Did you see any broken glass?' Of the students who had been asked about the speed at which the cars had 'smashed' into each other, 32 per cent responded that yes, they had indeed seen broken glass. In contrast, only 14 per cent of the students who had been asked about the speed of the cars when they 'hit' each other remembered seeing glass.

The only problem was: there had been no broken glass at all in the original video clip.[61] Rather chillingly, the more evocative word 'smashed' persuaded nearly three times as many students that they had seen something that actually never happened. By changing only a single word in a seemingly innocuous question, the researchers had managed to implant a false memory in triple the number of students.

Remember that the question was just posed on paper too. Consider the result the researchers might have got if they had asked the questions in person. Appreciating that body language and tone of voice can affect people's judgement, imagine if Elizabeth Loftus had asked with wide eyes and in a breathless, excited tone, 'About how fast were the cars going when they *smashed* into each other?' while smacking one fist into the palm of her other hand. Who knows? Subjects may even have been cajoled into believing they had seen blood and broken limbs.

Of course lawyers have long appreciated the supremacy of words. For good reason, lawyers are forbidden from 'leading the witness' by asking deliberately provocative questions. But thinking about my own car accident, did it really transpire the way I remember it? Or have the questions I've been asked and the words I've used in repeated retellings of the story blurred the memories? Perhaps the recollections that I have of the incident are no longer a true representation of what actually happened – I honestly can't say. The point is that the words we choose and the questions we ask can influence *other* people in situations outside of the courtroom too.

Say it and they will become it

A young woman is standing at a street intersection in a small French town. Dressed in a long dark overcoat but with a brilliant turquoise silk scarf wrapped loosely around her shoulders, she looks out of place. She turns her head from left to right and back again while her eyes dart even more frantically in search of … what? She swivels around several times. Her brow is furrowed and everyone in the vicinity can see that she's lost.

With increasing frustration, she finally musters up the courage to ask a passer-by, a middle-aged man, for help: 'Excuse me, sir, would you tell me the way … I'm looking for the cathedral.'

Given that just about everyone who lives in the town knows where the cathedral is, the man happily gives her directions. The youthful woman offers up two words of thanks and walks briskly in the direction of the cathedral, but as she leaves, her scarf flutters to the ground.

Will the man who helped her also pick up the scarf?

Well, the answer depends on exactly which two words the young woman used to thank her helper.

Of course this is another psychological experiment, this time dreamed up by Valérie Fointiat, a researcher in human behaviour at Université de Provence in France. When Fointiat's research assistant thanked passers-by with the words 'that's clear', 75 per cent of the people she approached for assistance chased after her with her dropped scarf. That suggests that around 1 in 4 people weren't bothered that the lost scarf would cause some anguish to the woman they had just helped. However, when she thanked passers-by with the words 'you're helpful', 90 per cent picked up the scarf and handed it back to her.[62]

Why should this be?

Fointiat explains that saying to someone 'that's clear' suggests that the person's action was helpful on that one occasion. However, saying 'you're helpful' is making a broader statement about the personality of that person; the label implies that the person is *generally* helpful as opposed to being of assistance only that once.

Why could *saying* that a person is helpful actually persuade them to become more helpful?

Consistent with the other studies we've already encountered on the power of words and labels, it seems that the research assistant's words moulded – at least for a few moments – how passers-by saw themselves. In particular though, the study highlights a phenomenon that psychologists have long observed about people's behaviour. People generally like to behave consistently.

Most of the time, consistency is seen as a positive trait. Think about synonyms for the word 'inconsistent': capricious, changeable, fickle, illogical, unstable, temperamental, erratic, flaky, unpredictable – the list goes on and none of it is great. We get frustrated when people change their minds back and forth. Someone who behaves inconsistently may even be criticised for being two-faced. On the other hand, a person who behaves consistently is seen as standing firm in the face of pressure, stable, rational, and even honest.[63]

So when we apply a label to someone else – even though it's a label they have not asked for or even consciously endorse – they become more likely to *be* that way. Tell people that they are 'helpful,' 'generous,' or 'kind' and they may go on to behave as if they really are.

Avoiding the downside of words

The criticisms and negative words we use may also have their own power – and not in a constructive fashion.

Say you have a friend or family member who is overweight. Calling him 'fat' – even in a jokey fashion – isn't going to make him lose weight. The research suggests it will simply encourage him to think of himself as fat. In order to remain consistent with this unwanted label, his brain at some primal level may be wondering: what do fat people do? Answer: they overeat and don't take any exercise. So your label may actually encourage more undesirable behaviour.

Or suppose you're a tenant and don't like the way you're being treated by your landlord. Complaining and telling her that you find her an 'angry and obstructive' person may help you to vent your feelings and make you feel good for a few moments. But your words may be more damaging than you intended. You may encourage her to think of herself as someone who is angry and uncooperative (at least to you). Before you know it, she may be losing her temper more and helping you even less.

A better alternative may be to choose words that motivate. To help an overweight loved one lose weight, you might say, 'You used to be so fit and healthy. You're just in a temporary slump and I know you can become that athletic person again.' With your landlord, you might be better off referring to the episode as a one-off rather than an example of a permanent personality flaw: 'I usually think of you as such a calm and considerate person, so I hope we can put this little incident behind us and work together again.' By using 'calm and considerate', you may invoke the principle of consistency to encourage your landlord to follow suit.

Emerging evidence by Dutch researchers suggests that we may not even need to apply a label to others to shape their thoughts and guide their behaviour. Simply getting them to think about the traits and behaviours associated with a particular label may have its own peculiar effects.

Behavioural change specialist Ap Dijksterhuis and his colleague Ad van Knippenberg at Radboud University Nijmegen in the Netherlands were inspired to investigate ways of influencing people's performance in a test of general knowledge. Their quest: to discover whether labels could boost people's performance.

They began by recruiting participants in their experiment to work their way through a multiple-choice quiz. Here are three examples of the questions they used. If you want to play along, I've put the correct answers in the notes at the end of the book. I have to admit that I didn't get all three questions right. I hope you do better![64]

- Who painted *La Guernica*? A: Dalí, B: Miró, C: Picasso, D: Velázquez.
- What is the capital of Bangladesh? A: Dhaka, B: Hanoi, C: Yangon, D: Bangkok.
- Which country hosted the 1990 football World Cup? A: the United States, B: Mexico, C: Spain, D: Italy.

Before administering the test, the researchers split the participants into two groups. One group was asked to bring to mind the notion of a typical professor. They were given a blank sheet of paper and asked to spend five minutes scribbling down the behaviours, life-style, and even appearance of this professor. The second group was asked to bring to mind a typical football hooligan and likewise asked to list their thoughts about how the thugs might behave, live and even dress.

I'm sure you can guess where the experiment is going. Participants who spent a few minutes thinking about a stereotypical professor answered 56 per cent of the test questions correctly. Participants who summoned up the idea of a football hooligan saw their scores plunge to only 43 per cent.[65]

That's a big difference! In a school exam, that could perhaps be the difference between a B grade and a C grade, between getting into a good university or technical college versus a so-so one. And remember that the participants spent a mere five minutes reflecting on either the professor or the football hooligan.

Why should this affect us in this way? A professor is a broad label for someone we think of as being über-clever; a football hooligan is a similarly sweeping label for someone fairly brainless. It seems that bringing to mind either a smart or stupid stereotype helps those traits within us to emerge at least a little bit too.

Before you test-drive the technique though, I'd like to point out another finding by the Dutch researchers. Perhaps a little surprisingly, the researchers didn't get as strong an effect when they asked people to think of behaviours and traits associated with either the word 'intelligent' or 'stupid'. Thinking about an abstract quality seemed to have less of an effect. It seems that we have to think of a specific type of person, a more concrete stereotype, to get the most benefit (or to wreak the most harm).

Using labels to boost people's performance

The Radboud University Nijmegen study suggests that we can harness the power of labels to good effect – not only for other people but also for ourselves. Spending a mere five minutes writing about a brainy person helped to lift participants' general knowledge scores whereas writing about a dim-witted thug curbed their performance. Students ranging from teenagers sitting a school exam to experienced managers studying for diplomas later in life may study for weeks or even months for big tests. The fact that a five-minute exercise may boost performance seems to me an absolutely worthwhile intervention.

Psychologists don't know for certain why this effect occurs. Perhaps writing about a professor motivated participants to concentrate harder. Or it may have opened up parts of their memory that would otherwise have been inaccessible. Ultimately it doesn't matter why the labelling effect happens. We can simply benefit from the fact that it works.

So how could we use it to influence people's behaviour and performance? The possibilities are endless, but here are a handful of examples:

- Buoy the confidence of colleagues before important meetings or a big presentation. Get them to think about the most confident person they know. Ask them to write down how that person behaves, what they look like, the gestures they make, and the way they sound.
- Help yourself to do well in tests and examinations. Just before the test begins, spend five minutes jotting down traits

and behaviours you associate with Nobel Prize-winning
professors.

- Encourage kids (and adults too) to do well in a sports game.
Get them to think of a sporting hero, their absolute idol. Ask
them to describe how the champion plays, how they look as
they give their best, and even how they feel.

- Calm yourself down and get into the right state of mind for
a tricky discussion with a troublesome colleague. Bring to
mind the most empathetic person you know or perhaps put
yourself into the shoes of a selfless humanitarian aid worker.

Of oaths and honesty

The online search giant Google's informal corporate slogan is 'Don't
be evil'. On its own web pages, the company explains that it aims to
be 'measured by the highest possible standards of ethical business
conduct'.[66] However, critics sneer and say that the motto is just a
collection of words, an ineffectual maxim put in place by a handful of well-intentioned but ultimately naive managers. After all, how
could a mere sentence have any meaningful effect on the behaviour
of their employees?

Of course behavioural scientists love to explore such questions.
And perhaps we can glean some answers from an ambitious study
carried out in 2008 by a research team led by Nina Mazar, a professor of management at Rotman School of Management in Toronto.
Mazar began by asking a group of students to take a five-minute test
of their numerical ability. The test consisted of 20 matrices, and as
a reward for their assistance, the researchers offered the participants

$2 for solving each matrix. Here's an example. You can give it a go if you like. Your task is to find two numbers that add up to 10. If you're wearing a watch or can see a clock, see approximately how long it takes for you to solve the puzzle. I'll put the answer in a note at the end of the book.[67]

1.69	4.81	4.57
1.82	4.67	3.05
5.06	4.28	5.82
6.36	2.91	5.19

Now imagine that was the first of 20 matrices and remember that you have only five minutes to solve as many of the matrices as you can. The first time I had a go at the matrix above, it took me over a minute to solve. Even assuming that I improved with each subsequent one, I doubt I would be able to solve more than four or five of them at the very most.

Going back to the experiment, remember that the participants were offered $2 to solve each one. But here's the twist. The academics said that they didn't need to see the participants' answer sheets – they would pay out $2 for every matrix that the participants *said* they managed to complete. In fact, the researchers explicitly told the students to fold up the answer sheets to take away and recycle somewhere. The research team had no way of telling how many correct answers the students had actually completed.

Taking them purely on trust, the researchers found that the students claimed they completed an average of 5.5 matrices correctly. Had the students been entirely honest though? Had any of them claimed to have solved more of the matrices than they actually had?

Of course the researchers couldn't tell for certain without looking at the participants' actual answer sheets. However, Mazar and her collaborators found another way to establish the participants' likely honesty. The researchers gave the same booklet of matrices to another group of participants, but this time asked to see their answer sheets before paying them the same $2 per matrix. This time, the participants only managed to complete an average of 3.3 matrices correctly.

Let's look at those results again. The first group who didn't have to hand in their answer sheets solved 5.5 matrices correctly. But the participants who handed in their answer sheets only scored 3.3 matrices correctly. Participants had been randomly allocated to either the first or second group so it was unlikely that the first group was more intelligent than the second group. Yet the first group claimed to have completed 67 per cent more matrices in the same amount of time? Hmm, suspicious. Not conclusive evidence of cheating, but certainly highly suggestive of at least a little massaging of the truth.

But the first two groups were merely the precursor to what the researchers were really interested in investigating. With a third group of participants, the researchers wanted to test the effect of taking an oath on their honesty. This third group was presented with the same booklet of questions and again told that they would be trusted to tell the researchers how many matrices they had solved correctly. However, on the top of the test sheet there was an additional statement that read: 'I understand that this short survey falls under [the university]'s honour system.'

The participants were instructed to sign and print their names below the pledge before starting the test. This time, the participants reported that they had solved an average of 3.0 matrices correctly. Remember that they weren't required to hand in their answer sheets; so even though they had the opportunity to lie about their performance on the test, the short statement curbed any proclivity they might otherwise have had to lie. The effect of the statement was all the more puzzling given that the university at which the students were tested didn't even have an 'honour system'.[68]

What does the study tell us about behaviour in the real world outside of the psychologist's laboratory? The researchers point to the fact that many people may cheat, lie, or act in dishonest ways when given the chance, when they don't think that they'll get caught. Indeed, surveys of cheating regularly find that around three-quarters of students admit to having cheated at least occasionally.[69] Outside of academic institutions, insurance companies estimate that they are defrauded out of billions of pounds every year by exaggerated claims. And most governments around the world reckon that they lose tens of billions of pounds, dollars, euros, and yen annually in tax revenues from the under-reporting of income by business owners. Dishonesty seems rife.

However, a simple reminder of the need to behave honestly may curb at least some people's tendencies towards deception and dishonesty. Remember in the study by Nina Mazar and her colleagues that the university at which they ran their study *didn't even have any honour system*. The mere reminder of the concept of honour was enough to steer people away from temptation.

Going back to the online behemoth that is Google, does their 'Don't be evil' slogan have merit? Yes, but only sort of. Mazar's study tells us that a reminder *immediately before* doing a task helped to promote honesty. I doubt that a general statement would be able to guide Google's employees for every minute of every hour of every day they're at work. Perhaps the phrase may help to remind them of the need to behave ethically and honestly every time they hear it – although the effect is likely to last minutes rather than even hours.

Putting pledges into practice

Doctors famously take the Hippocratic Oath, swearing to practise medicine ethically. Jurors swear oaths when they are asked to sit in judgement of defendants in court. Prime ministers and presidents pledge to use their powers for the betterment of the people of their countries.

Emerging evidence suggests that asking people to take an oath can have at least a temporary effect on their behaviour. We may genuinely be able to coax people to behave more honestly and ethically.

What kind of a pledge might we encourage people to take though?

In the spring of 2009, the students at Harvard Business School were derided when they announced to the world that they had put together an MBA Oath. This was at a time when the world was plunging headlong into a global recession precipitated by the financial sleights of hand carried out by a relatively small number of financiers and brokers, most of whom had MBAs. Cynics pointed out that the pledge was merely a shrewd marketing ploy, an attempt by savvy business students to shape public opinion about them. But perhaps we can harness the words within it.[70]

As I've mentioned, the research evidence does not suggest that a vow taken once can have lasting effects over a person's lifetime. But asking people to take an oath immediately before doing a particular task (e.g. taking an exam or test, going into a meeting, or serving as a juror in a trial) may genuinely encourage them to hold themselves to higher moral and ethical standards. Perhaps all professions and occupations could benefit from having an oath, to be repeated daily.

Sure, some people may mouth the words of any vow with not a hint of sincerity and continue with their heinous ways of doing things. However, many others may find that it provides them with the prompt they needed to steer clear of temptation, to step back from the brink. Given a morally difficult choice, a regular pledge may nudge them just enough so that they make the right decision.

I'm not saying that an oath will solve all that ails the world. But it might help a little. Taking the MBA Oath as my inspiration, I've adapted some of the statements. Given that these are based purely on my opinions, you may wish to revise the following phrases for any oaths you may ask the people around you to take:

- I will behave with honesty and integrity and will not advance my own personal interests at the expense of society.
- I will refrain from corruption, unfair competition, or business practices harmful to society.
- I will protect the human rights and dignity of all people affected by what I do, and I will oppose discrimination and exploitation.
- I will protect the right of future generations to advance their standard of living and enjoy a healthy planet.

Words matter. Both our own intuition and research tell us that people take oaths and pledges seriously. Encourage people to say the words and their behaviour may well follow suit.

Tapping into people's need for cognitive consistency

Let me ask you a couple of questions. Will you recommend this book to your friends or colleagues? (Say 'yes' – or 'no' – aloud if you're alone.) Will you look for other books that I've written? (Again, say 'yes' out loud if you can.)

Why have I asked you these two questions?

Let me transport you away for a few moments and I'll explain very soon. See in your mind's eye that you're on a beach right now. Even though it's summer, today is a weekday so the beach isn't at all crowded. The sun is out and the temperature is … perfect. You notice a woman in her mid-twenties unfurling a blanket onto the sand not too far from where you're relaxing. She turns on a portable radio and stretches out, but she can't seem to get comfortable and gets up. She walks off into the distance, perhaps to get a drink or because she's forgotten to bring any suntan lotion.

You return to your own thoughts briefly until you spot a tall man wearing a baseball cap approaching the woman's blanket. He turns his head left and right and left again, but his eyes are flicking around him even more quickly, perhaps somewhat furtively. As he reaches the beach blanket, he nonchalantly scoops up the radio and walks off with it. He doesn't even stop to switch it off.

No one seems to have noticed what you are pretty sure is a blatant act of theft. You're the nearest person to the incident and the young woman is practically a dot on the horizon. What will you do?

While I let you ponder how you would respond, let me explain that a researcher from the University of New York – an academic with the delightful name of Thomas Moriarty – orchestrated this precise scenario several dozen times on Jones Beach in New York. He found that most people were too wary to get involved, with only

20 per cent of the people nearest to the incident intervening to stop the would-be thief.

Moriarty then repeated the experiment with other beachgoers but instructed the woman on the beach blanket to address the nearest person to her first. When she said, 'Excuse me, I'm going up to the boardwalk for a few minutes ... would you watch my things?' a whopping 100 per cent of the unsuspecting subjects in the experiment intervened on behalf of the woman. They didn't just yell at the would-be thief from the safety of their blankets either; they got up and ran up to him, risking a physical confrontation to challenge him. Simply getting people to say 'yes' to a question seems to spur them into action.

But wait, you say: perhaps the unwitting subjects had an ulterior motive. Maybe they wanted to befriend the woman or were attracted to her. A reasonable point, but when Moriarty switched the genders of the beachgoer and the thief – so a young man left his radio unattended and a woman tried to steal it – 90 per cent of subjects still intervened on behalf of the stranger.

Neither were the heroes all athletic young men with the physical strength to confront the perpetrator. They were men and women ranging in age from a teenager aged just 14 to a man who turned out to be 70 years old.[71]

Why did the simple request from the total stranger have such a fiendishly powerful effect? Psychologists believe that making what seemed a harmless commitment triggered the subjects' need for cognitive consistency. The subjects who agreed to look after the belongings of either a woman or a man actually behaved in the way they said they would. Perhaps their minds computed: 'I agreed to look after her belongings, so I must actually go through with it and do what I said.' When it comes to the way the human mind works, it seems that there are no such things as idle words.

Using active commitment to secure action

Moriarty achieved remarkable response rates in his study – perhaps because there was only a short gap of mere minutes between subjects' promising to watch the stranger's belongings and their need to act upon their pledge. But other studies show that asking people to make a positive commitment can influence their behaviour for up to several days.

Behavioural scientists Delia Cioffi and Randy Garner approached students on campus asking them to participate in a sex education and AIDS awareness project to be conducted at local schools. The researchers told half of the students that they had to tick two boxes on a form if they wished to participate. They told the other half of the students that they simply had to read the form and to turn up at the appointed time if they wanted to get involved.

The researchers then waited several days until the students were due to turn up. Counting the tally of students who actually arrived for an alleged orientation session, they found that only 17 per cent of the students who had verbally agreed to participate in fact turned up. However, 49 per cent of the students who had ticked the couple of boxes on a form appeared as they had pledged.[72]

The study suggests that even the tiny commitment – ticking just two boxes on a form – seemed to boost the cognitive consistency effect. Their brains seemed to compute: 'I ticked those boxes, so I must be the kind of person who will actually turn up for this volunteering project.' Admittedly, only half of the students turned up. But that's still a three-fold improvement over the students who merely looked over the form and said they would.

The lesson? Moriarty's beach experiment tells us that we might get people to articulate their agreement out loud. So if you would like a customer to call you on the telephone, don't say, 'I look forward to hearing from you.' Ask instead, 'Will you call me back next week?' and get the customer to say 'yes'. If you're nearing the end of a first date and want a second date, don't say 'It would be great to go out again.' Ask: 'Will you go out with me again?' And don't take 'maybe' for an answer. Use your charm and good humour to get a 'yes'.

Many of us already ask for quotes in writing when we're dealing with folks we're not used to, or strangers such as salespeople. But perhaps we might also extend this principle to the rest of the people we deal with when we wish to urge them to do something. So don't ask a member of your family to take out the rubbish and clean the bathroom if you suspect they won't get around to it; you might get better results if you get them to spend the few seconds it takes to write the tasks down on a list of chores. Or if you want to motivate colleagues to take action – perhaps to speak up during team meetings or ask for a pay rise – urge them to write down a specific action that they promise to take.

In fact, whenever you're setting objectives, tasks or goals for others, do your best to get people to commit them to paper. You may triple your odds of getting them to follow through on their promises. It doesn't even matter if they never look back at what they've written. By activating the principle of cognitive consistency, you can enlist the support of people's unconscious minds to help turn their aspirations into action.

CHAPTER FOUR
from small steps
to big effects

'Tell me and I'll forget;
show me and I may remember;
involve me and I'll understand.'
Chinese proverb

When I first moved to London to start research for my PhD in psychology, I shared an apartment with a guy I'll call Timothy. I didn't realise it at the time, but now, with the benefit of hindsight and a greater grasp of the psychology of influence, I can appreciate that he was a self-taught master of persuasion.

He had a rather narrow focus when it came to his powers of persuasion though, because his favourite pursuit was seducing women. Unsavoury, I know. But, as someone who shared an apartment with him, I knew that he was remarkably good at it. What were the tricks to his frequent success?

When he was out relaxing with his friends and regaling us with tales of his conquests, he often revealed the secrets of his success as a lady-magnet. Amidst the noise and bustle of the capital's nightclubs and bars, he liked to lie about his occupation, telling women that he was a hairdresser (he was actually a banker). He explained that convincing women that he was a hair stylist allowed him to touch their hair and heads. He could run his fingers through their tresses making suggestions about new styles or perhaps treatments for dealing with split ends. As we discovered in Chapter Two: Secret Signals, physical touch can be an intoxicatingly potent tool for convincing people to comply with our requests.

Another of Timothy's favourite manoeuvres was to strike up conversations by asking strangers seemingly innocuous questions.

For example, he would deliberately set the time on his watch to be wrong and then ask women: 'My watch seems to have stopped working, do you have the time, please?' He maintained that even such an apparently innocent enquiry was often enough to break the ice and allow him to proceed with his full-blown seduction spiel.

At the time, I didn't really give much credence to his theories. But recent research has looked at this precise notion: do seemingly innocuous chat-up lines work?

In 2008, scholars from four different universities in France enlisted the aid of a handful of young men aged between 19 and 21 years of age to act as their assistants. Led by an influential researcher, Nicolas Guéguen, the scholars sent their helpers to a large French town with an unusual task: to approach unsuspecting women passers-by to ask if they would have a drink with them.

The researchers asked the assistants to dress casually. So imagine in your mind's eye a group of young men with fashionably tousled hair, wearing low-slung jeans and perhaps slightly rumpled shirts.

Hanging around on the boulevards and forecourts of a bustling shopping area, the boyish assistants were asked to look out for women of a similar age, in their late teens or early twenties, who were walking alone with a cigarette in their hands. Nearly 4 in 10 French women aged between 18 and 24 are smokers, so it wasn't difficult to find women either already smoking a cigarette or about to light one up.

The women were randomly divided into three groups. In the first, control condition, the bright-eyed assistants went up to the women and said: 'Hello, I'm sorry to bother you but I was wondering if you were busy now. If not, we could have a drink together if you have some time.'

How would you react if a total stranger sauntered up to you without warning and asked you if you wanted a drink? Perhaps not entirely unexpectedly, only a meagre 4 out of 120 women agreed to the requests.

You can see that being a research assistant isn't always an easy job. In this study they needed adamantine levels of resilience to keep going up to women only to get rejected again and again and again!

In a second condition, the assistants asked: 'Hello, I'm sorry to bother you, but would you have a light for my cigarette?' The assistants either thanked her for the light or said, 'It doesn't matter,' if she didn't have one. Irrespective of whether she had a light or not, they nonchalantly asked the same question: 'Are you busy now? If not, we could have a drink together, if you have some time.'

In a third condition, the assistants used a different pretext and simply asked for directions: 'Hello, I'm sorry to bother you, but I am looking for the Place de Libération.' Whether the unsuspecting woman was able to provide directions or not, the assistants again asked them if they would be willing to join them for a drink.

The hapless research assistants ended up approaching over 400 women before the researchers had enough data to analyse the effects of the different interventions. Both of the additional questions – either asking for a light or requesting directions – helped the assistants to be wildly more successful. In fact, *five times* as many women agreed to the drink than in the control condition.[73]

Timothy the seducing banker was right: asking women a question – almost *any* question, it seems – makes it much more likely that they will agree to go out with a man. But the study illustrates a more general point. When people invest a little effort in something – an idea, a cause, a relationship – they can be far more easily persuaded to invest a lot more effort in it later. In this case, when the French women had invested just a few seconds of effort in a conversation with a stranger, they were considerably more likely to continue with their investment.

Getting your foot in the door

Researchers have known for decades that getting people to agree to a small request significantly boosts the chances that they will say 'yes' to a much larger one. The technique was first showcased in the mid-1960s in an amusing experiment by Jonathan Freedman and Scott Fraser, a pair of psychologists at Stanford University.

The experimenters visited the homes of residents in a leafy neighbourhood in the city of Palo Alto, California, posing as campaigners for a group called Citizens for Safe Driving. Walking along the pretty streets filled with tidy homes and their carefully tended front lawns, their goal: to cajole homeowners to allow them to plant in their front yards a large sign advocating safe driving. To illustrate what the sign looked like, they showed the owners a photograph of an enormous sign reading 'Drive Carefully' in front of a house.

Only 20 per cent of homeowners agreed to the experimenters' request. But when I say the sign was enormous, it obscured most of the front of the home in the photo. Stretch your arms out to the sides right now – and then add a couple of feet. *That's* how big the sign was. Making the sign an even less attractive proposition, the words were daubed on it in an untidy fashion too.

However, the experimenters managed to get 76 per cent of a different group of homeowners to agree to have the same huge signs planted in their otherwise pristine front lawns.[74] How?

Two weeks prior to the visit from the Citizens for Safe Driving, the experimenters had sent a group of different campaigners to these homes. Explaining that they were from the Community Committee for Traffic Safety, these earlier activists asked homeowners to display a small sign saying 'Be a safe driver' either in the window of their houses or in their cars. And this one really was small, about the same size as the palm of your hand. The sign was so small and seemingly inoffensive that scarcely anyone said 'no' to the request; the researchers got a nearly 100 per cent uptake to the teeny, tiny sign. Yet two weeks later, it had worked its magic. When the second set of experimenters went to these homes, more than three-quarters of the homeowners who had taken the tiny signs were persuaded to embrace the giant-sized ones.

Freedman and Fraser gave their approach to gaining compliance a name: the foot-in-the-door technique. Knocking on people's metaphorical doors with a small offer that they can say 'yes' to means they're more invested in what happens next; it ensures they're more likely to throw the door wide open to a subsequent and much larger request.

Taking the French dating experiment and Californian 'Drive Carefully' study together, we can see what crafty salespeople have known for a very long time: getting people to make a small commitment may ultimately lead them to making more significant ones. Getting a customer to buy a single item from a store makes it much more likely that the customer will return for a larger purchase. Persuading your children to eat just one piece of broccoli sets wheels in motion that may eventually see them devouring whole platefuls of the previously hated vegetable. Getting people to engage in even the smallest, most innocuous action may ultimately have them agreeing to more monumental endeavours that they would never have otherwise done.

Yes, yes, yes

I like receiving free gifts when I'm shopping and many stores are more than willing to offer freebies, samples, and tasters in an attempt to encourage shoppers to spend money. Staff at the coffee chain Starbucks, for example, often walk around stores doling out bite-sized chunks of cakes and muffins. Of course I'm delighted to gobble them up. The servers in the Häagen-Dazs ice-cream parlours offer up little spoonfuls of ice cream to taste and I'm only too happy to accept them too. And the sales assistants at L'Occitane, a high-street purveyor of luxury skincare goods with stores world-wide from London to Hong Kong, offer customers a freshly brewed cup of herbal tea while they browse. However, I always say 'no'. The tea is usually too hot to drink immediately and I don't want to have to hang around in the store waiting overly long for it to cool down. But does it matter if we say 'yes' or 'no' to the initial foot-in-the-door offer?

In 2010, an international coterie of researchers from universities in Belgium, the Netherlands, and Norway decided to shed light on this very question in a cunning experiment. Led by Ghent University social scientist Mario Pandelaere, the team hired a panel of market researchers to make short telephone calls to people at home. Their goal: to gain the homeowners' consent to being contacted again to take part in future, possibly quite lengthy telephone surveys.

Of course most homeowners don't like being pestered by unknown callers. They've been working all day and want nothing more than to slump in front of their televisions or spend time with their families. So before making their rather bold requests, the market researchers asked the homeowners eight questions from one of two versions of a mini-survey.

A first, control version of the mini-survey was contrived to have participants shaking their heads in disagreement. These participants were asked to agree or disagree with controversial statements such as 'I think women may be paid less than men' and 'I think doping in sports should be allowed'. As expected, the researchers found that participants disagreed with many of these statements.

The second, experimental version of the mini-survey was designed to elicit agreement. Participants were asked to either agree or disagree with statements such as 'I think women should receive equal pay to men' and 'I think doping in sports should be forbidden'. Again, as anticipated, participants who were asked these questions tended to agree with most of the statements.

After being asked all eight questions, participants were finally asked whether they would mind being contacted again for future telephone surveys. Of the control group who had mainly disagreed with the initial eight questions, only 29 per cent said that they were happy to be contacted again in the future. However, 47 per cent of the experimental participants – remember they had mainly been asked questions that they'd agreed with – said 'yes' to being called up again for further polls.[75]

Getting people used to saying yes seems to have knock-on effects. Asking people an initial question or making a small request – so long as it's easy enough for them to say 'yes' to it – is a way of making a person an active, willing participant in a discussion. The foot-in-the-door technique encourages them to feel more invested in a relationship, helping a supplicant's later request to be viewed more favourably.

So if anyone from the head office of L'Occitane is reading this, I would suggest that they dispense with the cups of tea. Most custom-ers say 'no', which may lessen their chances of spending money in the store. My advice would be to tweak the first thing the sales assistants say to customers, perhaps even something like, 'Do let me know if I can help you, won't you?' to which customers would surely respond, 'Yes, I will.'

Getting to yes

The foot-in-the-door research suggests that we might pave the way towards making large requests of people with small requests first. If you want a customer to purchase 1,000 pallets of your product, a good start would be to get them to pay for just one. Even if the administrative hassle of shipping it over and billing for a single item doesn't quite seem worth it, you may win a small victory that will help you to shift more items later on.

Suppose your children don't want to go swimming but, for their own safety, you need for them to be able to swim properly. To bolster your chances of persuading them to visit the swimming pool, ask a series of other questions to get them used to saying 'yes'. 'You know that your best friends Maria and Alex will be going to the pool?' (Their likely answer: 'yes'.) 'Did you enjoy it that time that we went for ice cream after we'd been swimming?' (Their almost certain answer: 'yes'.) 'Well, how about we go swimming for just a little while?'

Or if you are hankering for a pay rise from your boss, work up to the big question. Perhaps create a staged approach with questions of increasing magnitude. Start with 'Would you agree that I did a good job on that project last week?' and then 'Do you remember that you said last month that I was one of the best people you've ever had working for you?' before making your suggestion: 'Can we put a date in the diary to review my performance and discuss whether I might be due a pay rise?'

However, you might do well to heed the results of the study by Mario Pandelaere. Your initial request or questions must be answered affirmatively. Having your initial questions declined could be fatal for your odds of getting a 'yes' to that really big question you're building up to ask. The best approach may be to ensure that your initial requests or questions will be easy for people to say 'yes' to.

From thoughts to behaviour

Most of us know the kinds of changes we should make in our life-styles, our day-to-day actions and habits, to live our lives more healthily. We know that we should spend a little more time on an exercise bicycle or pounding the pavements and a little less time sat on our sofas. We know that we should forgo that greasy bacon sandwich in favour of a more wholesome grilled chicken salad. We know we should cut back on the beer and wine and drink a few more glasses of water too.

Thing is: *no one* – whether it's ourselves or the people around us – likes to be told what they're doing wrong. So if we want to encourage people to change their behaviour in positive ways, how can we do it?

We've known for well over 50 years that cigarette smoking is bad for us. Yet millions of people around the world continue to smoke. Frustrated by the disconnect between people's rational understanding of the risks and their actual behaviour, Barbara Müller from Radboud University Nijmegen in the Netherlands conducted an experiment in 2009 to see if she could shape smokers' behaviour. Müller gathered a group of committed smokers aged from 17 to 47 in her laboratory and allowed them to have a cigarette while she explained the alleged aim of her study. She explained that she was measuring people's ability to weigh up the pros and cons of different arguments.

Half of the subjects were asked to write down as many arguments as they could think of as to why people shouldn't smoke. The other half of the subjects acted as a control group and merely read a pre-prepared list of arguments as to why smoking was undesirable.

Both groups were told that the second part of the task involved a computerised test. However, the experimenter apologised and said that there was a problem: a technical glitch meant that the subjects would have to hang around for around 15 minutes before they could be seated in front of the computers.

So the unsuspecting subjects waited and waited. Fifteen minutes passed and still there was no sign of the experimenter. And the clock continued to tick and tick and tick. I'm sure you can imagine how bored, frustrated smokers might react: tapping their fingers, glancing repeatedly at the time, biting their nails, maybe pacing around the room a little, but finally succumbing to having another cigarette.

In fact, there was no technical glitch. Really, there wasn't even a computer test at all – this was merely a pretext used by Müller and her team to have the subjects hanging around with nothing to do. The researchers were secretly using hidden cameras to spy on the subjects; they wanted to know how long it would take them to light up another cigarette. If a subject didn't have a cigarette within 30 minutes, the experimenters went in to tell the subject that the computer was still not working properly and that he or she was free to leave.

Only 36.8 per cent of the control group subjects who read pre-prepared arguments against smoking managed to last the full 30 minutes without striking up another cigarette. However, nearly double the number – 70.6 per cent – of the subjects who were tasked with coming up with their own arguments felt they did not need a cigarette within the same half-hour period.[76]

None of the reasons that the subjects came up with for themselves differed greatly from the arguments against smoking that the control group had read. And it's not as if smokers are generally unaware of the arguments against smoking. The only difference was that the control group had passively been presented with a list of arguments against smoking while the experimental group had actively generated a list of nearly identical reasons.

The implications of the study are huge. We know that people don't like to be told what to do. But when we involve them and ask them to spend a few minutes of their time generating reasons as to why they should do something, they can't help but become more emotionally invested.

Asking questions rather than giving instructions

Asking questions is a key tenet of both effective teaching at school and in the home as well as coaching within the workplace. Rather than telling people what to do, a good coach asks people to ponder why they might do something and how they might go about it. The more we can encourage people to invest time and effort in thinking about a behaviour or planning a task, the more likely they will be to follow through and actually do it.

Say you're a manager who wants an employee to be more organised. Rather than nagging by saying, 'You need to be more organised because …' you might get better results by asking, 'What are the reasons you might benefit from becoming more organised?' Once the employee has been won over to the need to stay organised, you could then ask, 'And what steps might you take to get a little more organised?'

If you want a friend to join you at the gym, don't lecture her about the fact that she's worryingly overweight. Ask her: 'Why do you think you need to lose weight?'

Or suppose you have a husband or wife who doesn't want to get out of bed before midday at weekends. Rather than hectoring them about their idleness, ask them what they might do with the mornings. As cheekily or charmingly as you like, you could ask, 'Can you give me three good reasons why we might get up a bit earlier?' With a twinkle in your eye, you could even throw in a bribe by suggesting, 'If you can give me three reasons, maybe I'll come up with a very good fourth reason too!'

I watched a friend argue with her teenage son a couple of weeks ago. Rather than acting as the parent and raising her voice while telling him to feed the dog and take the rubbish out, she might have had more success treating him as another adult for a few moments by asking him, 'Why do you think I'm asking you to feed the dog and take the rubbish out?'

CHAPTER FIVE
invoking the imagination and telling tales

'*Ideas come and go, stories stay.*'
Nassim Nicholas Taleb

A good friend of mine got married in the spring. Some eight months before, Louisa went to a bridal boutique on a leafy avenue in west London that specialises in high-end wedding dresses. With the aid of her bevy of bridesmaids, she found a dress she liked: a simple yet elegant strapless off-the-shoulder gown in cream-coloured taffeta. Her bridesmaids suggested that, with her mass of curly black hair and olive skin, the dress would make her look exquisite.

When she asked to try it on, the sales assistant ushered her into a cramped cubicle to pull on the dress. The assistant apologised that there was no mirror in the changing room, but explained that they would go into another room with better lighting where Louisa could see what she looked like in front of three mirrors.

The assistant helped to pin the dress up before steering Louisa into this other room. A small dais sat in the centre of the room and heavy cream-coloured sheets covered up three large mirrors. Windows above the mirrors flooded the room with warm, natural sunlight.

The assistant asked Louisa to close her eyes.

'Open your hands,' the assistant told Louisa.

Louisa felt a bouquet of fresh flowers being pressed between her fingers. The welcoming scent of roses filled her nostrils and she luxuriated in the smell as she heard the sound of the sheets being pulled away from the mirrors.

'Now imagine that it's your wedding day. It's a beautiful day and all of your closest friends and family have gathered to show you how much they love you. The man you want to marry, the love of your life and your future husband, is coming down the aisle towards you. He looks so handsome in his suit and you can see how in love with you he is. Now open your eyes and see how beautiful you will look to him.'

Louisa opened her eyes, looked at her reflection, and burst into tears of happiness. Oh, and she bought the dress too.

Clearly Louisa was won over by the bridal boutique's sales patter. She was so moved by the mental movie she had conjured up that she almost felt as if it was her wedding day. But is there something the rest of us can learn here? Can building a vivid picture in the mind really change minds and influence behaviour?

From a foot in the door to a toehold in the mind

Behavioural scientists believe that humans are the only animals on the planet capable of imagination, the act of envisioning things we've never seen before. Let's try an experiment right now. Take a second to imagine how it would feel to be on a manned mission to Mars. What would you be wearing? What would the interior of the ship look like? What might you be doing?

Even though no such spaceship currently exists, I'm sure you can conjure up an image of some sort. We can all visualise ourselves doing all sorts of things we've never done. You could dream of yourself winning a gold medal at the Olympic Games or clambering successfully to the top of Mount Everest. You could picture yourself being an international jetsetter, perhaps a playboy or an heiress. The list of what we can see in our mind's eye is endless and, for the most part, imagining ourselves in such situations is nothing more than a quotidian diversion. The saying goes that a picture is worth a thousand words and, when it comes to steering people's actions, it turns out that a mental picture can sometimes be as powerful as many of the most persuasive words.

One of the most illuminating studies on the workings of the imagination was conducted in the early 1980s. A group of psychology investigators headed up by W. Larry Gregory at New Mexico State University asked homeowners in the arid city of Tempe in Arizona about their attitudes to a relatively new development called cable television. At the time, cable TV was available only in certain large cities in the US; the citizens of Tempe didn't have access to it and probably considered the survey to be a harmless thought experiment.

A pollster – a young woman – knocked on the doors of homes across the city and explained to homeowners that she was canvassing opinions about cable TV (CATV). Before asking their opinions, she explained that she would read out a short paragraph giving them some background about the service.

One group of homeowners was asked to reflect on the merits of cable television when it eventually arrived:

CATV will provide a broader entertainment and informational service to its subscribers. Used properly, a person can plan in advance to enjoy events offered. Instead of spending money on the babysitter and gas, and putting up with the hassles of going out, more time can be spent at home with family, alone, or with friends.

A second group of homeowners heard a slightly different script:

> Take a moment and imagine how CATV will provide you with a
> broader entertainment and informational service. When you use it
> properly, you will be able to plan in advance which of the events
> offered you wish to enjoy. Take a moment and think of how, instead
> of spending money on the babysitter and gas, and then having to
> put up with the hassle of going out, you will be able to spend your
> time at home, with your family, alone, or with your friends.

After reading one of the two versions, the pollster asked the home-owners a series of questions, for example, 'How likely do you think it will be that CATV could become as popular as regular television?' She then thanked them for their participation and that seemed to be the end of the study.

Of course the research team had an ace up their sleeves. They knew that the arrival of cable television wasn't some distant, theoretical event. They had insider knowledge that the residents of Tempe would be offered the opportunity to buy subscriptions to cable television imminently.

Only a handful of weeks after the survey, cable television actually arrived in Tempe and the local cable company sent its salespeople out to entice homeowners into subscribing. When the researchers looked at which homes had taken up the offers, they discovered that 20 per cent of the homeowners who read the first version of the appeal signed up. However, an impressive 47 per cent of the homeowners who read the second version of the appeal signed up.[77]

Can you spot the difference between the two versions? Both talk about the benefits of being able to plan in advance. Both mention how the cable service would not only save money on babysitters and gas but also reduce hassle.

The differences are quite subtle. The first version talks about how 'a person' can plan in advance. The second asks readers to 'imagine' *themselves* experiencing those benefits. Go back through the two paragraphs and count the number of times the word 'you' appears in each and you'll see that the second version of the script tries to transport the homeowner into how it might actually feel to have cable as opposed to merely weighing up its merits from a hypothetical perspective.

The study is a scintillating demonstration of the power of the imagination. But what impresses me most about it is the potency of the second version of the script. For a start, the homeowners were contacted not merely a few days later but several *weeks* later to see if they were interested in subscribing to cable television. So the 'imagine' script had an effect that lasted not just hours or days, but weeks.

Plus the pollster didn't have to spend a half-hour selling the benefits of cable TV. She didn't even have to spend five minutes. The version that asked people to imagine themselves experiencing the benefits of cable took less than 30 seconds to read. The young pollster probably didn't even realise that her words might be persuasive. Yet they were, because the 'imagine' script yielded a subscription rate weeks later that was nearly two and a half times as high as she got from homeowners who merely heard a list of benefits. That's a pretty mind-blowingly powerful tactic for seeding thoughts in people's minds and ultimately changing their behaviour.

If gaining people's agreement to a small request is akin to getting a foot in the door (see Chapter Four: From Small Steps to Big Effects), then getting them to project themselves into a situation could be called getting a toehold in the mind. By harnessing the power of people's imaginations, we don't even have to seek an actual commitment. We don't need people to answer a token question as the researchers did in Nicolas Guéguen's dating experiment. We don't need them to agree to a small request as they did in Freedman and Fraser's safe driving study. Getting our peers to put themselves at the centre of their very own mental movies seems to activate some kind of principle of personal investment, with the consequence that they are more than twice as likely to be influenced to do something.

Why might this happen though? Why does picturing a behaviour make us more likely to do it?

Again, the relatively new science of brain imaging allows us to look inside the skull at what the brain is doing when people use their imaginations. Scientists in a 2006 study asked participants either to move their hands or to *imagine* moving their hands (but not actually move them) while seated in a magnetic resonance imaging machine. As expected, the primary motor cortex lit up strongly when participants moved their hands. However, the primary motor cortex still showed a smaller spike in activity when participants were asked to imagine moving their hands.[78]

As far as the brain is concerned, picturing a behaviour in our minds and actually doing it are more or less the same thing. Sure, imagining an action evokes significantly less activity in the brain. But the difference seems to be quantitative rather than qualitative. The mere act of imagining a behaviour may create a pathway that makes it easier for people to actually follow through to do the behaviour too.

Painting pictures to show the way

A solid body of evidence tells us that when people imagine a behaviour, it makes them more likely to engage in the behaviour. Getting a buddy to picture eating a tub of ice cream – peeling the lid off the container and lifting a spoonful of his favourite flavour to his lips – is more likely to send him to the shops to buy one. Asking a colleague to bring to mind how it might feel to take that job overseas may nudge her into accepting the posting. But wait a second, it turns out that there's an additional little trick to getting the greatest change in behaviour from people's mental movies.

Let's travel not so far back in time to 2004 and the eve of yet another presidential election in the United States. Democratic candidate John Kerry is fighting a close election against the Republican incumbent George W. Bush. Of course we know the eventual victor in the story, but one group of researchers wasn't really interested in who might win. No, they were exhilarated that this was a unique opportunity for them to test the effects of different types of mental imagery on people's behaviour.

The team's ringleader was Lisa Libby, a fresh-faced social psychologist with a tidy brown bob of hair and vivid blue eyes smiling out from under fashionable spectacles. An unorthodox teacher who has been known to use clips from the hit TV show *Sex and the City* in her classes at the Ohio State University, she and her colleagues spent several weeks before the election signing up participants for an online experiment on the psychology of the imagination. At 6.30 p.m. on 1 November – the eve of the election – the participants opened their email inboxes to find a new message from the researchers.

The participants had been randomly divided into two groups and told that they would be asked to imagine doing a certain action: they would be asked to imagine themselves voting in the upcoming election. Depending on their group allocation, participants received one of two different emails. Participants in one group read the following instructions:

You should picture doing the action from a first-person visual perspective. With the first-person visual perspective you see the event from the visual perspective you would have if the event were actually taking place. That is, you are looking out at your surroundings through your own eyes.

Participants in the second group read a slightly different set of orders:

You should picture doing the action from a third-person visual perspective. With the third-person visual perspective you see the event from the visual perspective an observer would have if the event were actually taking place. That is, you see yourself in the image, as well as your surroundings.

Participants in both groups were then told to close their eyes and use either the first- or third-person perspective to picture themselves voting in the upcoming presidential election. Close *your* eyes and try out both sets of instructions to explore the differences if you like. From a first-person perspective, you might see a ballot box, a voting slip, and a pen in front of you. You would see your own hands reaching forwards and putting a cross next to the name of your preferred candidate. You see your hands folding the voting slip up and stuffing it into the box. From the third-person perspective, you would see yourself as if you were a bystander nearby or a ghost floating above the scene. You would see your body walking into perhaps a small booth and closing a door or a curtain behind you. You see yourself standing next to the ballot box, deliberating for a moment – with perhaps a slight frown on your face – and voting.

It seems a trivial difference. Yet the researchers found a statistically significant difference in the numbers of participants who actually voted on the day of the election itself. Care to guess which set of instructions brought about more actual voting?

Of those who imagined the scene from a first-person perspective, 72 per cent voted. However, 90 per cent of the participants who pictured the scene from the out-of-body, third-person perspective ended up voting.[79]

Why might seeing ourselves in a scene make us more likely to turn it into reality?

The explanation may lie in the way we think about the behaviour of ourselves versus others. Psychologists call it the fundamental attribution error, having known for a long time that when we see other people doing something foolish, we tend to attribute it to their personality, their innate disposition. So we think of them as 'thoughtless' or 'reckless'. However, when we ourselves do something stupid, we are more likely to attribute our action to external circumstances. We may blame situational factors, for example that 'I was tired' or 'my friends were pestering me to make a decision'. Of course we do sometimes think 'I'm thoughtless' or 'I'm reckless' too. For the most part though, we tend to attribute other people's actions to their disposition, while we attribute our own actions to what's happening around us at the time.

We can extrapolate that discrepancy into the realm of our imaginations. When we see ourselves performing a behaviour from our usual first-person perspective, we may think of that behaviour as having been externally motivated, for example, 'I was in the area so it was no big deal to vote,' or, 'My brother was voting at the same time so I went along with him.' On the other hand, when we see ourselves performing a behaviour from a ghostlike third-person perspective, we may ourselves fall prey to the fundamental attribution error and end up associating that behaviour with what we believe is our personality, our innate motivations, our identities. So a subconscious part of ourselves may think, 'I saw myself voting so I must be the kind of person who is likely to vote,' with the consequence that we are more likely to end up voting for real.

From seeing to doing

It's for good reason that advertisers ask consumers to 'imagine yourself behind the steering wheel of a Mercedes', 'see yourself with younger-looking skin after just 30 days of using Olay', or 'dream of the sun on your skin and warm water lapping between your toes as you walk on a beautiful beach in the Bahamas'.

Say you're trying to persuade your partner that the two of you might buy a certain house together. Sure, a well-crafted argument about its location, price, and other attributes should be a part of your arsenal. But try adding in images to support your appeal as you wander around its interior: 'Here's where the stove would go and over there is where we'd put the breakfast table so we'd get all of that lovely sunshine coming in from those big windows ...'

We may be able to warn people off undesirable behaviours too. For example, many people already know that sunburn may lead to skin cancer. But get people to imagine how it might feel if you want them to slap on the sunscreen: '*Imagine* a surgeon having to cut into your flesh to dig out the patches of cancerous cells. *Imagine* having to go for scans every 12 months to make sure the cancer hasn't come back – or worse, hasn't spread to other organs in the body.'

From Lisa Libby's work, we know that the perspective people use to envisage a behaviour might change the persuasiveness of your message too. Getting people to see themselves from a third-person perspective rather than a first-person perspective may be a more effective tool for encouraging people to do what they see.

In practice, you may not always be able to control the perspective people use to imagine a scene. When you're trying to sell a product or service to someone – say in a TV or print advert – you can't necessarily dictate how they see the scene. Simply asking them to 'imagine' may still be better than merely describing the benefits though.

However, you may be able to encourage people to use the third-person perspective when you're working with them to control their future behaviour. Say you're a guidance counsellor helping teenagers to avoid drinking alcohol and getting drunk or from engaging in unsafe sex. You can ask them to picture scenes in which they say 'no' as if they were sat watching a movie in which they're also the star on screen. The same goes if you want to boost someone's confidence before a big presentation or want to help a friend to stick to her new exercise schedule or anything else the people around you want to achieve. Ask people to see themselves in the scene as if they're spying on themselves like a ghost floating in the sky and you may help them to actually achieve what they see.

Once upon a time

As citizens of the twenty-first century, we're bombarded daily with dozens if not hundreds of advertisements on posters, billboards, and the sides of taxis and buses. Having lived and commuted in London for over 10 years, I've developed a thick skin and usually pay scant attention to advertising. But, standing on a train platform one morning, one poster caught my attention. It was the story of Patrick, a self-described incurable optimist.

PATRICK
the incurable optimist

Here are his words:

> I have motor neurone disease (MND). I'm gradually losing the
> ability to walk, talk, eat and breathe. I won't see my daughter
> go to primary school and she won't remember me. I am dying –
> MND is killing me.
>
> I'm determined to use what's left of my life and my
> diminishing artistic skill to encourage others to do something
> optimistic every day. MND may be incurable but I am an
> incurable optimist. I know that through optimism we will find the
> cure to MND.

After reading it, I reached for a pen and piece of paper to note down
the website address. I felt compelled to log on to www.patrickthe
optimist.org later that evening to read more about Patrick's story
and make a donation to the Motor Neurone Disease Association.
Why did this one advert – out of the hundreds and thousands I see
every month – break through my defences?

An ambitious study by research psychologist Timothy Wilson at
the University of Virginia and Nancy Brekke at Lake Forest College
in Illinois may give us some answers. They invited a group of women
students to attend a lecture on safe sex, telling them that they would
be presented with information about two brands of condoms.
Afterwards, the students would be free to take samples of their
preferred brand away with them.

The research duo gave the young women two sources of information upon which to base their decisions. The first was an article on condom brands in *Consumer Reports*, a magazine run by a highly rated independent, non-profit organisation dedicated to helping members of the general public to make better decisions. The expert evaluation of the two makes indicated clearly that Brand A was superior to Brand B.

The second source of information was a handful of first-hand accounts allegedly written by actual students. For example, one of the students described a vivid occasion in which Brand A had burst while she and her boyfriend were having sex, causing her great distress over whether she was pregnant.

After weighing up both sources, the vast majority of the students – 97 per cent – said that the article within the pages of the highly vaunted *Consumer Reports* magazine represented a fairer comparison of the pros and cons of the two brands. They agreed that the balanced report was the more dependable source of information; they also said that they wanted their friends to choose Brand A based on the expert critique. No surprises so far. However, when the students were given the opportunity to take away samples of whichever brand they trusted more, 31 per cent of the students ended up taking Brand B. Despite the factual report in a reliable consumer magazine, one in three students was more swayed by the flamboyant first-hand stories.[80]

Putting it another way, the students knew that they *should* trust the nearly incontrovertible evidence presented in the impartial report. However, one in three of them couldn't help but be swayed by the first-hand accounts.

Perhaps we shouldn't be surprised that stories about specific individuals can exert such substantial pulls on people's behaviour. People have shared stories with each other about their exploits and those of others since long before the written word was invented. In countries and cultures all around the world, parents tell their children stories. Even young children who have barely learned to speak are spellbound by stories of brave princes and beautiful princesses on epic journeys in worlds populated by trolls and monsters.

The vast majority of the best-selling books of all time – including modern hits such as the Harry Potter books and Dan Brown's *The Da Vinci Code* – are essentially compelling stories. The best-selling book in recorded history is the Bible: a collection of stories about the creation of the world, God's relationship with humanity, and the trials of Jesus Christ. Yes, the Bible imparts lessons, but it does so through illustrative stories that evoke our imagination.

The condom study by Wilson and Brekke pitted stories *against* facts. And the stories won around a third of the time. Just think: if you marry together facts *and* stories, you'd make your arguments not merely compelling, but practically compulsory. There's a saying amongst journalists that facts tell but stories sell. Open up the pages of any newspaper or magazine to read an article and there's almost always a personal angle. There's a vignette, a case study, an anecdote, the story of a particular individual told in a great amount of detail as opposed to just a litany of facts and figures.

Here's another study that sheds light on why we are so moved by stories about individual people. Compare the following pleas from a humanitarian organisation asking people to donate money to a good cause. The first is what's known as a statistical appeal:

Food shortages in Malawi are affecting more than three million children. In Zambia, severe rainfall deficits have resulted in a 42 per cent drop in maize production from 2000. As a result, an estimated three million Zambians face hunger. Four million Angolans – one third of the population – have been forced to flee their homes. More than 11 million people in Ethiopia need immediate food assistance.

The second is known as an identifiable appeal:

Any money that you donate will go to Rokia, a 7-year-old girl from Mali, Africa. Rokia is desperately poor, and faces a threat of severe hunger or even starvation. Her life will be changed for the better as a result of your financial gift. With your support, and the support of other caring sponsors, Save the Children will work with Rokia's family and other members of the community to help feed her, provide her with education, as well as basic medical care and hygiene education.

In an experiment led by University of Pennsylvania researcher Deborah Small, people were approached on the street and asked for donations using either the statistical or the identifiable appeal. Which do *you* think elicited greater donations?

It's not a difficult question, is it? The statistical appeal throws up truly fearsome numbers. More than three *million* children in Malawi are facing food shortages. Three *million* Zambians may be going hungry. And a staggering 11 *million* Ethiopians need food aid. The numbers are so enormous that we lose track. We can't really comprehend what a million of *anything* might look like.

But we can picture one girl – we can *identify* with her. Many people who read that description of Rokia say that they see an image of a girl in their heads. We can't seem to help it; our imagination kicks in automatically. Predictably then, people who read the story of Rokia donated 76 per cent more money to charity than people who read about the faceless masses.[81] In terms of convincing people to open up their wallets, a torrent of facts was again beaten by the story about a single person.

The inseparability of stories and action

People have told stories since the dawn of human prehistory. Yet it is only in the last few years that studies using brain-scanning methods have illuminated exactly why stories may have such wide-ranging effects on our behaviour.

We've already seen that asking people to imagine an activity such as moving the hand activates the same parts of the brain that are responsible for controlling actual movement. But do stories have the same effect on the brain? In 2009, a team led by Nicole Speer at Washington University in St Louis tracked brain activity using fMRI scanners as participants read short stories. Participants read about the everyday activities of Raymond, a seven-year-old boy: he got up and ate breakfast, played with his friends in the school playground, and attended an English lesson followed by a music lesson.

The brain scans showed that different areas of the participants' brains lit up according to what Raymond was doing in the story. For example, when they read that Raymond walked over to his friend Susan's bicycle and pushed his jacket into the basket attached to her cycle, the areas of their brain associated with grasping hand movements flared up.[82]

Such studies demonstrate that it's not just imagining a behaviour that activates the corresponding area of the brain. Hearing a story also seems to tap into the same mechanism, activating the same parts of the brain that are associated with actually performing the behaviour. Again, the research shows that the level of activation while hearing about an action in a story is much less than the level we see in the brain when someone is actually doing the action, but the two are related.

So asking someone to imagine a situation doesn't seem all that different from telling them an involving story about it. The same parts of the brain spark up and, in doing so, make people more likely to act in certain ways. In the same way that physical exercise strengthens a muscle, the merest mental thought about an activity seems to strengthen the likelihood of performing it for real.

If I may speculate, I'd say that while the imagination is a powerful tool for influencing behaviour, stories might be akin to the imagination on steroids. Stories about real people can be incredibly persuasive because they not only harness the power of the imagination, but draw us in deeper. They provide us with little details that we couldn't imagine for ourselves. A first-hand account about someone's unbridled success or a cautionary tale about another's dismal failure can transport us elsewhere whether we want to be swept away or not.

Crafting persuasive stories

What makes for a truly persuasive story? If we want to change people's minds and influence their behaviour, how can we construct anecdotes that grab people's attention and don't let go?

Professor of education Mark Sadoski has been researching such questions for a long time. A man with a lithe energy and ruddy cheeks, it's only the shock of thick white hair and grey moustache that betray the fact that he recently celebrated his thirtieth year as an academic at Texas A&M University. In one study, he asked participants to read a booklet of 24 short paragraphs, warning them that they would later be asked to recall what they had read.

Here's an example of one of the paragraphs:

There are three general principles that form the basis of aerodynamics. First, moving air will push up against a surface placed at an angle to the airflow. Secondly, the force of the air under a moving object will propel it upward; and finally, the surfaces of an object will move toward a rapidly moving airstream above it.

Here's a different example:

Acceleration is the rate at which the velocity of an object changes. As a runner sprints off, his speed accelerates; when an airplane blasts down the runway and the passengers lurch backward in their seats, the speed of the plane is accelerating. Acceleration may be negative, as in an automobile when the driver suddenly jams on the brakes.

Each of the two passages tries to convey a key concept to do with physics, the science of how objects and forces interact in the real world. But can you spot the key difference between the two? The first is entirely abstract. So it talks about 'a surface' and 'a moving object' without saying what the surface might look like or what the moving object might be. In contrast, the second segment of text is considerably more concrete, using words that we can visualise with ease. We can see in our mind's eye a runner in sports kit hurtling down a track in a big stadium, an aeroplane tilting towards the sky with the passengers being thrown back in their seats, and a car screeching to a halt when the driver slams on the brakes.

When Sadoski asked the participants to answer a series of questions about the material, he observed that they found the concrete paragraphs not only easier to understand but also more interesting to read. When they were tested on what they could remember about the paragraphs, they also tended to recall more information about the concrete passages.[83]

Concrete details beat abstract ideas on nearly every important count then. If you think about it, what's more concrete than telling a story about a specific person in a richly described situation? Even the most basic of stories – like the one about Rokia, the African girl in need of aid – tends to be more concrete (and therefore easier to understand, more interesting to read, and more memorable) than any litany of facts or statistics. But I said concreteness trumps abstraction on *almost* every count; what we can't tell from Sadoski's research is whether it makes an argument more persuasive.

So let's turn to just one more study. Research partners Jonathan Shedler and Melvin Manis constructed a scenario in which a single mother named Mrs Johnson was being evaluated for her fitness to continue being the legal guardian to her young son. The researchers told their participants that they would hear statements made by various people involved with the family about Mrs Johnson's parenting skills and behaviour towards her child, a seven-year-old. Afterwards, the participants would have to judge whether her son could be left with her or taken into foster care.

The researchers deliberately assembled the audio recording so that eight statements supported Mrs Johnson's suitability as a parent and eight statements argued against it. This being another psychological experiment, however, the participants heard one of two similar versions of the recording.

In one version, all of the statements that supported Mrs Johnson had some extra, vivid detail attached to them, while all of the statements arguing against her had no additional details. In the other version, all of the statements supporting Mrs Johnson were merely unadorned facts, whereas all of the statements criticising her had a vivid, concrete detail attached to it.

Compare the following examples. Here's one with a vivid argument in favour of Mrs Johnson but a mere statement of fact censuring her:

A. Mrs Johnson sees to it that her child washes and brushes his teeth before bed time. He uses a Star Wars toothbrush that looks like Darth Vader.

B. The child went to school with a badly scraped arm, which Mrs Johnson had not cleaned or attended to. The school nurse had to clean the scrape.

This version has an unadorned comment supporting her parenting skills but a vivid titbit of detail slating her:

A. Mrs Johnson sees to it that her child washes and brushes his teeth before bed time.

B. The child went to school with a badly scraped arm, which Mrs Johnson had not cleaned or attended to. The school nurse had to clean the scrape, and in the process she accidentally spilled mercurochrome and left a red stain on the breast of her nurse's uniform.

After listening to one of the two versions, the participants were asked: 'According to law, a judge who decides in this case must act "in the best interest of the child". If you were the judge, how would you rule?'

The crucial facts of the case were equal in both versions of the recording. Only some of the minor yet colourful details varied between the two. Yet those minor details had an impact that was far from trivial. Participants who heard the vivid details supporting Mrs Johnson's case were more likely to decide that her son should remain with her. The participants who heard the vivid details arguing against her case were more likely to suggest that her son be taken into foster care.[84]

If you read the two sets of statements again, you'll see that the additional details are irrelevant to the case, totally immaterial. A good mother should get her son to brush his teeth. Whether he uses a plain toothbrush or one shaped like Darth Vader shouldn't matter. Similarly, a good mother shouldn't let her son go to school with a scraped arm. The nurse's clumsiness shouldn't factor into the question as to whether Mrs Johnson should be allowed to keep her son.

Yet the details *did* matter. When the participants heard more details, they found those facts correspondingly easier to remember and were more likely to judge Mrs Johnson's suitability as a parent in either direction.

Telling stories to win people over

Telling people a story may be an even better way of influencing people's actions than activating their imaginations and hoping that they fill in the blanks. Research clearly tells us that we might do well to use individual stories to influence people's behaviour. Remember the study by Timothy Wilson and Nancy Brekke of the students who read an independent report on condoms highlighting the superiority of Brand A over Brand B? One in three of the participants in the study ignored the expert report and was more influenced by a couple of anecdotal reports. To repeat: for a third of those participants, sensational stories trumped hard facts.

That doesn't mean that we should dispense entirely with facts and statistics. However, consider what we might achieve when we have stories, anecdotes, and retellings of events that *back up* our facts or statistics.

This is far from a definitive list, but here are some ideas as to how you could guide people's behaviour with stories and anecdotes:

- Cautionary tales. For example, rather than telling people about the risks of driving under the influence of alcohol, try to find a news cutting about a specific incident. Share the details with your audience about the driver's age, his occupation, the number of children he left behind, and the colourful details of the crash.

- Examples of good behaviour. If you want employees to focus on customer service, tell them about the time one particular employee took an elderly customer home in his own car because she suddenly felt too unwell and didn't think she'd be able to take the bus home. Or bosses often want their employees to be 'more creative'. But what does that mean in practice? Give people a handful of concrete examples so they can picture what creativity looks like. Stories may help to take the guesswork out of how people are supposed to behave.

- Highlighting the benefits of a product or service. Say you run a hotel. Rather than describing what guests could do, why not have three or four testimonials explaining what guests actually have done; perhaps a testimonial from a young man who talks about the jet-skiing and scuba-diving he did and a testimonial from an older woman talking about the massage and beauty treatments she enjoyed at the spa. A third testimonial might come from an older couple, talking about the tours they did to nearby sights. Stories may make products and services come to life and become so much more appealing than a dry list of options, features, and benefits.

- Making you *more* memorable. When I meet people at conferences, I could describe myself by saying to people that 'I'm a business psychologist, which means that I interview candidates on behalf of organisations and coach senior managers' and leave it at that. But I find that it helps to give an example or two by mentioning what I've been working on recently. So I usually add something like: 'Last week I interviewed some candidates on behalf of a major German bank to decide who should become the new managing director of their private equity division. One of the candidates came across extremely confidently to the point of arrogance, but on detailed questioning, I suspected that he had exaggerated some of his experience. And this morning I coached a thirty-something advertising executive who's starting up his own agency. He's ultra-confident and personable but wanted some help in building up his profile and networking more effectively.' The research suggests that even those little examples may help to get across what I do more effectively than merely cataloguing what I offer.

Here's the crunch though: *remember to include concrete, vivid details* in your stories. The little, seemingly trivial details and factoids matter. Even though you might not think they're important, research tells us that it makes stories easier to understand, easier to recall, and ultimately more persuasive too.

So avoid describing a man as 'athletic' as it makes your audience have to do a little work to see him in their minds. You'd be better off saying that he 'goes to the gym four times a week' or that he 'has broad shoulders and biceps that bulge from his sleeves when he wears a T-shirt'. Describing a house as 'large' could mean a number of things; say instead that it has 'six bedrooms and three bathrooms'. A 'happy' girl is harder to picture than saying that 'the girl laughed so much that you could see the fillings in her back teeth'.

When it comes to telling tales that not only educate but also effect behaviour change, those tasty titbits of detail can make a big difference.

CHAPTER SIX
friendship and favours

'*If you would win a man to your cause,
first convince him that you are his sincere friend.*'
Abraham Lincoln

It won't surprise you to hear that most people are more easily swayed by friends and the people they like. But what causes one person to like another? What helps to accelerate the process by which two people become friends?

In the summer of 1969, a young man with inky black hair named Stephen accompanied an elderly friend on a visit to a hospital in Birmingham. His friend needed a blood test but didn't feel very confident about the prospect of talking to the doctors so Stephen agreed to liaise on his behalf.

Roaming the maze-like corridors of the hospital, Stephen and his friend couldn't find the right department. Eventually, they gave up and decided to ask for directions.

By chance – or perhaps by design – Stephen approached a slim, rather pretty nurse for help. She had long black hair tumbling down to the small of her back and he couldn't help but notice how distractingly attractive she was, so he introduced himself and found out that her name was Judy.

The blood test turned out to be fairly routine and Stephen escorted his friend home. But he couldn't get the thought of the charming young nurse out of his head.

Three weeks later, he was still thinking about her and decided to track her down. With a not inconsiderable amount of detective work, he managed to get Judy on the nurses' phone to ask her out on a date.

The next weekend, they went to see a movie. As they queued outside the cinema on a bright summer's evening, they chatted. And, as people do on dates, they got talking about their birthdays. Stephen asked Judy when her birthday was.

'The second of August,' she replied.

'You're joking. You're making it up,' he said.

'No. Why would I make it up?' she replied in astonishment.

'Because that's my birthday too,' he explained.

True, Stephen was several years older. But what were the odds? What a coincidence that they had the same birthday!

They went on a few more dates and their relationship bloomed. As the weeks turned into months, they continued to grow closer and closer, falling in love. As the leaves turned red and brown in the autumn, Stephen asked Judy to marry him and they became husband and wife only weeks before Christmas.

So what does that have to do with the psychology of influence and persuasion? Before I explain, let me say that the story of how Stephen and Judy got together has a rather special resonance for me. I'll tell you why: a handful of years after they got married, they conceived a child together. And they named him Robert – although nearly everyone who knows him calls him Rob. That's me. Because Stephen Yeung is my father and Judy my mother.

To some people, the fact that Stephen and Judy had the same birth date was nothing less than destiny, the fickle finger of fate telling them that they were made for each other. Others might shake their heads and call it no more than a happy coincidence. But as we'll discover, such flukes and twists of fate may point to further tools we can all use not only to cement our relationships with friends, business partners, and even lovers, but also to become more influential and persuasive.

Similarity and soft spots

Psychologists are always interested in ways of predicting how people will behave. So imagine for a moment that you've signed up as a volunteer for a scientific study on astrology. You arrive at the psychologist's laboratory to discover there's already another participant waiting there: a man with dark hair and a tanned face who's about the same age as you or maybe a few years older. The two of you sit in silence while the experimenter explains that it doesn't matter whether you're a believer or a sceptic about astrology. The study is designed to test the claim by astrologers that personality is related to one's birth sign. Does being born under the sign of Aquarius or Gemini, Leo or Sagittarius, or indeed any other star sign really shape the person that you have become?

The experimenter, a middle-aged woman with thin lips and grey hair scraped back in a tight ponytail, asks both you and the other participant to fill out forms with details about yourselves. You scribble down your address, occupation, date of birth – the usual stuff.

The experimenter points to a stack of 12 folders, each labelled with one of the signs of the zodiac, and explains that you will each receive a different personality test depending on your particular astrological sign. She asks the other participant: 'Could you tell me your birthday please?'

The other participant calls out his birthday and, to your surprise, your fellow participant has exactly the same birthday as you! So when the experimenter asks you for your birthday, you can't help but grin when you say that you have the same birthday too.

The experimenter acknowledges the coincidence with a nod but otherwise seems disinterested. She gives you each a personality test to complete. The questions are straightforward and you only take a handful of minutes to complete the short questionnaire. When both you and the other participant have finished, the experimenter thanks you both for your time and excuses you.

You and the other participant gather your belongings and depart. Walking down the corridor to the exit, he takes his backpack off his shoulder and pulls a sheaf of papers from it. A little hesitantly, he looks at you and opens his mouth to speak. It's the first time the two of you have spoken.

'I'm doing an assignment at the moment and I've been asked to find someone who doesn't know me to critique my essay. I wonder if you could read this eight-page essay for me and give me one page of written feedback on whether my arguments are persuasive and why?'

You're busy. You can think of plenty of things you'd rather be doing. But this guy seems so sincere. You're torn. What are you going to do?

Of course this is another psychological experiment and this alleged other participant is in fact a confederate in league with the experimenter. But when this study was conducted by Jerry Burger, an acclaimed professor of psychology at Santa Clara University in California, the genuine participants didn't know that they were being tested surreptitiously.

Participants had in fact been randomly assigned to one of two groups. With one half of the participants, the confederate simply looked across at the genuine participants' birthdays and claimed that he had the same birthday. With the other half of the participants, he used his own birthday, which was never the same as that of the genuine participants.

When the participants heard that the confederate had a birthday that was different to their own, only 34 per cent of them agreed to read his eight-page essay and critique it. After all, he was more or less a total stranger. The participants had only met him less than an hour ago. However, when they believed that they shared the same birthday, nearly twice the number – 62 per cent – agreed to the same request.[85]

The confederate hardly said anything and acted the same way with all of the participants. However, the fact that half of the participants believed that they shared the same birthday – such a seemingly trivial similarity – contrived enough of a connection that they were swayed to agree to his request.

Burger, a man with a perpetual smile and brown hair combed into a jaunty quiff, is a veteran researcher with decades of experience peering into the psychology of compliance. In a follow-up experiment, he and his team enlisted women subjects to take part in a study supposedly exploring the nature of creativity. Yet the creativity story was surreptitiously a pretext to get subjects into the department of psychology one at a time.

Each subject completed the alleged experiment on creativity – its details don't really concern us – and then left the laboratory. Outside of the building that housed the psychology department, the subject was ambushed by a woman saying that she was a volunteer collecting donations on behalf of the Cystic Fibrosis Foundation. Her name badge bore the logo of the Cystic Fibrosis Foundation.

With half of the subjects, the volunteer used her own name on the name badge. With the other half of the subjects, the volunteer had been briefed by the experimenters and used the same first name as the subject on her badge.

How would you react if you came across a charity worker looking for donations who had the same first name as you?

Most of the subjects that the volunteer approached handed over a small donation. But when she pretended that her name was the same as that of her subjects, she collected more than double the amount – 107 per cent more on average.[86]

The volunteer didn't even have to draw attention to the name on her badge. Subjects automatically noticed it, creating an instant connection, an affinity that was enough to make them considerably more amenable to the volunteer's request.

When we're weighing up whether to do someone a favour, we should be deciding on how much time we have, how much effort and cost is involved, and what we might get out of it. We *shouldn't* be influenced by incidental details such as their birth date or name. But we are. Taking the two studies together, we can conclude that similarity – even the kind of superficial commonality concocted by having the same birthday or the same name – promotes some kind of bond, which makes people more receptive to being influenced.

So maybe the fact that my parents Stephen and Judy shared the same birthday really did draw them together just that little bit more. Without that shared birthday, would they have got together anyway? Of course we can only speculate. But if they hadn't continued with their relationship and got married, I wouldn't exist and you wouldn't be reading this book!

Harnessing the effects of similarity

Plenty of studies have established that people like each other more and are more positively predisposed to their requests when they feel they have things in common.[87] Remember that this has been demonstrated in experiments in which the similarities were seemingly trivial – sharing a birthday or having the same name – and the participants had only known each other for a matter of minutes.

Consider how much more persuasive you could become if you can uncover real commonalities with the people you meet. So whether you're looking to make friends at parties or to turn prospects into customers at a business event, ask lots of questions when you meet people. Find out where they were born and grew up, where they went to school and university, and whether they're fans of football or rugby or cricket or athletics or any other sport. Of course you don't want to sound like a police interrogator – you may need to share something about yourself occasionally too – but don't stop there. Keep going and enquire politely what they do for a living, where they've worked before, what they enjoy doing for fun, and what their favourite TV shows, books, films, and restaurants are – you get the idea.

Once you discover that you genuinely share the same interest or background, say so. 'Oh, I studied economics at university too.' 'I can't stand reality TV programmes either!' The more you both have in common, the stronger the pull you'll generate. And the good news is that you won't have to fake it. The psychology of similarity means that it's not just going to be the people you meet who will like you more – you'll genuinely like them more too.

If you need to persuade a particular person or group of people to seeing things your way, then think about what you wear on those occasions too. Experiments show that both men and women are more inclined to do favours for people who dress like themselves.[88] So if you need to give a talk at an oil refinery to a group of workers wearing boiler-suits and hard-hats, don't do what my colleague and good friend David once did: he wore his smart £500 suit, a white shirt, and an Armani tie. Dress down for the occasion. Or even if you're an artist or fashion designer used to wearing vintage clothes and artfully distressed jeans, make a special effort when you go to see your stuffy bank manager.

Recognise too that you may sometimes benefit from drawing on the support of other people. Say you're trying to persuade a six-year-old boy to brush and floss his teeth regularly. Well, you and other adults may not be the most effective role models. If you can, find a way to bring the boy into contact with another six-year-old boy who can talk about why he cleans his teeth unfailingly.

The force of social obligation

We like what we know. And what we know more than anything is ourselves. So it makes sense that we like people who are like ourselves and that we're more open to being persuaded by them. But there's an even more powerful force that trumps the effects of mere similarity and liking.

In the late 1960s, Dennis Regan was a young psychologist studying for his doctorate at Stanford University. A lot of research was being done at the time on the effects of liking on persuasion, but Regan wanted to do something different. In a classic experiment, he enrolled pairs of participants at a gallery for a study on 'aesthetics'.

Imagine that you're one of the volunteers and let's see how you'd react. So you arrive at the psychology department to be greeted by a prim secretary at a reception desk. She smiles and invites you to take a seat in the reception area.

A few minutes later, another person comes along. In his early twenties, he tells the secretary that his name is John and that he's here for the study on 'aesthetics'. The secretary greets him, tells him to take a seat too and says that the experimenter will be along in a couple of moments.

As you're waiting, the secretary gets up from her desk a couple of times to go to a nearby filing cabinet. Then she shakes her head and scurries out of the room. Perhaps she has forgotten something or is running an errand, but whatever it is, she is in a hurry.

You carry on waiting and then, as you're starting to get bored, the secretary's phone rings. Both you and John look at each other. After five or six rings, John saunters over to the desk and picks up the phone.

He listens to what the caller is saying, his head nodding a couple of times.

Shockingly, he sneers down the phone: 'Nah, there's no secretary here.'

Another pause and this time he rolls his eyes skyward. His voice gets louder and, almost spitting down the phone now, he says: 'Look, I don't work here, lady, for chrissake … Just call later.'

He slams the phone down, clearly cutting the caller off in mid-flow.

As he walks away from the desk back to his seat, you avoid eye contact. You're not a nosy person but you couldn't help but notice the exchange and you definitely don't want to let on how rude you found his behaviour. What an obnoxious jerk!

Anyway, moments later a man appears, introducing himself as Dennis, the experimenter. He leads you and John into a small room where he explains the purpose of the study. He will show you photos, reproductions of famous paintings, and ask you to rate them on various scales.

The research itself is very straightforward. You look at each photograph and then tick on a series of scales how you feel about the painting. Actually, it's not just straightforward, it's rather dull. But you get on with the task and finish it easily enough.

As you get towards the end of the photos to rate, John motions for your attention. When you look up, he passes you a scrap of paper that he seems to have torn from a notebook. The experimenter has his head down. On it, he has scribbled the following words:

Would you do me a favour? I'm selling raffle tickets for my high school back home to build a new gym. The tickets cost 25 cents each and the prize is a new Corvette. The thing is, if I sell the most tickets I get 50 dollars and I could use it. If you'd buy any, would you just write the number on this note and give it back to me right away so I can make out the tickets? Any would help, the more the better. Thanks.

How many tickets would you want to buy from him? Not many, I'd guess. You've not exchanged a single word with him. Actually, the only time you even heard him speak was when he was being tetchy and unhelpful on the secretary's phone.

The scenario I just described was more or less the basic set-up for Dennis Regan's experiment. Each time a true participant turned up, he was paired up with John, who was – surprise, surprise – secretly an accomplice hired by Regan to play the part of another participant. Regan was interested in whether participants' dislike or like for John influenced the number of tickets they were willing to buy from him.

Half of the true participants got to meet 'nasty John' who sneered his way through the call on the secretary's phone. The other half met a much more pleasant version of John. When 'nice John' answered the phone, he listened to the caller and explained in a friendly tone that he was sorry, but he didn't work in the building and didn't know where the secretary was.

When Regan tallied up the number of raffle tickets that participants were willing to buy, he found that participants bought significantly more tickets from 'nice John' than 'nasty John'. Not exactly a groundbreaking result, is it? That accords with what we would expect, that we are more open to persuasion by people we like. But that was only the start of the experiment.

With another two groups of participants, Regan again asked John to play both the nice and nasty roles. But this time he also gave the participants a breather halfway through rating the paintings. During the break, the experimenter announced that he needed to get something from his office, leaving the two participants alone.

During the unexpected lull in the experiment, John slipped out of the room and returned with two bottles of Coca-Cola. He said to the true participant: 'I asked the experimenter if I could get myself a Coke, and he said it was OK, so I bought one for you too.'

Then, as before, John slipped each participant his hand-scrawled note, explaining that he was trying to shift enough raffle tickets to win a prize.

To summarise then, there were actually four conditions in the experiment:

1) 'Nice John' behaved pleasantly on the phone, but didn't buy any bottles of Coke.

2) 'Nasty John' behaved unpleasantly on the phone, and didn't buy any bottles of Coke.

3) 'Nice John' behaved pleasantly on the phone and bought the participant a bottle of Coke.

4) 'Nasty John' behaved unpleasantly on the phone, but bought the participant a bottle of Coke.

As I already mentioned, participants who met 'nice John' in condition 1 bought more raffle tickets than those who met 'nasty John' in condition 2. We already know that people are more open to persuasion from people they like and participants who saw John behave rudely liked him less and therefore bought fewer tickets from him.

What about conditions 3 and 4 when John did an unsolicited favour for the participant though? Well, when 'nice John' was pleasant on the phone *and* bought the participant a bottle of Coke, participants did indeed like him *even* more. The additional bottle of Coke made participants buy still more tickets from him. But the same thing happened in condition 4 too: even though John had behaved in a thoroughly boorish and obnoxious manner, participants still felt *compelled* to buy more tickets from him. In fact, participants who met 'nasty John' bought the same number of tickets as those who met 'nice John'. The gift of the bottle of Coke eliminated the effects of John's meanness or likeability.[89]

Spelling it out then, the need to repay a favour seems to override the extent to which we like other people – even when the favour is not only unexpected but unwanted. Let's stop for a moment to ponder the implication. It suggests that doing people a favour may be a more winning method of influencing them than having to strike up a rapport, establish what we have in common, and all of those other techniques.

What's more, research by sociologists in different cultures around the world suggests that the need to repay a favour – even when the favour is unwanted *and* we don't care much for the person who did us the favour – seems to be almost universal.[90] Whether you're reading this book in India or Italy, Singapore or South Africa, Honduras or Hong Kong, you'll almost certainly find that doing someone a favour will make them feel grateful or guilty but ultimately indebted to you and more open to being influenced by you.

Social scientists argue that the need to reciprocate favours may have been instrumental in the survival and evolution of the human race. We aren't a solitary species; we've always needed other people around us to survive. Our ancestors rallied together in clans and tribes and they needed rules – such as the norm of reciprocation – to ensure the survival of the whole group, not just one or two individuals.

A team led by James Rilling, an anthropologist at Emory University in Atlanta, Georgia, has gathered support for the notion that we may have evolved to reciprocate, to return even unwanted favours. Rilling and his associates asked pairs of participants to play a game in which they could either choose to compete or cooperate with each other to win cash prizes. Similar games have been used by social scientists for decades to investigate when and why people choose to work together, but Rilling's study in 2002 did something that hadn't been done before: he used brain-scanning equipment to monitor brain activity as the participants weighed up their options and made their decisions. When the participants chose to cooperate, several areas of their brains lit up that are commonly associated with the processing of reward.[91] Even though they could sometimes have won more money by competing, the participants got more of a mental reward, a psychological high, by cooperating. That suggests that our very brains may be hard-wired to trust others, to cooperate, and reciprocate favours. No wonder we may still respond to unwanted favours from people we dislike.

The absurdity of reciprocity

People's profound desire to reciprocate even unwanted favours leads them to behave in sometimes fiercely irrational ways. To illustrate the illogical consequences of the norm of reciprocity, let me take you through a study completed by the University of Michigan that attempted to improve response rates to telephone surveys in the United States.

A little background first: the Survey of Consumer Attitudes is a monthly telephone poll of American consumers' expectations about the economy and their own financial situations. Telephone interviewers are allocated randomly generated telephone numbers to call in order to make the survey as representative of the nation's attitudes as possible. The results are important because they are scrutinised by both government and non-governmental agencies for the purposes of economic planning.

As you might expect though, the telephone interviewers often have a hard time convincing the people they call to take part in the survey. After a long day at work, the average homeowner wants to relax, maybe cook some dinner or play with the kids, not talk to a total stranger about how much they earn, how much they spent on food and fuel, and how much they expect to spend on their next holiday. So experts from the University of Michigan were drafted in to investigate ways of boosting response rates.

If you were asked to help an organisation to increase the number of people at home who would agree to take part in a telephone survey, how would you go about it? Perhaps you'd consider offering people incentives for their participation. In 1996, the telephone interviewers did indeed start offering payments to a sample of randomly chosen households. They began by offering $5, upped it a couple of months later to $10, and even tried promising $20.

The result? Nothing. Offering even $20 to homeowners made almost no difference to people's willingness to participate. That not only disappointed but surprised the researchers. Remember that this was 1996 and $20 was around three times the minimum hourly wage. The fact that almost nobody was willing to exchange a half-hour of their time for what it might have taken them three hours to earn seemed to indicate that people valued either their leisure time or privacy immensely, that their cooperation couldn't be bought.

The following year, the researchers changed tack. They tried sending letters to homeowners, informing they that someone would call on behalf of the Survey of Consumer Attitudes. They thought that a brief letter would make the subsequent call less intrusive. But the letter made no difference either. The people at home who received a letter remained unimpressed and were no more likely to take part in the survey than people who were called with no advance notice.

Finally, in 1998, the researchers decided to try a different financial incentive. Some homes were sent a standard letter telling them that they would be receiving a call from the Survey of Consumer Attitudes. But a separate sample of homes was sent the letter along with a crisp $5 bill, thanking them in advance for taking part. And this time it did have a significant effect. Compared to the proportion of homeowners who agreed to take part in the survey after being sent the standard letter, an additional 16 per cent of homeowners who received the $5 bill agreed to take part.

That seems irrational. People in 1996 were offered incentives of up to $20 as a reward for participating but spurned the offer. Yet the inclusion of much less money – a mere $5 bill – nudged the response rate up by 16 per cent.[92]

The homeowners could easily have seen the $5 bill as a free gift. There was no legal contract forcing them to take part in the survey. They could have pocketed the cash and hung up on the telephone interviewers when they called. But they didn't. The norm of reciprocity was so monstrously powerful that a significant proportion of them felt compelled to participate in the survey even though the gift had been unasked for.

Another study highlights even more strongly the clout that the need for reciprocity holds over us. Researchers Jeannine James and Richard Bolstein offered different incentives to the owners of small businesses in the US for completing a postal survey on the topic of business insurance. They found that business owners who were offered $50 for sending in a completed questionnaire were no more likely to do so than their counterparts who were not offered a cent. These were busy business professionals, after all. However, the inclusion of *a single dollar* did increase response rates.[93]

Sounds crazy, doesn't it? Absolutely, grotesquely ridiculous. That people would turn down $50 as a reward for doing something yet feel almost enthralled into responding when sent a measly dollar. Yet taken together, the two studies illustrate the strength of the norm of reciprocity. When asked to take part in either a phone survey or a postal survey, people felt compelled to participate – even when the gift had been totally unasked for.

Of course many organisations have caught on to the fact that even tiny gifts can create a feeling of indebtedness. Many charities send out freebies – car stickers, little key chains, free Christmas cards, personalised address labels – in the hope of soliciting donations. Insurance companies often include free pens with their mailouts in the hope of getting homeowners to get in touch for at least a free quote.

Savvy individuals know how to put reciprocity into play too. In high-end restaurants, they appreciate that the best way to secure a table on a busy night is to press a folded-up note into the maître d's hand. And in many cultures, business just doesn't get done without upfront incentives – although some disgruntled suppliers may think of these as unfair, extortionate, and unnecessary bribes.

Doing favours without doing favours

Doing someone a favour to secure a favour hardly seems a revolutionary method for influencing people. But there is a way to appear as if you're doing someone a favour without handing over cash or any sort of gift or incentive at all. It's all in phrasing your request in the right way.

Play along with me and picture that you're walking on the street enjoying the sunshine when a charity fund-raiser steps in your way with a friendly but beseeching smile. He's wearing a shirt and tie but has teamed it with jeans and scuffed tennis shoes, perhaps to demonstrate that he's a cool and funky individual.

He explains: 'Hi, I'm Luke and I'm working for Dr Chung at the Institute of Mental Health not far from here. He's coordinating a volunteer mental health programme to be staffed by non-professionals. We're recruiting people to work as voluntary unpaid counsellors or clerical office workers in a community mental health agency for two hours once on a single afternoon or evening.'

He pauses for a moment to let the information sink in. Then he asks, 'Would you like to be considered for such a position?'

Hmm. I'm not sure I would say 'yes' if a total stranger pounced on me to ask me the question. I'm busy and can think of plenty of things I'd rather be doing with a free afternoon or evening. Indeed, only 29 per cent of people who were asked more or less the same question agreed to sign up as a mental health volunteer.

Yet the charity crusaders managed to sign up nearly three times as many people, a massive 77 per cent of the people they talked to by asking just one other question first. How?

On this occasion, they started by making a very different request: 'Hi, I'm Luke and I'm working for Dr Chung at the Institute of Mental Health not far from here. He's coordinating a volunteer mental health programme to be staffed by non-professionals. We're recruiting people to work as voluntary unpaid counsellors in a community mental health agency.'

So far so straightforward. But here's the twist: 'The position would require two hours of your time per week for a minimum of two years. You would be assisting regular staff members in their duties. Would you like to be considered for such a position?'

That's ridiculous! Two hours of your time per week for a minimum of *two years*? Surely you misheard?

Seeing the look of disbelief on your face, the disappointed volunteer continues: 'Well, I'm also recruiting volunteers for another position which would entail two hours once on a single afternoon or evening working as a voluntary unpaid clerical office worker in a mental health agency. Would you like to be considered for this position?'

Well, that seems more reasonable. You can't dedicate two hours a week for two years to the cause, but perhaps two hours on a single occasion wouldn't be so bad. And the participants in the study thought the same thing, allowing the charity workers to boost extraordinarily the numbers of people they signed up for the two-hour stint of volunteering.[94]

The technique has been called the 'large-then-small' request strategy by some academics and the 'rejection-then-retreat' manoeuvre by others. But it is perhaps best known as the 'door-in-the-face' technique: slamming a figurative door in a requester's face because of too large an initial request seems to make people more likely to agree easing the door ajar to the comparatively smaller request that follows it.[95]

I hinted that this is still a procedure that harnesses people's need for reciprocity. So how does that work? The secret is that people seem to regard concessions as favours. The subjects in the study we just covered thought that the charity worker genuinely wanted to recruit someone to work for a couple of hours a week for two years. When they heard the second, smaller request, they thought that the charity worker was backing down, conceding, and doing them a favour by dropping the larger request and only asking them to volunteer for a mere two hours on a single occasion.

People make compromises all the time. A union representative negotiating with the chief executive of a business may demand a 12 per cent pay rise for workers, but secretly be willing to settle for 5 per cent. A salesperson begins by introducing you to the hyper-expensive state-of-the-art wares in his catalogue but seems content on selling you something from the middle of the range.

A smart teenager may ask her parents if she can stay out until 2 a.m. on a Saturday night. She knows that if she starts her bargaining by asking to stay out until midnight, she may be told to be home by 10 p.m. So she increases her initial demand by saying that all of her friends will be out until two or maybe even three in the morning. Of course she gets the door slammed in her face from the ridiculousness of the request to begin with. But then she can appear to back down, to show how reasonable she is in compromising and agreeing to return home by midnight.

Claus Ebster is a business and marketing professor at the University of Vienna whose forte is identifying ways of selling products more effectively. A burly middle-aged man with puppy-dog eyes, Ebster put together a charming experiment that shed further light on the face-in-the-door effect. He began by setting up a makeshift stall to sell home-made cheese to passers-by. However, he chose a curious location for his business, putting the stall just outside a mountain lodge 5,065 feet above sea level in the Austrian Alps; and the passers-by were hikers navigating a treacherous path through the rocky terrain.

Possibly the last thing the passers-by expected was a hut outside a mountain lodge touting cheese. But the enthusiastic salesperson – a woman – gamely asked the perhaps rather surprised hikers: 'Would you like to buy a piece of homemade cheese produced here? How about this piece which weighs a pound? It costs four euros.'

Only 9 per cent of the climbers agreed to take the cheese. After all, they weren't even offered a taste of the cheese. What if it was awful? Plus they'd have to carry it all the way back down the side of the mountain.

With another group of hikers, the saleswoman used the door-in-the-face technique, asking: 'Would you like to buy a piece of home-made cheese produced here? How about this piece which weighs two pounds? It costs eight euros.' All of the mountaineers slammed the metaphorical door in the seller's face by declining the request, so she asked a second question: 'Would you like to buy a smaller piece which weighs only one pound? It costs four euros.'

As expected, backing down from the initial request made the saleswoman seem more reasonable; 24 per cent of these hikers agreed to buy the cheese.

So far that's entirely consistent with what we know about the door-in-the-face technique. By making an initial demand that is too sizeable for people to agree to, we can increase the chances that they will accept a later request. When we make a concession in the size of our request, people make a concession by agreeing to it. We invoke the norm of reciprocity without having to part with cash, gifts, or actual favours.

However, in a third set-up, the saleswoman emphasised the concession that was being made. After the hikers rejected the initial request to buy the larger, two-pound lump of cheese, she admitted: 'Well, two pounds is probably really too much. After all, you have to carry the cheese all the way down to the valley.'

When the experimenter then asked if the climbers would like to buy the smaller one-pound cheese, 40 per cent of them said 'yes'.[96]

From Ebster's study, we learn that we can boost the effectiveness of the door-in-the-face technique even further by *making it clear that we are making a concession*. Backing down from an initial, supersize request and appearing to be more reasonable encourages people to listen to our second, smaller request. But we can magnify the effect even more by pointing out how reasonable we're being.

It's the thought that counts

At the start of the chapter, we established that similarity and the perception that we have things in common with people makes them like us. However, helping them – either by doing them a genuine favour or appearing to do them a favour by making a concession from an initial, large request – makes them crave returning the favour even more.

When it comes to doing favours for people though, it seems that it's not the size of your favour but – ahem – what you do with it that counts. In the spring of 1998, Monmouth University researcher David Strohmetz and his collaborators asked a waitress in a busy restaurant to take a key role in an experiment on the effects of favours on customer tipping. They gave the waitress a small wicker basket filled with pieces of individually foil-wrapped chocolates. They also gave her a stack of four index cards, each of which asked her to do something different when she presented the bill to diners in the restaurant. As she approached each table, she picked one of the shuffled cards at random, which told her what to do at the table.

The first card (the control condition) asked the waitress to deliver the bill as usual, which established a baseline for how much customers would normally tip after an otherwise unremarkable meal. The other three cards, however, instructed her to offer each diner on a table either one or two pieces of chocolate from her basket. So did more chocolates result in bigger tips?

When she offered each customer a single piece of chocolate, her tips grew by 3 per cent. The small favour on her part merited a rather trivial return gesture from the customers.

When she allowed each customer to choose two pieces of chocolate, her tips grew a little more. On average, she earned 14 per cent more per table. Over the course of a week, an extra 14 per cent could really add up.

The fourth, final card had a special instruction on it for the waitress. With a quarter of the customers, she offered each customer one piece of chocolate and then walked away. But after a pace, she stopped and swivelled on the spot – apparently changing her mind – to offer her customers an additional piece of chocolate. So, while she still only gave the customers two pieces of chocolate each, she seemed to have acted in an uncommonly generous fashion. The idea was to make the customers believe that the waitress was only supposed to give out a single piece of chocolate per person, but that she had decided to do them an extraordinary favour. In return, they paid her favour, her apparent generosity, back by tipping her 21 per cent more.[97]

That's an essential discovery because it shows us that, when it comes to winning people over, it's not the absolute size of the favours or concessions we make that matters. It's the *perceived* thoughtfulness or generosity of the gesture that counts. The study on the side of a mountain demonstrates that telling people that we're making a concession boosts their willingness to be persuaded. Highlighting our helpfulness makes people more aware of the favour, which subsequently encourages people to be more amenable to persuasion. And Strohmetz's study of the waitress again illustrates that it's when people are prompted about the significance of our gestures that they are most willing to pay us back.

So if you want to be persuasive, don't just do favours for people. Make sure they know that you're doing them a favour. Spell out the fact that you're making a concession and you will almost certainly find people will be more amenable to helping you out in turn.

Plaudits and puffery

Some people love getting their hair cut while others see it as a necessary evil, a chore. Whatever your views, do you think you would be swayed to tip more heavily if your barber or hair stylist complimented you?

John Seiter, a professor of speech communication at Utah State University, and his colleague Eric Dutson set out to answer this very question. They asked two women hair stylists in a unisex salon to either compliment or not compliment their customers. Rather cleverly, the research duo gave the hair stylists three pennies marked with the numbers 1, 2, or 3 to ensure that they complimented the customers in a genuinely random way, irrespective of how the customer actually ended up looking. Moments before finishing a hairstyle, each stylist put her hand in her pocket to pull out a coin. If the penny was marked with a 1, the stylist gave no compliment. The number 2 indicated that the stylist should say, 'Your hair looks terrific.' If the number 3 popped out, the stylist remarked, 'Any hairstyle would look good on you.'

Before we discuss the results, let's think about it a little. When the hairdresser made the admiring comment, 'Your hair looks terrific,' wasn't that really a tribute to her own flair as a hair stylist, a compliment to herself rather than to the customer?

And if someone said, 'Any hairstyle would look good on you,' surely that's too transparent. Surely people would simply shake their heads in annoyance that they were being flattered so insincerely.

But it didn't matter. Compared to the control condition in which the stylists made no compliment, saying, 'Your hair looks terrific,' resulted in 40 per cent higher tips. Even when the stylists gushed, 'Any hairstyle would look good on you,' customers still handed over tips that were 37 per cent bigger.[98]

It's not only hair stylists who benefit from complimenting their customers either. In a separate study also led by John Seiter, waiters and waitresses were asked to praise all of the diners on certain tables by making the bright and breezy comment, 'You all made good choices!' after they placed their orders. Yes, I know that sounds more than a little cheesy. But hey, it worked. Compared to a control condition in which they didn't pay their customers any compliment after taking their orders, the waiters and waitresses gained significantly bigger tips.[99]

If you think about it, a compliment is simply another type of favour, a small gift that costs nothing to give. Most people enjoy feeling good about themselves; they welcome admiring comments from friends as confirmation that they have made the right choices. 'That's a lovely dress,' 'Thank you for dinner – you're such a good cook,' 'You've done such a great job in refurbishing this house!'

Of course people may relish receiving genuine compliments from friends, people whose opinions they respect. But can't people tell that some compliments aren't totally honest, that they're delivered with an ulterior motive?

We might argue that customers in hairdressing salons are pre-occupied with how they look. They've paid money to look good so they're willing participants in receiving praise. Perhaps diners in restaurants are also looking forward to enjoying their meals so they're again more than happy to receive praise for the choices they made. But surely there must be occasions when people can see through comments that are transparently obvious flattery – mustn't there?

In a clever experiment, marketing researchers Elaine Chan and Jaideep Sengupta at Hong Kong University of Science and Technology asked participants to read a brief leaflet sent to them by a new retail store that was patently interested in courting their custom. The researchers explained that this was a real store and a real pamphlet. However, for reasons of confidentiality, they had changed the name of the store. Here's what the leaflet said:

> Don't Miss the Grand Opening of PerfectStore!
> Our store will feature a wide array of clothing brands, including several famous American, European and Japanese designer labels.
> We are contacting you directly because we know that you are a fashionable and stylish person. Your dress sense is not only classy but also chic. As someone with exceptional taste in

clothes, you will enjoy the designs featured in our new collection,
featuring 'must-haves' for the coming season.

The flattery in that final paragraph is so transparently obvious that it's enough to make anyone sick, right? Read the paragraph again if you don't believe me.

The researchers then presented the participants with a second leaflet about a different retailer called RovoStore. The letter was deliberately constructed to mention similar information. The only thing missing was the transparent flattery.

Immediately after reading the two flyers, half of the participants were told that they could choose to take a store coupon worth 50 Hong Kong dollars (about £4) from only one of the two retailers. Despite the fact that the leaflet from PerfectStore was almost desperately sycophantic – 'Your dress sense is not only classy but also chic' – 60 per cent of the participants still plumped for the coupon from PerfectStore. It seemed that at least some of the participants had been swayed by the overtly flattering message.

The other half of the participants were sent away and told to come back three days later. On their return, they were again presented with the same choice. Did they want a voucher from PerfectStore, which had said nice things about their dress sense and style, or from RovoStore? This time, 80 per cent of the participants chose the coupon from PerfectStore.[100]

Interpreting the results, the researchers suggest that the participants simply remembered that they liked one store (PerfectStore) more than the other. The flattery had induced a small amount of goodwill in them. The fact that the flattery was clearly aimed at getting them to visit their store and buy products from the store didn't matter.

So yes, people may be able to tell when they're being flattered insincerely. But especially with the passing of time, they forget the insincerity and just remember that there was something they liked about the person or organisation that paid them a compliment. And that's enough to steer their behaviour. Put simply then, flattery works.

Compliment or obsequiousness?

The research suggests that paying someone an admiring comment is doing them a small favour. It invokes the norm of reciprocity, making them more open-minded about the requests we may make of them.

Many people have a niggling voice at the back of their minds telling them when flattery may have an ulterior motive, for example when a shop assistant says, 'That outfit is perfect on you!' Clearly there is a sales commission to be earned if a customer buys the outfit. However, the research suggests that people don't mind mildly ulterior motives. Even in hair salons, restaurants, and shops in which the flatterer obviously has an economic interest in saying nice things, people are happy to accept the compliment and pay it back.

I'm not advocating that anyone should deliver total falsehoods to people in an attempt to manipulate them. Saying, 'You look so slim, have you lost weight?' when you think someone has actually gained weight will not only make you feel incredibly uncomfortable, your insincerity may leak out in your non-verbal signalling, your body language too. But if you can genuinely say something positive about someone – perhaps 'That's a lovely colour on you,' or 'You were so helpful the last time I phoned you up for advice' – then why not do it? People enjoy being complimented. And if a genuine compliment makes them more amenable to your requests and suggestions, doesn't everybody win?

CHAPTER SEVEN
the perils of prizes

'*Far and away the best prize that life offers
is the chance to work hard at work worth doing.*'
Theodore Roosevelt

I once worked with a vibrant television producer I'll call Imogen. She had everything going for her: she was blessed with a smile that reminded me of a young Julia Roberts circa *Pretty Woman* and a career that seemed destined for the top. What was the secret of her success?

She confided in me that she grew up in a household that was run somewhat like a military academy. Imogen's late father was a distinguished pilot, a wing commander in the Royal Air Force. He travelled extensively around the world to wherever his overseers sent him, but on his brief jaunts home, he insisted on using a system of merits and demerits to guide the behaviour of Imogen and her two younger brothers.

Merits were awarded for actions such as helping their mother with laying the table for dinner, tidying their bedrooms, and mucking out the stables. The children could win points for doing well in sports such as rugby and cricket for the boys and hockey for Imogen; they also won points for other activities such as performing in school plays, volunteering at church, and passing music exams. But the best way of earning merits was for achieving good grades at school. Ultimately, points made prizes: points were turned into pocket money at the end of each month.

The wing commander's ambition was to instil the values of hard work, discipline, and respect into his three children. It had worked for him and he believed that he could pass this legacy on to them.

So did the system work? Did his three children turn out as role models of virtue?

It certainly seemed to have benefited Imogen. She studied political science at university and then beat off a lot of competition to secure a coveted job at the BBC as a junior TV researcher. She worked her way up extremely quickly, becoming an assistant producer then a producer and director. Before she had turned 30, she was lured away to join an independent television production company in a more senior role. And she became an executive producer only a couple of years later.

Perhaps only one in 40 or 50 people who starts work in television manages to ascend to the lofty ranks of becoming an executive producer. Many others languish in the lower grades and eventually decide that they can't compete with the endless supply of fresh-faced early twenty-somethings who continually flood into the industry. Most of the executives I know tend to be far older too; Imogen is probably 10 to 15 years younger than the average executive. Her wing commander father would be proud of her.

The same probably can't be said for Imogen's two brothers. The older brother decided to take a year out to travel abroad before going to university. One year turned into two and then three and then four. To fund his lifestyle, he has taken various menial jobs, including working as a barista at a coffee chain, serving drinks behind the bar of a pub, and driving a van delivering dry cleaning to customers at home.

Imogen's youngest brother graduated from university with a third class honours degree in tourism and business studies. But he struggled to find work so had to move back into the family home. The last I heard, he was still living at home.

The wing commander's system of merits and demerits had mixed results. Imogen continues to soar, but her two siblings haven't done so well. But what does research tell us about the effectiveness of using bonuses, prizes, and other incentives to influence people's behaviour?

The true price of awarding a prize

The average children's nursery can often look more like a war zone than a classroom. Visit one and you'll no doubt see some of the kids running around, shouting and screaming. A few may be drawing or painting quietly. Others may be clambering over items of furniture or bashing toys against other toys or perhaps the furniture. But that's part of being a kid: children love to explore their environments, make up games, and test to destruction anything and everything that's not locked away in a cupboard safely out of reach.

At one particular nursery in Stanford, California, the kids were free to do pretty much whatever they wanted. They had building blocks to play with. They had easels for painting and housekeeping toys if they wanted to pretend that they were cooking dinner or cleaning the house. They had access to an outdoor playground so they could run and chase each other and get their faces dirty and their knees scraped as little kids inevitably do.

Occasionally though, the teachers introduced additional activities into class. So one day a teacher gathered the children around the classroom tables to draw pictures on sheets of paper with crayons. On another day, the teacher asked them to cut pictures from magazines – with child-safe scissors, of course – and glue them together to create collages to present to their adoring parents.

In the barely contained mayhem of this nursery, a Stanford University psychologist named Mark Lepper and his collaborators set out to test the effects of prizes on children's behaviour. They wanted to understand: how much more effort would kids put into a task if they get rewarded for it?

Lepper asked the teachers at the nursery to introduce a completely brand-spanking-new activity to the class: drawing with marker pens on sheets of creamy white artist's drawing paper. While the kids had painted with brushes and drawn with crayons, they had never been allowed to draw with coloured marker pens before, so this was a totally fresh experience for them. Naturally, most of the children relished the opportunity to do something new. But after only an hour, and to the disappointment of many of the children, the materials for this new activity were whisked away.

A few days later, a research assistant came back into the classroom and, taking the children one at a time into a separate room, invited each child to draw some further pictures with the marker pens. Half of the children were put into a control group and were asked to draw pictures just as they had done before. After only six minutes – remember that these are very young children with short attention spans – the research assistant thanked each child and took away the materials again.

The other half of the children were assigned to an experimental group, in which they were offered a prize for drawing their pictures. The research assistant explained that he had some special awards for children who drew really good pictures. Each award was merely a sheet of card with the words 'Good Player Award' on it with spaces for the child's name and school engraved on the front next to a big gold star and a red ribbon. But remember that these were nursery school kids. The children ranged in age from around three and a half to five years, so the award was a big deal to them. Their eyes widened and their faces lit up as they drew their pictures, spurred on by the prospect of being able to show the prizes off to their friends and parents. As with the control group, the children were given six minutes to create their masterpieces. Immediately afterwards, the research assistant complimented each child and handed over the award.

The real crux of the experiment came a week later when the investigators returned to the nursery for a final time. When all of the kids were gathered in the classroom for one of their usual free play sessions, the researchers put the same marker pens and sheets of paper out on the communal tables. Now the children were faced with their standard array of options; they could run around in the playground, play with their usual toys, or return to the special marker pens. Without drawing attention to the pens or the paper, the researchers quietly observed the amount of time the various children chose to spend drawing. To what extent would the prizes that the researchers gave to half of the class affect the kids' behaviour?

The researchers came to a stunning conclusion – one they didn't expect and a result that turned conventional wisdom about both education and parenting on its head. The kids who were rewarded for their pretty pictures chose to spend *less* time drawing than those who weren't rewarded. The children who weren't told about the prospect of any prize continued to enjoy drawing, but the children who were given awards seemed reluctant to carry on without the promise of further honours. The initial award *reduced* the children's motivation rather than spurring them on to greater heights.

But that's not all. The investigative team also asked a group of independent art aficionados, who were unaware of the goals of the study, to evaluate the quality of the children's handiwork. The pictures drawn by the children who were rewarded tended to be rated as less competent, less skilled than those drawn by the unrewarded children. In other words, the rewarded children didn't just spend less time drawing when given a choice in the matter; they seemed to put less effort into their art too.[101]

Lepper and his colleagues conducted this pioneering piece of research in the early 1970s and their findings were called into question at the time. Surely they were mistaken, said other researchers. But multiple groups of investigators all over the world have since come to the same conclusion. When children are doing something that is innately interesting, handing out awards and rewards typically *reduces* their motivation to continue. Their natural interest seems to be replaced by a hunger for compensation. And when they don't receive any, they feel fed up and discouraged. The lesson is unmistakable: if you want to *crush* children's intrinsic motivation – their innate enthusiasm for an activity – reward them for it. Putting it another way, we might be wise to avoid bribing, incentivising, or otherwise rewarding children to do things that we believe are truly important.

If a reward doesn't work, what does?

It's not only children who may end up being discouraged and put off from innately enjoyable activities when they receive rewards. Quite a lot of research – not just a trickle of studies over the years but a veritable torrent of them – tells us that adults may similarly become demotivated from intrinsically interesting activities when they are rewarded. Awards and bonuses can end up putting people of *all* ages off.[102]

I want to stress that this research is based on tasks that are *intrinsically interesting* – in other words, activities that are at least a little bit fun to do for their own sake. The research says nothing about the effects that offering prizes may have on tasks that are a complete chore to do – such as cleaning toilets, scrubbing floors, or picking litter up off the streets. Having said that though, the research may have weighty implications for the way many sporting stars are incentivised.

Suppose we take a handful of amateur athletes who currently enjoy participating in a sport. They do it because they get a buzz out of it. Perhaps they swim because they enjoy pushing themselves to see how much faster they can swim 100 metres. Or they play football or rugby or tennis or anything else because it's fun. They drive themselves to get fitter, faster, and better. They take pleasure in stretching themselves and seeing their skills develop and grow. Or they take pleasure from the camaraderie of being in a team.

Now imagine that we offer to pay them huge sums of cash for their participation. We offer them bonuses when they do well and prizes for truly exceptional achievement. Most people – including the bosses of sports teams and coaches of top athletes – may *think* that's the way to get the best out of their sporting supremos. However, that only works so long as the prizes and bonuses keep coming. Say the team loses a game and its members don't get their bonus. The research tells us in no uncertain terms that the athletes may almost instantly feel less motivated; they may suddenly come to view their sport as a chore, no matter how much it may have given them a kick to begin with.

That doesn't mean that we shouldn't pay professional sports-people. Of course we live in the real world and there are huge sums of money to be made by athletes at the top of their game. However, the research suggests that we shouldn't make money the main focus of these athletes if we wish to keep them motivated and moved to give of their best.

If we shouldn't wave fistfuls of money at athletes – or indeed *any* adults engaged in intrinsically interesting activities – then how can we motivate them?

Thankfully, the research doesn't leave us in the lurch. Rather than simply telling us that rewards don't work, investigators have begun piecing together methods that we *can* use to motivate people and persuade them to work hard.

Maarten Vansteenkiste, a tall and lean Dutchman with a tangle of curly brown hair, is something of a luminary in the field of motivational research. Currently a professor of psychology at Ghent University in Belgium, he continues to investigate ways of tweaking goals and environments in order to spur people on to persist longer with whatever they are doing. In a landmark series of experiments, Vansteenkiste and a squad of investigators compared the effects of different goals on people's behaviour. We're going to look at two of their experiments.

In the first experiment, students on a marketing course were told by their professor that they would be studying a text on communication styles. Vansteenkiste divided the students into two groups. Half of the students – let's call them group I (for 'intrinsic goals') – were told that 'carefully reading the text about communication styles can contribute to your personal development'. For this group then, the students expected that learning about communication styles would benefit their personal growth. They were doing it for their own interest and betterment rather than any external reward. The other half of the students – group E (for 'extrinsic goals') – were told that 'carefully reading the text about communication styles can help your chances of getting a well-paid job in the future'. In other words, the prospect of future, external rewards was highlighted prominently for this group.

To measure the ways in which the different goals affected the students' motivation, Vansteenkiste and his colleagues measured a number of variables. Immediately after reading the text, all of the students were tested on their recall of the subject matter. They were again tested on the material two weeks later. What's more, instructors graded the quality of each student's participation in small-group discussions. Aggregating their performance across the two tests and the group discussions, the research team found that the group I students who had been told to study the text for their personal development performed much better in the tests, gaining average grades that were 24.5 per cent higher than those achieved by the group E students.

In addition, the research team conceived a clever way to investigate the students' ongoing interest in the communication topic. They asked the professor in charge of the class to offer four further opportunities for the students to learn more about the topic:

- Immediately after the initial lecture, the professor offered all of the students a handout with additional reading material on the topic. The research team made a note of which students came to the front of the class to pick up the handout.
- Three days after the initial lecture, the professor also offered all of the students a second handout of further reading material as well as some optional homework. The professor explained that the homework would not count towards their course grade, but that the students could do it if they found the topic interesting and wanted to learn about it in greater depth. Again, the researchers kept a log of which students decided to do the optional homework.
- Another two days later, a visiting expert came to run an optional seminar on communication styles. The researchers again kept a tally of which students turned up.
- Fourthly, the researchers gained permission to check which of the students went to the college library to read up on the topic. The students had to present their

electronic swipe cards to gain entry to the library, so
this information was easy enough for the researchers
to access.

Analysing the results, Vansteenkiste and his colleagues found that
the group I students, who had been instructed to read about the
topic for their own personal development, seemed to have more
interest in it. The group I students took up an average of 3.98 out of
the four opportunities to learn more about the topic. The group E
students only took up 2.57 of the same opportunities.[103]

The study was revealing in two ways. Firstly, the students who
read about a topic because they thought it would benefit their
personal development absorbed more of the information. In both
objective tests of their recall and independent assessments of their
class participation, they outperformed students who were told to
read the material because it would help them to secure high-paying
jobs later on. The study also showed that the 'personal development'
I group remained much more interested in the topic, voluntarily
seeking out more reading and assignments to further their knowledge. Given various options to learn more or less about the topic,
the 'well-paid job' E group simply weren't that interested.

Before I explain the implications of the study, let me introduce
the second of Vansteenkiste's experiments, which again compares
the effects of intrinsic versus extrinsic goals, although this time for
a less cerebral task. In this second experiment, Vansteenkiste and
his cadre of researchers persuaded a local school to let him test the
effects of intrinsic versus extrinsic goals on pupils' willingness to
involve themselves in a newly introduced form of physical exercise.
As part of their regular physical education classes, 15- to 16-year-old
pupils were given a one-off taster session on Tai-bo, a cross between
Taekwondo and boxing.

Half of the pupils were assigned to an 'intrinsic goals' I group and told that Tai-bo could help them to get physically fitter and stay healthy. The other half of the pupils were assigned to an 'extrinsic goals' E group and told that Tai-bo could help them to avoid gaining weight, which would help them to look more physically attractive and appealing to others. As before, the pupils who had the intrinsic focus not only received better grades from their teachers, they also volunteered to take part in more optional Tai-bo activities afterwards.

What can we take away from the pair of studies?

The first study by Vansteenkiste's team demonstrates that intrinsic goals assist people to learn more effectively when they're given topics to read about from textbooks. The second study shows that intrinsic goals also help people to perform better when given physical tasks to do. And these are just two examples, because study after study shows that setting people intrinsic goals helps them (and us) to get more out of what they (and we) choose to do in life. Focusing on doing a task or learning new material for its own sake and because it's fun is motivating and seems to pay off in all sorts of ways.

Setting goals that motivate, not discourage (part I)

Although many bosses, organisations, and parents seem to govern by using the old-fashioned carrot and stick method, research suggests that it's not actually terribly effective. A conclusive mass of research suggests that most people are by nature inquisitive, self-motivated, and eager to learn and succeed. They find the process of learning inherently gratifying and rewarding. They don't need rewards waved in front of them to spur them on.

Psychologists distinguish between two types of goals:

- Intrinsic goals are aims or aspirations that satisfy innate human needs. Most people enjoy learning and the feeling that they're making progress; they like to feel competent and in control of their lives. They also enjoy spending time with people they like and building warm, supportive relationships. When people seek to improve themselves or learn about a topic for its own sake, they may be said to be engaged in the pursuit of intrinsic goals.

- Extrinsic goals are aims and ambitions that depend on external rewards or consequences. So the pursuit of wealth, recognition, and fame are extrinsic goals. Competing to win a prize or beat other people is an extrinsic goal. Wishing to appear physically attractive or popular is an extrinsic goal because it depends on the reactions of other people too.

Of course we all pursue a mix of intrinsic and extrinsic goals in life. You may want to get a salary hike at work (an extrinsic goal), but you may play a sport because it's fun (an intrinsic goal). However, a mounting body of evidence suggests that intrinsic goals are naturally more motivating than extrinsic ones. People who are set intrinsic goals tend to work harder at mastering a skill or topic than those who are set extrinsic goals. And their motivation stays higher for longer.

There are other reasons for focusing more on the intrinsic side of matters too. Research by psychologists Tim Kasser and Richard Ryan at the University of Rochester in New York suggests that the relative balance between the two sets of goals can have powerful effects on people's well-being. Namely, people who place more emphasis on intrinsic goals tend to experience higher levels of psychological well-being than those who place more emphasis on extrinsic goals. Those who put more stress on the pursuit of extrinsic goals tend not only to be more anxious and depressed but also to report more physical complaints and ailments.[104]

In reality, it may not always be possible to set goals that are entirely intrinsic in nature. However, we would be wise to emphasise the intrinsic qualities of tasks and de-emphasise their extrinsic qualities whenever we can.

So if you want to persuade colleagues to help you with a project, highlight how 'fascinating' it will be and how much they will broaden their minds and grow as individuals. You don't need to remind them that they are being paid to do the job anyway.

If you wish to encourage your sons and daughters to study hard and do their homework, try to find a part of the topic or an angle that might inspire them to learn more. Avoid mentioning how important it is for them to do well in their exams to get good jobs.

Accentuating the intrinsic aspects of goals is a good start. But it turns out there's another trick we can use to boost the motivation of the people we know too.

In the research paper by Maarten Vansteenkiste and his colleagues that we already discussed, he and his team also tested the effects of two types of language when asking participants to engage in various activities:

- Language that emphasises free choice, such as 'you can', 'you might', 'if you choose', and 'we ask you to'.
- Language that implies more coercion, such as 'you should', 'you have to', 'you'd better', and 'you must'.

In a third study, Vansteenkiste and his team asked young teacher trainees to learn about recycling, the arguments for and against it, the methods available for recycling, and ways of encouraging the teachers' future pupils to recycle more. For half of the trainees, the researchers emphasised the trainees' freedom of choice by saying, 'You can decide to learn more about recycling strategies.' For the other half of the group, the researchers made a more coercive statement by recommending, 'You should learn more about recycling strategies.'

The distinction between 'can decide' and 'should' seems a small difference, an almost petty quirk of language that might seem more interesting to bookish grammarians and linguistics experts than people in the real world. But it turned out to be a significant one. In this third study (as well as others), Vansteenkiste's team found that using language to emphasise participants' free choice spurred them to recall more about a topic when they were tested on it. It also made them more likely to want to learn more about the topic.

In explaining the result, Vansteenkiste suggests that language that emphasises people's free choice reinforces their sense of control; it reminds them that they are doing an activity or a task because they wish to – and not because they must – which seems to add to the intrinsic thrill of doing it.

Setting goals that motivate, not discourage (part II)

Pulling together all of the pieces of the jigsaw then, we have two tactics we can deploy to boost people's motivation, each of which has two options. You can either choose intrinsic versus extrinsic goals. But you could also use language that emphasises choice or coercion. How can we use that in practice though?

Say you want your partner to do some exercise. Focusing on fitness makes it an intrinsic goal, whereas focusing on appearance and attractiveness is an extrinsic goal. Using both the intrinsic/extrinsic goals distinction as well as choice/coercion language gives us four permutations to try:

- Intrinsic goals emphasising choice – 'Exercising would help to keep you fit and you might enjoy it.'
- Intrinsic goals emphasising coercion – 'Exercising would help you to keep fit and you should do it.'
- Extrinsic goals emphasising choice – 'Exercising would help you to lose weight and look good and you might enjoy it.'
- Extrinsic goals emphasising coercion – 'Exercising would help you to lose weight and look good and you should do it.'

Setting an extrinsic goal that also invokes a sense of coercion is likely to dampen down people's motivation the fastest. But setting an intrinsic goal that calls attention to their free choice in the matter is most likely to ignite their dormant motivation to go running or visit the gym.

You get the picture. I'd say that you *should* use this technique, but maybe I'll just suggest that you *might* want to use it instead.

Money makes the world go around
– or does it?

Of course, we can't always rely on the intrinsically appealing nature of a task to persuade people to help us out. Some tasks are either incredibly dull or unpleasant – or both. Say you need to send a letter to several thousand prospective customers. I doubt that stuffing letters into envelopes and sticking stamps on the front of them would deliver much of an intrinsic thrill to the majority of the people you know. And if you need to get your household drains unclogged, good luck finding somebody to do that for free.

In the real world, we usually need to pay people wages and salaries to work for us. And many employers offer cash bonuses and other financial incentives too. But does more money lead to more productivity?

To answer the question, let me introduce to you Sebastian Kube, a professor of economics at the University of Bonn in Germany. A slight, wiry man with a mop of floppy brown hair, Kube is one of a new generation of economists more interested in the behaviour of genuine people in real situations than macroeconomic issues such as the interrelationships between inflation, unemployment rates, and international trade. In May 2007, Kube spotted a unique opportunity to explore the effects of different incentives on work productivity. His university's library happened to be recruiting students to catalogue its collection of books. Students were being offered a fairly generous €12 an hour for three hours of their time to sit at a computer, entering the details of as many books as they could onto the university's computer system.

Kube urged the university librarians to let him run a quietly radical experiment on the students. Without letting the students know that they were being treated differently, he assigned them to one of three groups. The first group acted as a control group and was paid the advertised rate of €12 per hour to enter the books' author(s), title, publisher, year, and ISBN number into the electronic database. The second group was told on their arrival at the library that they were going to earn *more* than they had expected. These lucky students were told that they'd be taking home a €7 bonus – equivalent to a 20 per cent pay rise – simply as a thank you for their assistance. A third group was told on their arrival that they would not only earn the basic €12 an hour but would also walk away with a gift-wrapped thermos bottle worth €7, again as a thank you for their help.

The precise nature of the work meant that Kube and his colleagues could tell exactly how many books' details had been entered into the computer system by students in each of the three groups. So what happened?

The group that was offered the unexpected pay rise of 20 per cent worked no harder than those who earned the baseline €12 an hour. *More pay led to no more productivity.* To many traditional economists who believe that people respond in a rational way to incentives, that's a smack in the teeth.

The group who were given the gift-wrapped thermos flask did work harder though. On average, they entered an impressive 30 per cent more book details onto the database. It seemed that a gift-in-kind equivalent to €7 spurred the students to work harder than the same amount in hard cash.

Looking for flaws in his own experiment, Kube wondered if the group that had been offered the thermos flask might perhaps have overestimated its value. So he recruited a fourth group of students for the same three hours' work. Again, they were hired for €12 per hour and given the thermos flask as a thank you for their help. However, this time the students were told the precise value of the flask.

Measuring their productivity, Kube and his colleagues observed that the students still worked as hard as the group of students that had not been informed about the price of the flask. The gift was equally effective at inspiring greater productivity from the students, irrespective of whether its value was flagged up or not.[105]

Given the choice of a cash bonus or a thermos flask as a token of appreciation for your work in entering book details onto the university's database, which would you have preferred? When Kube asked a separate group of students which they'd prefer, 159 out of 172 people (92.4 per cent) said they would opt for €7 in cash rather than the thermos flask. After all, some people might already have owned a similar flask; others might never drink hot drinks. Still others might prefer to use disposable cups for their hot drinks. The point is: cash is significantly more useful. We can buy what we like with cash.

However, one of the paradoxes of our behaviour seems to be that we work harder when offered gifts instead of cash bonuses. Kube and his colleagues suggested that people may perceive gifts as being a signal of kindness, and that people respond more to kindness than they do to cash.

The truth is that we don't know exactly why gifts drive performance up more than money. It just happens. The lesson here is that if we're paying people a salary to work anyway, giving them more money may not get greater levels of commitment and productivity from them. But a gift might.

Understanding the pros and cons of gift-giving

Kube's study suggests that gifts may be a powerful and somewhat underused tool for incentivising the people around us. However, other work by James Heyman, now a professor at the University of St Thomas in Minnesota, suggests that there is a big 'but' when offering people presents in lieu of payment for their aid.

In a series of experiments, Heyman and his collaborators compared the effectiveness of small gifts in motivating people to persist with a boring task. And when I say that the task was boring, it was quite mind-numbingly dull.

Envision being brought into a dimly lit room and sat in front of a computer. On the screen there's a light grey circle on the left side and a dark grey box on the right. An experimenter explains that your task is to use the computer mouse to drag the 'ball' into the 'box'. Once you've done that, the circle will disappear and a new circle will appear on the left. And guess what? You have to drag that one across the width of the screen onto the square too.

Best of all, you get to do this lovely new task for three whole minutes. Oh joy! I'm sure you can barely contain your excitement at the prospect and are already wondering if you can buy the software to enjoy the game at home.

Heyman paid some of his participants $4 for three minutes of their time to establish a baseline for how hard they would work. With two other groups of participants, he offered them an upfront gift: one group was given a big bag of edible jelly beans as a thank you for their participation; the other group was given just five edible jelly beans.

Would the bag of jelly beans incentivise people to work harder? Would the mean-spirited gesture of a mere five jelly beans be spurned by the participants and make them slacken off?

In fact, neither outcome happened. Both of the jelly bean groups worked equally as hard as the participants who were paid $4 in cash. Irrespective of the size of the gift, all of the participants remained equally motivated.[106] That suggests that it's the *gesture* behind a gift that motivates performance, not its size. Great news for cheapskates around the world looking for cost-effective ways to boost performance!

But Heyman wanted to explore one more question: would the size of the gift matter when people are told about the value of the gift? In a second study, Heyman gave other groups of participants a challenge to solve a series of numerical puzzles. Take a look at the example below. Each puzzle consists of 12 numbers on screen. Your job is to pick as few or as many of them as you like to add up to 100 in total. I'll put the answer in a note at the back of the book, but I'll give you a hint: the person who started on this example is on completely the wrong track.[107]

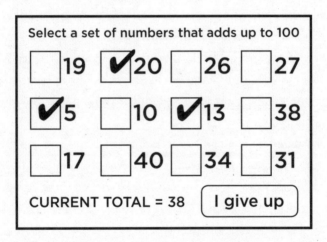

The participants were instructed that they would be presented with a dozen such puzzles and that they could spend as much time on them as they liked. Once they'd had enough though, they were told to click the 'I give up' button on the screen. In return for their help, the participants were given upfront either a large gift (an entire box of luxury Godiva chocolates – yum!) or a small one (a single candy bar). However, in contrast to his first experiment, Heyman told his participants the value of the gifts before they started the task. The box of chocolates was worth about $5; the candy was worth around 50 cents.

What the researcher didn't tell the unsuspecting participants was that there were only five puzzles to tackle and only the first four puzzles were solvable. The fifth one was deliberately unsolvable because Heyman craftily wanted to investigate the effects of the gifts on participants' persistence. Would the value of the gift affect their perseverance when presented with a vexing challenge?

The results showed that one group worked much harder than the other. The group that was told that the small gift wasn't worth much ended up quitting significantly sooner. Being told that their gift was worth a measly 50 cents seemed to erode their willingness to stick with the task.

So where does this all leave us exactly?

Heyman's first study suggests that even small gifts – a mere five jelly beans, for example – can be motivating. However, when people are explicitly told the value of gifts, they seem to make mental calculations as to whether they are being paid appropriately for their time and effort. When Heyman offered some of his participants a $5 box of chocolates, they ran the numbers and decided that it was still worthwhile, so they persisted at the numerical task. However, when he told a second group of participants that their candy bar was worth a paltry 50 cents, those participants decided that it wasn't worth their while to persist and they gave up all too easily.

That suggests that we should be extremely careful about mentioning the value of the gifts we give others. So long as we don't mention the cost of an item, it's the gesture of gift-giving itself that is motivating – not its value. But mention its value and people seem to make a wholly different kind of judgement, weighing up whether we're being sufficiently generous or not. If they decide that we're being cheap and that they're being paid an unsatisfactory rate, their motivation may plummet.

CHAPTER EIGHT
the peculiar power of circumstantial persuasion

'The truth is not simply what you think it is;
it is also the circumstances in which it is said,
and to whom, why and how it is said.'
Vaclav Havel

A few years ago, my cousin Annette and her husband had to make a difficult decision about the health of their daughter Milly. They live in Canada so I couldn't be there physically with them, but through a series of frantic emails and late-night phone calls in which we sometimes ended up saying nothing for several minutes, I shared a little of their worry and pain. Of course we can never appreciate the same level of anxiety when it's not one of our own children, but even as I brought the episode to mind to type these words, I realised that my brow was furrowed and my jaw was clenched.

One morning when Milly was nearly three years old, she started coughing while she was having breakfast. Her parents rubbed her back, made appropriate cooing noises, and watched as the momentary coughing fit passed. After all, kids often wolf down their food and sometimes a tiny bit can go down the wrong way.

But over the next few days, the coughing got more severe. At first Milly's parents thought that the juicy bits in her orange juice were causing the problem. But they soon discovered that she was coughing after a glass of milk or water too.

Her parents wasted no time in taking her to see a doctor, who referred them to a specialist, who insisted on a variety of uncomfortable and worry-inducing medical tests. After several fraught weeks, they were told that some of the acid from Milly's stomach was making its way into her lungs, putting her at risk of infections such as pneumonia or worse.

Unfortunately, Milly's condition deteriorated over the course of several months despite the doctors' best efforts. To save her life, the doctors made an incision across her belly to attach a feeding tube, a piece of plastic hose, directly to her stomach. I'm sure I don't have to tell you how invasive and obviously distressing this was for the sweet little girl.

Even that didn't help much and Milly continued to get worse. Finally, the doctors presented her parents with two options. One, they could wait another six months to see whether Milly got better on her own. But the risk of waiting was that Milly could literally forget how to eat and swallow normally. Pushed to estimate the risks to Milly's health by her parents, the doctors reckoned there was a 30 or 40 per cent chance that the delay could cause her further developmental problems.

The second option was a surgical one. The doctors could operate to try to fix the problem. But the operation had its own risks: a botched procedure could result in health complications and there were no guarantees that it would work. The doctors reckoned that the operation had a good – but not great – success rate, which they judged at 70 to 80 per cent.

In their position, what would you have done?

After many consultations with other doctors, countless sleepless nights, and innumerable hours poring over Internet websites for information about Milly's condition, Annette and her husband eventually chose to take the surgical route. It wasn't an easy decision and the path to recovery wasn't quick, but it seems to have worked out. Milly is now a relatively healthy six-year-old and although she still needs to have regular physical therapy, she's able to eat more or less normally and do almost all of the other things that kids like to do.

It could easily have been so very different though. The doctors had presented Milly's parents with two options:

(a) Keep the feeding tube in, which had up to a 40 per cent risk of causing developmental problems, or

(b) Pursue a surgical option, which had up to an 80 per cent chance of success.

But what if the doctors had presented the options slightly differently? The following are the same options – at least from a statistical standpoint – just flipped around to emphasise success rather than failure for option (a) and failure rather than success for option (b):

(a) Keep the feeding tube in, which meant a 60 per cent chance that Milly could get better on her own with no developmental problems, or

(b) Pursue a surgical option, which had a 20 per cent chance of failure and further complications.

Would the way the options were posed have made a difference?

Thankfully, we can't turn the clock back – not that anyone involved would want to in any case. However, research tells us that the way information is presented makes a big difference.

People don't always consider information in a rational and cool-headed fashion. When it comes to making weighty decisions, they *shouldn't* be influenced by trivial changes in the way facts are presented or choices are phrased. Yet they are. And the fact that people do find themselves swayed by contexts and circumstances such as the mere phrasing of options sheds light on not only the inner workings of the human psyche but also on ways in which we can exercise influence over people's decision-making, about everything from energy conservation and financial planning to matters to do with their health and even the goods they put in their shopping baskets.

Matters of life and death

Barbara McNeil has a warm, round face and wears oversized spectacles that wouldn't look amiss on a kindly librarian. Yet her appearance belies her formidable position as the head of the Health Care Policy Department at Harvard Medical School and a celebrated professor of radiology at Brigham and Women's Hospital. In the early 1980s though, she was just a young radiologist with a yearning to understand how to help patients make more informed decisions about their own treatments. In an instrumental study, she posed a variety of scenarios to participants in a series of experiments. You can play along and see how you would decide if you like.

A gaggle of researchers asks you to ponder a hypothetical scenario. They ask you to imagine that you have been diagnosed with lung cancer, one of the most aggressive forms of cancer. Unfortunately, the fearsome disease also has a rather poor prognosis so you can't afford to sit back and do nothing. You have a choice of two treatments, either surgery or radiation therapy. However, the two have quite different risks:

(a) Surgery: of 100 people having surgery, 90 live through the post-operative period, 68 are alive at the end of the first year and 34 are alive at the end of five years.

(b) Radiation therapy: of 100 people having radiation therapy, all live through the treatment, 77 are alive at the end of one year and 22 are alive at the end of five years.

Which would you choose?

Take a moment and read the choices again if you like. Let's think about it. For many friends I've asked about this, the critical bit seems to be what happens after five years. They don't really care that slightly more people are alive after a year after radiation therapy. They intend to be around longer than that, so the fact that roughly 3 in 10 people who elect for surgery are alive after five years as opposed to only 2 in 10 who choose radiotherapy tends to swing their votes. Indeed, when McNeil and an elite gang of researchers posed this exact scenario to participants, she found that only 18 per cent of them chose radiation therapy.

But then she tried presenting the same options in a different way:

(a) Surgery: of 100 people having surgery, 10 die during surgery or the post-operative period, 32 die by the end of the first year and 66 die by the end of five years.

(b) Radiation therapy: of 100 people having radiation therapy, none die during treatment, 23 die by the end of one year and 78 die by the end of five years.

Now which one would you choose? Of course you're on to the ways in which the mind sometimes works, so you probably wouldn't change your decision. After five years, 66 out of 100 people who choose surgery are dead whereas 78 out of 100 people who choose radiation therapy die. From an objective, rational, purely statistical standpoint, the options are identical. The frame has just been changed from one of percentage survival rates in the first scenario to percentage death rates in the second. But this seemingly minor revision of wording in the second pair of options persuaded 44 per cent to choose radiation therapy.[108]

That's a big deal. Apparently, the advantage of radiation therapy over surgery stands out more when people consider the risks of immediate death for the two options. No one dies during treatment by radiation therapy, but 1 in 10 dies under the surgeon's knife.

Many experiments can be rightly criticised for relying on university students as their participants. A curmudgeon might argue that of course university students can be tricked by a change in how a pair of options is phrased. They know nothing of life and they're too young to know any better. However, McNeil and her collaborators didn't just pose the two scenarios to immature students. She also presented the same scenarios to experienced doctors as well as actual clinical patients and found exactly the same thing: the framing of the options led to significantly different choices.

The disparity seems to stem from the different ways in which the participants thought about losses versus gains. When people were told to consider the two choices from the perspective of what they could gain, i.e. how long they could live, they overwhelmingly opted for surgery over radiation therapy. However, when asked to weigh up the options from the angle of what they could lose, i.e. their risk of dying, more people were lured into choosing radiation therapy.

What is most unsettling is that the participants weren't changing their minds over something relatively inconsequential like what they fancied for lunch or the kind of house they wanted to buy. This was literally a decision about life and death.

When it comes to such major decisions, we would hope that our fellows could make cool-headed decisions about the right course to take. But they don't. People seem to process the ideas of loss and gain in different ways. And the fact that people are swayed in their decision-making by the framing of options suggests that something fairly elemental is going on, something that hints at the mysterious mechanisms of our minds.

Evolutionary psychologists contend that our species may have evolved to pay much more attention to losses than gains. To consider the arguments, let's cast our minds far back to prehistoric times. When our ancestors had enough food to feed themselves and their families for a few days, they had little reason to accumulate more. This was tens of thousands of years before refrigerators and freezers would be invented. Having more food was simply wasteful, as it would have spoiled. So the concept of having 'more' may not have been much of a motivator for our distant forebears.

However, consider the impact of having 'less'. This was a time when our ancestors didn't have to worry about problems such as overeating, obesity, and high cholesterol. Hunting wild animals for meat and foraging for berries and fruits, our prehistoric predecessors had barely enough to eat. When they didn't have enough food, they simply starved.

While 'more' may have been moderately helpful, having 'less' could have been fatal. So those amongst our ancestors who were more acutely attuned to the notion of 'less', to the possibility of loss, gained an advantage. By reacting more strongly to the risk of losing food or having it taken from them, they were able to protect their food and, ultimately, prevent themselves and their families from starvation and death. Those who didn't react strongly enough to the prospect of loss and the concept of having 'less' may have withered away, their genes lost for ever.

Intuitively, that makes sense. It sounds plausible that our minds may have developed with certain innate tendencies such as a special sensitivity to loss rather than gain. In support of the idea, evolutionary psychologists such as Martie Haselton at the University of California, Los Angeles, and Daniel Nettle at the University of Newcastle point out that many of our fears and preferences may be hard-wired. They note that 'we are predisposed to fear spiders and snakes rather than elements of our contemporary environment that are in fact much more dangerous, such as electrical outlets. We are predisposed to fear injured or diseased people and contamination of food supply, when in fact road traffic and obesity are much more likely to kill us.'[109]

Research using fMRI scanners in the laboratories of neuroscientists lends further credence to the idea that loss aversion is written in the brain's primal architecture. In a study published in 2007, Joshua Weller at the University of Iowa and his colleagues invited patients who had suffered various types of brain damage to play games of chance in which they stood to gain or lose real sums of money. The researchers noticed that patients who had lesions to the prefrontal cortex – the front, topmost part of the brain – showed impaired decision-making when it came to considering both potential gains and potential losses.

However, patients with damage to the amygdala – an ancient almond-shaped structure of the brain that we share not only with other primates but most animals including birds and even lizards – showed impaired decision-making only when it came to decisions involving potential gains. Their ability to weigh up the possibility of loss seemed mostly intact, suggesting that the brain is wired to protect its ability to evaluate loss much more than its ability to consider gains.[110]

Taking all of that together, we can know fairly conclusively that people pay more attention to losses than gains. How does that help us to influence them?

Focusing on loss and gain as methods of persuasion

The fact that people are more fearful of losing something than they are interested in gaining something may seem a somewhat obscure notion. So let's cover a few practical examples of how it can be used.

Most governments around the world these days are urging citizens to conserve energy. Using less energy doesn't just save the environment, it also saves people money. So we can phrase a request to people to use less energy either in terms of the saving they could make (i.e. 'Use less energy and you could save £2 a week!') or the loss they could stop incurring (i.e. 'Use less energy because you're currently losing £2 a week!') But would it really make a difference?

Yes. In a pilot study, investigators found that homeowners who were told that they were losing money every day were 55 per cent more likely to apply for government-backed schemes promoting energy efficiency.[111] Again, people responded more powerfully when exactly the same offer was phrased in terms of loss rather than gain.

In another study, customers of a credit-card company who had applied for a credit card but not used it were telephoned by the company who stressed either the advantages of using the card or the disadvantages of continuing to pay by cash. Customers who were told about the ways in which they were losing out were twice as likely to use their credit cards as those who were told about the gains to be had by paying by card.[112]

Whenever we present people with two choices, we can encourage them to favour one more than the other. Say you run a car-cleaning company that offers two service options: a quick service, and a full service that is the same as the quick service but also includes waxing and buffing your car to an incredible shine. The quick service costs £40 while the full service costs £50. If you want more people to choose the full service, explain that the quick service is cheaper because it is a 'discount' as compared with the full service. However, if you would like more people to go for the quick service – perhaps it involves a lot less work so you can service many more cars every day – then say that the full service incurs a 'surcharge' of £10. People don't like to feel they're losing out, so the idea of an extra charge will scare more of them away from the full service.

You can apply the same logic to most choices or decisions. For instance, suppose that you want to persuade your colleagues to let you carry out a project that could save the company £20,000. What's the best way to get support for your proposal? Traditionally, we would point out the benefits of doing the project; however, the research suggests that we explain instead that the company stands to lose £20,000 if the scheme doesn't get the green light.

Or if you want to persuade your boss to let you buy some new computers that you reckon could save members of the team up to 15 minutes a day, think about how you phrase it too. Rather than talking up the saving, mention that the team is currently losing out on 15 minutes of productivity every single day until you implement the upgrade. Is it sneaky? Perhaps a little. But that's human psychology for you.

Great expectations

Do you like the occasional glass of wine? On a hot summer's day, consider how a glass of cool white wine might taste as you take a sip. Perhaps as an accompaniment to a Caesar salad. Or if it's winter, a bottle of Chilean red might go rather well with a hot stew. Perhaps you're a fan of wines from California, New Zealand, or Australia. Or you might prefer more traditional vintages from France or Italy. You probably know how much you're comfortable spending too. Sure, some of the more expensive wines taste lovely, but they're not for everyday drinking. Whatever your tastes though, you probably know what a good wine tastes like. But are you *sure* you know what you like?

Over a period of around nine months in 2007 to 2008, Robin Goldstein, an American food and wine critic, carried out a series of clever wine taste tests with over 500 participants. The vast majority of the participants in the tasting sessions had no formal training in wine; however, they were mainly well-educated individuals aged from 21 to 88 years who worked in the food and wine industry. So they had above-average experience of fine wines.

Each participant was given a range of wines to taste that varied in price from a measly $1.65 to an eye-watering $150 per bottle. However, here's the clever bit. The wines were decanted from their bottles and presented in what scientists call a double-blind proced-ure: neither the person serving the wine nor the taster knew anything about the wine other than its colour. So no one was told about the types of grapes that made up the wine, what country it came from or, most importantly, how much it cost.

Upon sipping the wine, each person was asked: 'Overall, how do you find the wine?' The participants were asked to choose one of only four options, saying that the wine was 'bad', 'okay', 'good', or 'great'.

Now Goldstein isn't a scientist by training. So he enlisted the support of a crack team of economists to analyse his data for him, which included professors from Harvard and Yale universities as well as the Research Institute of Industrial Economics in Sweden. And they discovered that there was in fact a negative correlation between enjoyment and the price of a wine. Putting that into plain English, it means that, on average, most people enjoy more expen-sive wines slightly *less*.

To spell out exactly what this means, consider we have two wines, A and B. Wine B costs 10 times as much as A. On average, people rate the more expensive wine B as 4 per cent *less* enjoyable than wine A. That's not a great deal, but it was statistically robust. So we can rule out the suggestion that this might have been a chance discovery, a fluke. Remember that the data were scrutinised in depth by a panel of highly distinguished economists too. So there's no debating the result: when most of us pay more for a wine – a *lot* more, in fact – we may actually enjoy it marginally less.[113]

That fact surprises most people. Many people I've told about this simply don't believe it. Most people – especially the well-educated and often wealthy clients I have – think they're reasonably good at telling exceptional wines from merely adequate ones. And they say they can definitely distinguish a poor wine from an average one.

But remember that this was a double-blind study, the gold standard of research. Neither the person who poured the wine nor the participants giving the ratings knew anything about the price or alleged qualities of the wines.

When the rest of us try wines, we are heavily influenced by what we know about them. For a start, if we bought the wine, we know whether it was cheap or expensive. We may have read a review about the wine or even the little note in the wine shop or supermarket telling us what we should expect; even its bottle may be shaped in a more refined fashion and the label may imply traditional skills that have been honed over several generations. In other words, the pleasure we get from consuming wine depends not only on inherent qualities such as its taste and smell but also on external factors such as its price and our expectations.

Our faithful friend the fMRI brain scanner comes to the rescue yet again, providing us with further insight into why we like the wines we like. Hilke Plassmann, a German woman with enviably unlined skin and long blonde hair, is now a professor of market-ing at INSEAD, the leading business school based in Fontainebleau, France. Earlier in her career, Plassmann and her colleagues invited adults to take part in a study allegedly to investigate the relationship between degustation time (i.e. the amount of time that people take to savour a drink) and brain activity. Strapping the participants into the fMRI, the research investigators explained that the participants would taste five different Cabernet Sauvignons. To distinguish them, the researchers said that they would call out how much they cost.

However, all of this was merely a cover story as the researchers were secretly interested in the impact of *beliefs* about wine prices and brain activity. Despite having said that there would be five different wines, the wily investigators actually only had three different wines, two of which would be presented twice. Here's the order of the wines as well as what the researchers said about each wine:

- Wine 1 was described as having cost $5.
- Wine 2 was described as having cost $10.
- Wine 3 was described as having cost $35.
- Wine 4 was actually the same wine as wine 1, but this time described as having cost $45.
- Wine 5 was the same as wine 2, but this time described as having cost $90.

As the researchers expected, participants rated the pleasantness of the wines in line with the stated prices. As the wines seemed to get more expensive, people said that they tasted better. So they said they enjoyed wine 4 more than wine 1, even though they had been the same wine. They also rated wine 5 more than wine 2. However – and here's where the brains scans come in – it didn't appear as if the participants were lying in order to impress the researchers. A part of the brain called the medial orbitofrontal cortex also buzzed with more activity when the participants thought that the wine was more expensive.[114]

That tells us something we might not have expected about the workings of the human mind. The participants weren't relying on what their taste buds were telling them to judge how much they liked each wine. Without the conscious awareness of the participants, their brains seemed to use the information about price to overrule the physical taste sensations they actually experienced. It was as if the participants' own brains were conspiring with the researchers to convince the participants that they really were drinking more expensive wines. Putting it another way, both blind tests and brain scans demonstrate that our experiences are heavily determined by our expectations.

Many other studies confirm similar effects, so we know that it's not just the price of wine that has this effect. For example, in a paper published only a few years ago in 2009, London Business School investigator Marco Bertini and his colleagues conducted a coffee tasting with a twist on a university campus. On the first day, they asked passers-by – who included not only students but also professors and administrative staff – to taste and rate the quality of their coffee on a 10-point scale (where 1 indicated very low quality and 10 very high quality).

On the second day, the researchers gave participants the opportunity to add one or more spices to their drinks, such as cloves, orange peel, sweet paprika, and cardamom. None of the participants chose to add any of the curious spices to their coffee, but the fact that the spices were presented in elegant crystal containers boosted participants' ratings of the coffee by 23.7 per cent as compared with the first, control day.

On the third day, the researchers presented the same range of optional extras, but this time in broken Styrofoam cups. Again, even though none of the participants actually ended up adding a spice to their coffee, the cheap setting was enough to influence their subjective experience of it, sending ratings of the coffee plummeting by 13 per cent as compared with the first day.[115]

That's good news for coffee chains such as Starbucks that offer customers freebies like cinnamon or grated nutmeg to sprinkle on their cappuccinos. Even if customers don't use them, their perception of the drinks served at the establishment may still shoot up.

But the broader point is that, again, context matters. It's not only price that affects our experiences and how much we enjoy what we consume; the setting and ambience matter too.

Bringing the background to the fore

A friend of mine is a bit of an über-cook. Marietta rides her bicycle to a local farmer's market early in the morning, long before her children rise to get ready for school, to pick the choicest ingredients, which she turns into amazing dinners. I enjoy eating whatever she cooks. But now that I understand the research on contexts and settings, I have to wonder: is the food really so unreservedly good?

After all, she knows how to dress a dinner table too. She has leather coasters and placemats on the table plus candles and low vases stuffed with crocuses, daffodils, or whatever other flowers she may have cut from her garden. And we always eat from elegant bone china and drink wine from crystal glasses.

In reality, the setting probably helps good food to taste better. No one can make bad food taste great just with a handful of fancy accoutrements. But if you want to persuade your dinner guests that you're a great cook, invest in a nice tablecloth, good-quality glasses and silverware. In fact, this is a lesson we can all apply more broadly to whatever we do.

If you're in business and offer customers a product or service, then you may wish to think carefully about how you price it. Yes, pricing something too high may make it too expensive for many customers. But pricing it too low could backfire too; it may ward customers off who believe that the quality of the product or service must be poor. I have no sure-fire solutions when it comes to correct pricing, only a warning that cheaper isn't automatically better.

It's not only the perception of products or tangible services that may be affected by their price either. One study from 2008 showed that people were more likely to follow advice when they had paid for it than when exactly the same advice was provided at no cost.[116] When people pay for information or guidance, they seem to become more emotionally invested in it. So you may want to think twice before offering your opinions for nothing. If offering advice is the mainstay of your work and your aim is to influence someone's behaviour with your recommendations, you may often be better off charging at least a token fee for your opinions than giving them away for nothing.

The little details matter too. Even children as young as three to five years of age may be affected in their judgements by the expectations they have. In a 2007 study, child health researcher Thomas Robinson and his fellow investigators challenged young children to taste five pairs of foods and drink packaged in either unbranded or McDonald's branded packaging. The packaging was otherwise identical. For example, one pairing offered the children two chunks of a McDonald's hamburger, partially wrapped in either a white McDonald's wrapper clearly displaying the company logo or a plain white wrapper of the same size and material. Another pairing offered the children two baby carrots placed either on top of a McDonald's French fries bag or on top of an unbranded but otherwise identical plain white bag.

In results that will horrify many parents but delight fast-food purveyors, the children said they preferred the taste of the food that came in the McDonald's packaging. On average, the children favoured the branded food in four out of five pairings.[117]

For good reason then, retailers and advertisers pay immense attention to their brands, the details of what they offer. Most luxury retailers, for example, obsess over tiny details ranging from the carrier bags they provide – preferring thick paper bags with perhaps ribbon or rope handles over flimsy plastic bags – to the rare scents they waft around the stores.

The old proverb warns that we shouldn't judge a book by its cover. But people do. All the time. People have too many decisions to make to waste hours poring over every little decision. So they rely on shortcuts instead. They assume that a bottle of wine that cost £30 should taste better than one that cost £5. When an item of clothing comes with the label of an upscale store, people may genuinely enjoy it more than the exact same item with a cheaper label stitched on the inside. Even eating a meal in an upmarket restaurant in a fashionable part of town may make the food itself more pleasurable than eating an identical meal on the high street.

Branding, packaging, the little details, ambience, and price all matter. Perhaps they shouldn't, but they do. People truly experience what they are led to expect. When they anticipate that something will be good or enjoyable, they are much more likely to confirm their own expectations. That *something* could be a product such as a foodstuff or a drink. It could be a film they intend to watch or nearly any service they intend to try, such as making a trip to the hairdresser, hiring an accountant, or visiting a physiotherapist to sort out a sports injury. The lesson: if we want to make a good impact and persuade people that we offer a quality product or service, the research tells us that we do need to sweat the small stuff.

The power of paper

We know that how a message is presented matters. People don't just pay attention to the content of a message, the facts or information within it, or the product or service they're evaluating. Features of the background and the ways in which a message or product or service are presented count too.

So let me ask you a question: do you prefer to type emails or do you prefer to write letters? Do you prefer to send documents as attachments or to print them out and put them in the post?

Perhaps you may have a business proposal to send to a customer. Or maybe you're thinking of sending an invitation out to friends to invite them to your birthday party or anniversary celebration. If your intention is to influence or persuade people, you may wish to take note of research done by educator P. K. Murphy and her colleagues at the Ohio State University.

The team from the university's School of Educational Policy and Leadership asked groups of undergraduate students to read two controversial articles taken from *Time* magazine either on printed paper or from a computer screen. One of the articles, 'First and Last, Do No Harm', covered a recent decision by American courts to legalise doctor-assisted suicide for terminally ill patients. The second article, 'Dividing Line: Why We Need to Raise Hell', looked at arguments for and against moves to improve the integration of black and white children in poor areas of America.[118]

The researchers asked one group of participants to read the two articles on a computer screen. A second group of participants read a paper print-out of the same two articles. I'm sure you won't be surprised to hear that your choice of medium matters. Care to hazard a guess as to which is more persuasive: old-fashioned paper or computerised text?

One thing stayed the same across both computer monitor and paper: both groups of participants reported that their knowledge of the two topics increased. But those who had read it from a computer screen reported that they had found the articles less interesting and more difficult to understand. They also said that they found the authors less credible.[119]

Why might this be though? After all, these weren't elderly people with little familiarity with computers. The subjects in the study were young tech-savvy twenty-first-century undergraduates who reported spending an average of nearly 13 hours a week on computers, surfing the Internet, emailing, and typing up assignments.

The researchers couldn't say for certain why people find paper easier to understand and more credible and persuasive. Perhaps it's because the vast majority of people today learned to read from old-fashioned books comprising words and pictures on paper when they were children. In 20 or even 10 years' time, whole generations may be learning to read from computers and digital tablets such as Apple's iPad and Amazon's Kindle. But for now, words and pictures on paper are still the dominant – and more persuasive – way of getting a message across.

Persuading in print

The advantage of paper over a computer screen doesn't even take into account the specialness of receiving a letter. Most of us use email so readily because it's easy. You don't have to dig out your address book to write the address on an envelope. You don't have to put pen to paper or fill up the printer with fresh sheets. You never have to worry about having the correct postage either. You type and hit SEND. But perhaps it's precisely this ease that makes online communication less persuasive. We know that it takes less effort to send an email, so does that mean that recipients may put less effort into reading them too?

Certainly, I know many people who dread opening their email inboxes, especially when they've been away from work for several days. They roll their eyes and shudder at the prospect of the many dozens if not hundreds of emails that may lie in wait. They talk about wanting to sort through their emails so they can get on with the more important things they have to do.

In contrast, most of us receive relatively few letters. We can always tell bills and boring bank statements from the prim white envelopes they come in. But genuine letters are rare occurrences to be cherished.

If you want your communications to be even more persuasive, think about the font you use too. When I started my own business, I confess to having frittered away more than a few hours debating with colleagues the corporate font that we wanted to use for all of our documents. Thing is: it matters.

In a study published in 2008, University of Michigan doctoral student Hyunjin Song and psychology researcher Norbert Schwarz wanted to see if they could motivate a group of students to carry out a simple exercise routine. They asked two groups of participants to read an identical set of instructions printed in one of two different fonts. Here, you can take a look at the instructions and the fonts they actually used. This one's in 12-point Brush font:

Tuck your chin into your chest, and then lift your chin upward as far as possible. 6-12 repetitions.

Lower your left ear toward your left shoulder and then your right ear toward your right shoulder. 6-10 repetitions.

And this one is typeset in 12-point Arial:

Tuck your chin into your chest, and then lift your chin upward as far as possible. 6–12 repetitions.

Lower your left ear toward your left shoulder and then your right ear toward your right shoulder. 6–10 repetitions.

No contest which set is easier to read, is there? But would the different fonts have other, unintended consequences?

After letting the two groups of participants read one set of instructions each, the researchers asked them a series of questions. Participants who read the exercise instructions in the more ornate typeface said they were more reluctant to try out the exercise. They believed that the regimen would take more time, that it would drag on for longer and be more boring. More importantly, they admitted that they were significantly less eager about the prospect of incorporating it into their day-to-day lives. The ornate font was ultimately less persuasive.[120]

Apparently the participants mistook the ease of reading the instructions with the ease of following them, of actually doing the exercises. Those who struggled with the over-elaborate font seemed mentally worn out simply by the effort of deciphering the instructions.

The lesson from this study seems to be that we should choose simple fonts. But before we decide that simple fonts are always better, let me tell you about another font-based study by a Princeton University research team led by Connor Diemand-Yauman.

Imagine you've been drafted into an experiment and given 90 seconds to learn the distinguishing features of some made-up animals. For example, here are some facts about a 'Norgletti':

- Two feet tall
- Eats flower petals and pollen
- Has brown eyes

On the other hand, here are some features that typify the 'Pangerish':

- Ten feet tall
- Eats green, leafy vegetables
- Has blue eyes

The experimenters gave half their subjects similar lists to learn in a **plain Arial font**. The other half was asked to read the same facts in either **Comic Sans MS** or **Bodoni MT**. Fifteen minutes later, subjects who read about the animals in boring old Arial scored 73 per cent in a test of their recall; subjects who read in one of the more unusual fonts scored 87 per cent.

Sometimes what works in a sterile laboratory doesn't transfer to the real world. But Diemand-Yauman and his team found that the effect of uncommon fonts did transfer to learning amongst students at a local high school. The researchers asked for permission to play around with the fonts used by the teachers in their classrooms – both their written handouts as well as their PowerPoint slides. Over the course of up to a month, and studying students in classes taking subjects ranging from English and History to Chemistry and Physics, the researchers observed that students who were exposed to obscure fonts such as **Haettenschweiler** or *Monotype Corsiva* actually performed better in their exams than students who continued to learn using the teachers' normal materials.[121]

So what should we choose? A simple font or an unusual font? Answer: it depends. If your goal is to persuade people to try something out – and they have completely free choice over whether to do it or not – then the first study by Song and Schwarz suggests that a simple font may be most effective. However, if you want to encourage people to absorb information more effectively, say for a test or exam – and you're more confident that they won't just give up on the task entirely – then an unusual font might be worth a go.

Appreciating that pictures really can paint a thousand words

Here's another, rather succulent idea. If in doubt, don't worry about the words at all. Just add a picture to your missives.

In a paper published in 2010, Marianne Bertrand and other economists from a variety of powerhouse institutions including Princeton, Yale, and Chicago universities persuaded a bank to participate in an experiment looking at the effectiveness of different mailshot letters in winning back former customers. The bank already had one standard letter it used to try to convince customers to take out its short-term loans. Using this basic template, the researchers worked up multiple variations of the letter to send out to over 53,000 of the bank's ex-customers. For instance, some of the letters mentioned monthly interest rates as low as 3.25 per cent while others offered sky-high rates of up to 11.75 per cent.

The investigative team also made other tweaks to the letter, for example modifying the wording of the offers (e.g. offering a 'special rate for you' in some letters and 'a low rate for you' in others) and tried including a prize giveaway ('Win 10 cellphones up for grabs each month!') in some letters but not others. They also incorporated a small photograph of either a smiling man or a woman in the margin of some letters, and no photo in others. Their goal: to find out the combination of factors that led to the most persuasive letters.

Over the course of the subsequent weeks and months, the economists tracked which permutations of the letter were most successful at getting customers to apply for loans from the bank. Their first observation: as they expected, more of the customers got in touch for loans when the interest rate was lower than higher. That makes perfect sense. People rationally evaluate the offer and decide whether they're happy with the cost of paying back the loan.

Less expected was the effect of incorporating a photo in the margin of the letter. The researchers were mildly surprised to discover that a letter that included a photo of a smiling woman (but not a man) increased response rates too. It didn't matter if the customer receiving the letter was a man or a woman: the photo of the smiling woman was equally effective. In terms of effectiveness, the economists estimated that the photo was about as persuasive as dropping the interest rate by 2 per cent.[122]

Of course no one in their right mind would consciously let a picture of a smiling woman influence their assessment of a loan's merits. From a rational point of view, it doesn't make sense. People ought to be making up their minds based on the cost of the repayments or the attractiveness of the loan compared to those of other lenders. The photo shouldn't make a difference. But it did. As we've seen time and again in this chapter, another detail that should have been irrelevant actually made the offer more persuasive.

The seemingly innocuous photo – the kind of cheerful headshot that organisations can buy from stock photography websites for less than the price of a round of drinks – could have cost some customers quite a bit of money. Or, the other way of looking at it is that the inclusion of the photo helped the bank to push its profits up by 2 per cent.

From a practical point of view, the results of this study have already given me an idea. The next time my colleagues and I update the website of the consultancy that we run, we're going to include a few more smiling faces. Actually, make that quite a few smiling faces.

When less is more

Choice is a good thing, right? Consider if you visited a café and they only served one type of drink, say a white coffee with one spoonful of sugar. No, you can't have a black coffee or a white coffee with more or less sugar. No, you can't have a cup of tea or a hot chocolate. And God forbid that you might want something crazy like a cold drink.

Or imagine that you have a craving for ice cream. You probably have a favourite flavour or perhaps a couple of flavours that you return to again and again. But picture going to the supermarket to pick up a tub only to discover that it only stocks vanilla. No chocolate. Nothing with nuts or fruits or a caramel swirl. You can have any flavour you like – so long as it's vanilla.

Most people enjoy having options, alternatives to choose between. And we're not just talking about choice over what to eat or drink either. Most people prefer to feel that they have choices in life, that they're free to live where they wish, pursue a career that interests them, and socialise with the people they like. The opposite of having choice would be to feel powerless, to be forced to do something, to be coerced down a single path.

But can choice ever be a bad thing? Is there such a thing as *too much* choice?

To find out, let's look at a trio of simple experiments conducted by psychologists Sheena Iyengar and Mark Lepper (we encountered him earlier in Chapter Seven: The Perils of Prizes, looking at the effects of prizes on children's motivation to draw pretty pictures). In the first experiment, the research duo set up a tasting booth within Draeger's Market, an upmarket grocery store in Menlo Park, a wealthy suburb in California. The researchers chose Draeger's Market in particular because the chain was renowned for its extensive choice, at the time offering an array of around 75 kinds of olive oil, 250 varieties of mustard, and 300 types of jam.

On a busy Saturday, the researchers set up a tasting booth offering customers the chance to sample jams from the exclusive range of Wilkin & Sons (Purveyors to Her Majesty the Queen). For the first hour, customers were allowed to choose from six jams. For the second hour, customers were allowed to choose from 24 jams. For the third hour, the selection was restricted to six jams again, and so on throughout the day.

Did the number of choices affect customers' behaviour?

The short answer: yes. But perhaps not in the ways we might expect. When more jams were on display, a greater proportion of customers stopped at the booth: 60 per cent of customers who sauntered past the 24 jams decided they wanted to taste one or more of them. Only 40 per cent of customers who passed by the restricted range of six jams felt compelled to have a taste. This suggested that people find more choice inherently appealing.

However, the customers' actual buying behaviour showed a counterintuitive effect. Only 3 per cent of customers who strolled past the 24 jams actually purchased a jar, whereas a comparatively gargantuan 30 per cent of customers who walked by the limited selection put their hands into their wallets.[123] Having more jams on display made people *less* inclined to make a purchase. Not just a little less likely to buy either, but *10 times* less likely. Wow.

Given that stores presumably want people to buy products rather than just sample the freebies, that's an eye-opening result. When it comes to encouraging customers to buy, it seems that more is less: having more choices can lead to fewer sales.

The second of Iyengar and Lepper's trio of experiments was a chocolate-lover's dream. Envisage entering a room and sitting at a table in front of a display of luxury Godiva chocolates. You can see that some of them are lavish dark chocolates, some milk chocolates; a few are white chocolates and still others are swirled, beautifully made creations you've never seen before. Each of the exquisite chocolates has a name plaque next to it, indicating that there are chocolates with sumptuous-sounding names such as 'Grand Marnier Truffle' and 'Strawberry Cordial'.

An experimenter explains: 'We're doing a marketing research study that examines how people select chocolates. What I would like you to do is take a look at the names of the chocolates and the chocolates themselves, and tell me which one you would buy for yourself.'

Not only did the experimenters allow subjects to eat the individual chocolate they picked out, but they also offered them a box of Godiva chocolates as a thank you for participating in the study. Now that's the kind of experiment I'd like to take part in!

Of course, the experimenters were again interested in the effects of range of choice on behaviour. So half of the participants sat in front of a display with six different chocolates; the other half were presented with an assortment of 30 chocolates.

Timing how long it took for participants to make their decisions, the experimenters noticed that those who were offered six chocolates took an average of 9 seconds to make up their minds. Those offered 30 chocolates took much longer – 24 seconds – to make up their minds. That's not too remarkable, given that the second group had many more chocolates to peruse and name cards to read too.

However, the final question that the experimenters asked was the most telling. When the experimenters ask the participants how they felt about the number of options, those offered 30 chocolates said that there had been 'too many' to choose between. On the other hand, the participants who were offered six chocolates said that the number of alternatives was 'about right'.

Taking the two studies together, Iyengar and Lepper's research suggests that we may suffer both cognitively and emotionally when confronted with too much choice. People experience choice over-load and may actually prefer not to have too many choices. In the chocolate study, they took longer to decide and felt that the number of choices was excessive. In the jam study, passers-by who were presented with more jams ended up being put off and less likely to buy any.

But it's perhaps the third in the trio of experiments by Iyengar and Lepper that has the most far-reaching implications. This time, the researchers experimented on 197 unsuspecting students enrolled in an introductory social psychology class at an American university. In addition to attending regular lectures, the students were required to attend smaller weekly discussion groups led by teaching assistants.

One week, the students were told that there would be no discussion group. Instead, they were asked to watch the film *Twelve Angry Men*, a classic movie in which a single dissenting juror (played by Academy Award-winner Henry Fonda) gradually convinces his fellow jurors that the murder case being presented in court isn't as clear-cut as it initially seemed.

The students also received a set of instructions: 'After watching the movie, you can obtain two extra credit points on your next midterm examination by writing a response paper to the movie. The following is a list of possible questions you can write about. Papers should be approximately one to two pages typed, double spaced, and are due Tuesday, December 3, in class.'

As I'm sure you can by now guess, the students were divided into two experimental conditions. Some of the students were given a mammoth list of 30 essay topics; others were given a more manageable list of six essay topics. By chance, the students had already been divided at the start of the semester into 10 discussion groups. So five groups received the option of writing one of 30 essays, while the other five groups chose from the list of six.

Given that this was an optional assignment, the investigators were particularly interested in how many students would hand in an essay. As the researchers predicted, more choice led to lower uptake: 74 per cent of the students who chose from six topics handed in an essay; only 60 per cent of the students who chose from 30 topics could be bothered with the assignment.

However, the researchers weren't done. When the students were first told about the movie and the assignment, they were told that they could gain 'two extra credit points' simply for handing in an essay. The teaching assistants who led the discussion groups also reiterated that their performance on the assignment would not be graded. In other words, a lazy student could afford to put less effort into the essay and it wouldn't matter. Likewise, a diligent student wouldn't get any extra marks for researching and writing a fabulous essay.

Of course the sneaky researchers assessed the quality of the papers anyway. They asked two further trained research assistants who were unaware of the aims of the study to mark all of the papers on two criteria, both the content of the essays as well as their technical proficiency, i.e. their spelling and grammar. When that was done, the researchers compared the grades received by the students and again witnessed an advantage for the students asked to choose from only six essay topics. Their essays not only had better content but also had better spelling and grammar.

Remember that all of the students were told by their teaching assistants that their papers would not be graded. So the advantage of the students choosing from six topics seemed to stem from a greater level of intrinsic motivation in the topic. Those who were presented with 30 topic choices put less effort into their work.

Taking the three experiments together, we can conclude that choice isn't always a good thing. Too much choice can be a mental maelstrom: overwhelming, bewildering, an assault on the senses.

From a rational point of view, that doesn't make sense. Given only a limited selection, what if the item or choice we really want isn't there? Surely having more choice means we're more likely to find the alternative that suits us best. But that's not how the brain works.

We know how tough it is to multitask, to juggle lots of tasks and ideas in our minds at once. When that happens, people forget things and make mistakes. Our brains only have so much processing power and, when faced with a context of too much choice, can suffer from overload, paralysis, and indecision.

Turning less into more

Iyengar and Lepper's trio of experiments together paint a fairly conclusive picture. People don't seem to cope terribly well in the context of having too much choice. In the chocolate study, people took longer to make a decision and complained about having too extensive a choice. At the jam tasting booth, too much choice made people choose not to choose; they were unable to make a decision and ended up less likely to make a purchase. And in the essay study, people's motivation as well as the quality of their work dropped when they were faced with too much choice.

Restaurant owners, retailers, and other businesses that offer products and services directly to customers may want to take notice. A restaurant, for example, may wish to think about the number of dishes it serves. Somewhat counter-intuitively, customers may be happier with a reasonable number of dishes to choose between rather than too many; they may spend less time deliberating over what to order *and* enjoy their visit more.

The same goes for professional advisers such as stock brokers and financial advisers too. A pensions adviser who offers clients dozens and dozens of investment opportunities may perversely end up winning over fewer clients than a less diligent adviser who can only offer a handful. Presenting a smaller list of recommendations may be the way to go.

If you're coaching colleagues or advising friends on the best way to tackle a problem or conundrum, you could really help them out by reducing their options as swiftly as possible. Rather than asking them about what might work as a solution, try to close some doors for them by asking them what definitely won't work. Get them to discount a handful of ideas and you may help them to feel more motivated about pursuing the one they eventually choose. You may end up helping them to deliver a stronger solution too.

CHAPTER NINE
instant influence: speedy techniques for persuasion in a hurry

'*Persuasion is often more effectual than force.*'
Aesop

My ultimate goal as a psychologist would be to find a grand unified theory of influence and persuasion – an all-encompassing model of how and why people can be influenced and persuaded. In pursuit of this Holy Grail, I've organised the first eight chapters of this book into eight major themes that allow us to understand why certain methods and manoeuvres may help us to become more influential.

These eight broad themes cover much of what behavioural scientists know about how people's minds work and why they may be captivated by certain techniques. But the reality is that the human mind is remarkably, breathtakingly complex. It works in myriad mysterious ways, and some of those ways don't necessarily fit into the framework of explanations we've created. So in this final chapter, I'll present a final five tactics that may allow you to perform some crafty feats of influence and persuasion.

That's not all

When I was shopping in a department store on London's Oxford Street over the summer, a voice over the public address system announced: 'There will be a free knife giveaway on the third floor in the kitchenware department. Simply watch a 10-minute demonstration of our new range of StaySharp blades and you will receive a free knife as a thank you for watching!'

Oh, a free knife, I thought. I was shopping for a friend's wedding present, but who was I to turn down a free gift?

I wandered over to the kitchenware department to where a middle-aged chef in a white apron was standing behind a kitchen work surface on a slightly raised dais. The spotlights beaming at him gave his eyes a manic sparkle. When a crowd of several dozen shoppers had gathered, he began performing a demonstration with a set of three knives. I'm sure you'll be familiar with the kind of show he put on if you've ever watched an infomercial on television. He demonstrated how sharp the blades were, how easily they sliced through all manner of unruly vegetables, and how handy it was having knives of different lengths for different purposes. He talked non-stop, pointing out how much time he was saving in the kitchen given how quickly he was doing all his preparation. No struggling with dull knives for him!

Towards the end of the demonstration, he addressed the audience: 'Now, before I give you each a free knife, will you stay and listen to the amazing offer I have for you?'

The crowd nodded obediently.

'The set of knives normally sells at £29.99. But we've got an amazing offer for you today. Not only do you get the standard set of three knives but we'll also throw in a free paring knife. And because we negotiated a special deal with the manufacturer, we can give you a free bread knife too. That's not all though. The department store has also kindly decided to sweeten the offer with a free chopping board too.'

He dropped his voice to a conspiratorial whisper: 'Between you and me, I'm not sure how they're making any money from this at this kind of price.'

Then, in a brighter voice, he hit us with his request: 'Now, who would like to own not only the set of three that I've been demonstrating, but the two extra knives and the chopping board too?'

A handful of customers dutifully queued up to hand over their money.

Listening to his practised sales patter, you'd think that no one would fall for that kind of a yarn. Of course the department store made money from the promotion. But research shows that the 'that's-not-all' technique genuinely works.

Making a good offer irresistible

People like to feel that they're getting a bargain. In the first of two experiments Jerry Burger, a veteran researcher in the field of influence and persuasion at Santa Clara University, set up a stall selling cupcakes and cookies at an art fair. Half of the customers who approached the booth were told straightaway by the seller that a cupcake and two cookies cost 75 cents. Every other participant was told that each cupcake cost 75 cents – but then a second cupcake seller pretended to interrupt the first seller to say that they had an offer on: anyone buying a cupcake could get two cookies for free too! While only 40 per cent of people who were told upfront about the price of the overall package made a purchase, 73 per cent of people who were told that the cookies were 'extra' decided to buy.

Before I explain the implications of that first study, let me tell you what Burger did next. He again set up a cupcake stand, but this time with a different offer. Some participants were told that each cupcake cost 75 cents. Other participants in the 'that's-not-all' condition were initially told that the cupcakes cost a dollar – but then a second seller again interrupted the first seller to tell the customer that the booth was closing soon and that they were reducing the price to 75 cents. This time, 44 per cent of the people who were initially told a 75-cent price made a purchase; 73 per cent of the people who thought they were getting a bargain made a purchase.[124]

So what does that mean? The first of the two experiments demonstrates that people can be tempted by giving them the perception that they're getting more than they expected. The second experiment shows that the effect isn't just limited to giving people more value; people can also be persuaded to open their wallets when they think they're getting a discount.

The that's-not-all technique may work because people feel like they have negotiated a bargain and are wringing a better deal from the seller than the seller had initially intended. Or, because the seller seems to be doing the customer a favour by either offering more or a discount, the customer may feel compelled by the norm of reciprocity to respond by making a purchase. Unfortunately, the research hasn't been done to tell us exactly why the practice works. It just does.

You can deploy the that's-not-all technique by presenting a product at a particular price and allowing the customer to think about that initial price. Only *then* might you improve the deal either by offering more goods or add-ons for the same price or dropping the price by offering a discount. Whichever tactic you choose, your offer may suddenly seem much more compelling.

Being reasonable

Shortly after finishing university, I decided I wanted to backpack around the United States, so I flew to Boston, Massachusetts, and travelled by train all over the vast country. About midway through my eight-week tour, I ended up in a youth hostel in New Orleans, Louisiana, and I remember going for a dip in the hostel's swimming pool one evening. There was a handwritten sign next to the pool saying 'Do not swim until after 8 p.m.', but it was well past seven o'clock and no one was around and it had been such a hot and sticky day, so my friends and I thought nothing of peeling off and jumping into the pool.

A few minutes later, the sounds of our laughter and tomfoolery brought a caretaker out. Without any anger, he explained in a southern drawl that the pool probably wasn't safe for us to swim in yet. He'd dumped a fresh batch of chlorine into the water to disinfect it and the chemical might not have dissipated enough. Duly reprimanded and a little embarrassed, we got out to go and shower.

Years after that little incident, I came across a paper with an interesting finding: there is a magic word which, added to the sign, might have guaranteed our compliance. Let me explain.

Back in 1978, Harvard University psychologist Ellen Langer and her colleagues conducted a deceptively simple yet illuminating study by hiring two experimenters (one male and one female) to hang around near a photocopier in the library at the City University of New York. When an unsuspecting person approached the photocopier to use it, one of the experimenters immediately dashed over to ask to use the photocopier first.

Sometimes the experimenters said, 'Excuse me, I have five pages. May I use the Xerox machine?' Faced with this rather blunt request, 60 per cent of the unknowing subjects in the study agreed to let the experimenter jump ahead to use the machine.

However, the experimenters managed to boost their success rate to an impressive 94 per cent by adding a few extra words to their request. How? What was their secret?

They asked: 'Excuse me, I have five pages. May I use the Xerox machine, because I'm in a rush?'

If you were faced with someone who was in a rush, I'm sure you would let them go first too. So no surprises that the vast majority of subjects – 94 per cent of them – let the experimenters jump the queue.

To test the power of the word 'because' though, Langer's team also tried a different request that tacked on a rather circuitous explanation: 'Excuse me, I have five pages. May I use the Xerox machine, because I have to make copies?'

Er, you have to make copies? What kind of a tautological, inane explanation is that? You're not going to use the photocopier to make a phone call or brew a coffee, are you? However, even this obviously bogus line of reasoning was still enough to make 93 per cent of the subjects give way to the experimenters.

Langer and her colleagues suggest that the word 'because' has its own special power. Most of the time, the word is followed by a good reason, so many people get conditioned into agreeing to requests when they hear the word 'because'.

Going back to the New Orleans hostel pool then, the caretaker could have kept us out of the pool by adding almost any explanation. Perhaps 'because the pool is being cleaned' or 'because I put chlorine in the pool' might have done the job.

However, the power of the word 'because' isn't limitless. Langer and her team decided to repeat the experiment, but this time making a larger request, asking to photocopy 20 copies rather than five.

This time, the experimenters found that only 24 per cent of the subjects ahead of them at the photocopier agreed to let them jump ahead when they made their basic request. Remember that this was the late 1970s when photocopiers were still a relatively newfangled and barely reliable technology. So apart from the fact that the task was going to take four times longer, the copier was also much more likely to jam, run out of ink, or otherwise stall.

When the experimenters gave the good reason and explained that they wished to cut ahead 'because I'm in a rush', 42 per cent of subjects let them push ahead. That's still nearly twice the number of subjects who let the experimenters go first when no reason was given, suggesting that giving a reason is definitely a good idea, no matter what the size of the request.

However, when the experimenters gave the meaningless reason 'because I have to make copies', only 24 per cent of the subjects let them cut ahead.[125] In other words, when it came to a larger request, giving a poor reason was as bad as giving no reason at all.

Langer and her colleagues argue that the word 'because' is enough to increase persuasion even without a good reason only when the stakes are low. It wasn't much of an imposition to let someone go ahead in the queue when he or she only had a handful of copies to make. But when there were 20 copies to be made, the word 'because' lost its potency: having *a* reason wasn't good enough, people needed a *valid* reason to agree to the request.

Because

The message is clear: to make our requests as compelling as possible, use the word 'because' and have a robust reason to go along with it. That may sound blindingly obvious, but we're all prone to occasional forgetfulness when we're busy or preoccupied by other thoughts. We may simply overlook giving adequate reasons for why we want people to do what we ask of them.

Occasionally, we may think the reasons for our requests are patently clear. But we have to remember that the people around us aren't telepathic – they can't read our minds and know why we want them to do what we ask them to do!

It takes just a few seconds to tack a good reason onto the end of our requests. Asking colleagues or friends and family to help with a task 'because I'm really busy and could do with the help' could make all the difference between them ignoring the request and agreeing to lend a hand.

When it comes to warning our children about what they should or shouldn't do, a reason may help too. Parents say, 'Don't play with matches,' and 'Don't run across the road without looking.' But 'Don't play with matches *because* you may set the house on fire,' and 'Don't run across the road without looking because you could get injured,' may be far more effective at gaining our children's compliance.

The world's largest cosmetics and beauty company L'Oréal always finishes its TV commercials with the line 'Because we're worth it.' I wonder if the people in their marketing department have been studying the psychology of persuasion ...

The 'pique technique'

You have to pity the research assistants who work for psychologists sometimes. In yet another study conceived by the fiendish mind of Jerry Burger, the connoisseur of human behaviour who uncovered the that's-not-all technique, four research assistants were asked to approach strangers to beg for money! Burger and his fellow investigators were well aware of the physical risks for the research assistants; they went to great pains in their write-up of the experiment to mention that the research assistants worked in pairs 'for safety reasons' and kept at least three feet (one metre) away from the strangers at all times.

This all happened only a few years ago in 2007. The research assistants were all dressed casually and stationed at an outdoor shopping area in the San Francisco Bay Area. They were instructed to watch people walking by and to approach individual passers-by – in other words total strangers – with a fairly standard begging question: 'Excuse me, can you spare any change?'

If you've ever watched a genuine panhandler begging for change, I'm sure you'll agree that it looks like dispiriting work. Most people say no. And in this experiment, only 18.8 per cent of the passers-by, the unwitting subjects in the study, handed over any money. The research assistants would also have had to ask a lot of passers-by for money if they were to get rich. On average, the passers-by that stopped handed over just seven cents each time.

However, Burger and his band of researchers had a theory: they wondered if a specific and unusual request might provoke the curiosity of more people. So they asked their hapless research assistants to pester other passers-by with a very particular request: 'Excuse me, can you spare 37 cents?'

Realising that many of the passers-by might naturally ask, 'Why?' the investigators briefed the research assistants to respond in one of two ways. Half the time, they gave a vague reason by saying, 'Because I need to buy some things.' The other half of the time, they gave a more specific reason: 'Because I need to buy a stamp.'

Approaching over 300 people in total, the results showed a clear pattern. When the research assistants asked for 37 cents but weren't asked for a reason, 25.9 per cent of the strangers handed over an average of 10 cents each. That's a conspicuous improvement – nearly twice as much money – over the standard approach of simply asking for 'any change'. Not only was a higher proportion of passers-by willing to hand over money; they gave more money each time too. So asking for a peculiar amount did seem to provoke the curiosity of the subjects in the study.

The investigators behind the study explained the finding by suggesting that the quirkier request may have piqued the curiosity of more people – hence dubbing it the 'pique technique'. The argument goes that most people get into habitual patterns of responding. For example, if someone asks them for money, they automatically say 'no'. It's a way of saving time and reducing the amount of energy that our brains have to expend on conscious thought – a vestigial hangover from ancient times when our earliest forebears benefited from having not just bodies but even brains that made all possible efforts to conserve energy. However, unusual requests seem to tiptoe past people's defences and persuade them to consider the requests on their own merits.

But the results became more interesting when some of the perplexed strangers asked *why* they were being asked for money. When some of the subjects asked, 'Why?' they were told: 'Because I need to buy some things.' Even this vague reason led to more generosity, with 70 per cent of them handing over an average of 37 cents each. Most impressively though, when the strangers asked, 'Why?' and were given the specific reason: 'Because I need to buy a stamp,' this time 87.1 per cent of the subjects handed over an average of 38 cents.[126]

In other words, giving *a* reason – 'Because I need to buy some things' – persuaded the subjects in the study to be a little more generous. But providing a specific and perhaps seemingly more valid reason persuaded the subjects to be the most generous.

Hopefully that reminds you of the work done by Ellen Langer at the library photocopier. When her experimenters gave *a* reason – even a nonsensical or just blindingly obvious one – they helped to increase their chances of success in trying to barge in to photocopy a few documents. But they were most successful in jumping ahead when they gave a *sensible* reason.

Will you spend 138 seconds reading this box?

Most people are eminently capable of blocking out the requests and messages they hear. However, research on the 'pique technique' suggests that we may be able to get their attention by phrasing requests in unorthodox ways.

Say you run a shop or store of some kind. Any store can offer discounts of 'one-third off' or 'up to 50 per cent reductions'. But why not try an unusual number that will make people stop and scratch their heads? Try offering '23 per cent off all items' or 'up to 51 per cent off selected items' and you may find people coming in off the street to ask why on earth your store is offering such curious discounts.

Along similar lines, a group of European researchers approached strangers asking them to buy lottery tickets from them. When they told potential customers that each ticket cost 'three and a half euros', they managed to make a sale 25 per cent of the time. However, when they explained that a ticket cost '350 eurocents', they boosted their success rate to 43 per cent.[127] It sounds ridiculous, but if we ever need to raise funds or borrow money from friends, we might be better off stating our requests in pennies rather than pounds. Extending the implications, consider how you could use it if you work for a humanitarian cause, for example. Rather than asking for a donation of £10 or some other round number, why not ask for £12.83? But remember the additive power of the word 'because'. If you can find a way to justify your request – perhaps it's the price of a new plough for a remote African village or the monthly salary you'd pay a poor Indian family to keep their young children at school – you may find even more people amenable to your appeal.

Or imagine you're asking a buddy to lend you his car. Rather than asking to borrow it for the weekend, ask to have it for 42 hours. At the very least, he'll want to hear why you need it for such a specific length of time. By the time you've explained your reasoning by using the word 'because', he may well be hooked.

Perhaps the broader and more essential point is that *many of the techniques in this book may actually have additive effects*. Jerry Burger's 'pique technique' helps to boost our chances of success, but so too does giving a good reason, as discovered by Ellen Langer. Rather than using the tools within this book individually, think about how you could combine the power of multiple techniques to improve your influence and persuasiveness.

The 'Luncheon Technique'

Working as a corporate psychologist, I'm effectively a consultant, someone who needs to persuade organisations to hire me. Over the years, I've taken dozens and dozens of clients out for lunch, often to celebrate the end of a successful project. But in gathering research papers for this book, I discovered that I'd been getting it wrong: I should be taking clients out for lunch when we're getting to know each other.

In the late 1930s, psychologist Gregory Razran asked a group of experimental participants to rate the extent to which they agreed or disagreed with a range of political statements. Telling them that he wanted to give them time for a break from looking at the long list of tedious political slogans, he invited them to enjoy a free lunch. While they ate though, he asked them to look again at some of the political statements – just a subset of the overall list they had already rated. When he later asked the participants to rate for a second time their approval of the entire list of statements, he found that they tended to agree more with some of the statements: the ones the participants had heard again during the meal.[128]

Nutritionists often say that 'you are what you eat'. But it seems that we might be able to extend the adage to how people think too: 'You are what you think while you eat.'

Why should this happen though? Razran reasoned that eating is an innately pleasurable activity, so any thoughts we entertain or arguments we hear while we eat may become associated with those pleasant feelings too. In support of this idea, research investigators James Dabbs and Irving Janis from Yale University fed one group of experimental subjects *while* they listened to persuasive messages; they fed a separate group of experimental subjects first and *then* asked them to listen to the same statements. Comparing the degree to which subjects in the two groups changed their attitudes, the researchers found that only the subjects who heard the messages while they ate became more likely to endorse the statements. Subjects who ate first and then heard the messages didn't exhibit a significant shift in their attitudes.[129]

The implication is clear: if you're trying to sway the judgement of the people around you, buy them lunch. But make sure that you present your arguments while you eat. The mere presence of food and the fact that people are satisfying their carnal needs may be enough to make them more amenable to your suggestions.

Reminding people of their choice

Research backs up what we've long suspected: people hate being told what to do. Point out to friends that they drink too much alcohol or eat unhealthily and they are unlikely to thank you for it. Explain to a colleague that he's doing a task in an ineffective and time-consuming fashion and he may snap that he likes doing it that way. Warn a surly teenager not to take drugs and you may end up making the prospect even more enticing.[130]

But using that reverse psychology may help us to persuade more people to agree to our requests. French investigators asked research assistants to ask passers-by on a street whether they would be willing to take part in a short market research survey lasting around five to eight minutes in length.

The sprightly assistants approached passers-by with one of two introductory spiels. In a control condition, the research assistants stopped people by saying: 'Sorry, Sir/Madam. We are currently conducting a survey …' Using this standard script, 75.6 per cent of the people they approached agreed to take part in the survey.

However, with other passers-by, the research assistants mentioned straightaway that the participants were free to refuse the request: 'Sorry, Sir/Madam. I have something to ask you but you are free to accept or refuse. We are currently conducting a survey …' On these occasions, the proportion of people who took part in the survey jumped to 90.1 per cent.

What's interesting is that the phrase didn't materially change anything about the situation. After all, the participants in the control condition were still free to embrace or decline the request; it wasn't as if the research assistants had pinned them down to force them to complete the survey. When the participants heard the phrase 'but you are free to accept or refuse', it was only their *perception* that had changed. But that alone was enough to coax more of them to take part in the survey.

Hopefully the implication is clear. The phrase 'but you are free to accept or refuse' may seem a bit cumbersome, but it's been proven to be effective in a variety of different settings.[131] Highlighting people's freedom of choice in matters may be a wise lesson we can all learn then – but only if you want to, of course …

Helping people to feel in control

In Chapter Seven: The Perils of Prizes, I explained that phrasing instructions using language such as 'you can' and 'if you choose' led to greater participation in various activities than instructions using more coercive language such as 'you should' and 'you must' (see the boxes 'Setting goals that motivate, not discourage (part I)' on page 193, and 'Setting goals that motivate, not discourage (part II)' on page 197). The more we try to pressurise people, the *less* likely they may be to do what we ask of them. The fact that the additional phrase 'but you are free to accept or refuse' encourages people to go along with a request is entirely consistent with that research.

My own experience suggests that it's the sentiment that matters rather than the precise wording. I used the technique myself only last week. I had been doing interviews with radio stations and newspaper and magazine journalists in the Far East to promote my last book *The Extra One Per Cent: How small changes make exceptional people* (Macmillan). After a long week, I was checking into a flight from Singapore's Changi Airport back to London Heathrow. I wanted to carry my small suitcase as hand baggage rather than checking it in (so that I could avoid having to wait at the carousel when I got back to London). Unfortunately, the check-in assistant told me that the weight allowance was 10 kilograms and my bag was too heavy. My bag wasn't just a little too heavy though. It was nearly double the allowance at 18 kilograms.

Beaming her my warmest and most imploring smile, I said: 'I didn't realise that you had a weight allowance. I appreciate that this is totally at your discretion and of course you can refuse my request but you would really help me out if I could on this one occasion take my bag as hand luggage rather than checking it into the hold. May I please take it as hand luggage?'

The check-in assistant looked at me for several seconds. And then she said yes!

CONCLUSIONS
practising principled persuasion

'*With great power comes great responsibility.*'
Uncle Ben

I'm a fan of comic books so I hope you'll forgive a pop cultural reference here. The 2002 hit movie *Spider-Man* made over $820 million at the worldwide box office. That was nearly a decade ago so, taking inflation into account, it's nearly the equivalent of a billion dollars in today's money, or $1,000,000,000 if we're writing out all the zeros. In the movie, Peter Parker starts out as an unassuming student who is bitten by a radioactive spider to be transformed into the amazing Spider-Man. When he first discovers that he is super-fast, agile, and superhumanly strong, he begins to use his new-found powers for personal gain, to compete in wrestling matches for big cash prizes. But then his kindly Uncle Ben is gunned down by a criminal.

His uncle's last words as his life ebbs away are a caution to gangly young Peter: 'With great power comes great responsibility.' And only then does Spider-Man decide to dedicate his life to doing good.

What's my point?

The principles within this book form the basis of a powerful armoury for influencing and persuading others. If you incorporate all of the techniques into your repertoire, you'll be on your way to becoming a grand master of influence, a black belt in persuasion. You could use your new-found skills to manipulate people against their will, making them comply with your wishes and do your selfish bidding despite whatever reservations they may have. You could use the psychological insights from this book to foist unwanted products on customers. Or you could inveigle colleagues or your children or friends into doing as you ask even though they may later realise it's not what they wanted to do.

But if you're going to rip people off, you may need an inexhaustible supply of friends and family, colleagues and customers. Because that's a short-term strategy which only works if you aren't worried about having relationships of any longevity – *if you never have to see people again*. Perfect for the con artist or thief, the grifter and the door-to-door salesperson.*

For the majority of us, we don't want to (or maybe can't) get away from our friends and family. We work with the same colleagues from one day to the next. We want to foster long-term relationships with suppliers and clients and customers rather than having to chase after new ones all of the time.

To demonstrate how much this all matters, let me introduce you to an experimental game that psychologists use all around the world to investigate human behaviour: the ultimatum game. Let me explain the rules and you can play along with me if you like.

The two-player, two-stage game is fairly straightforward: two people have to agree on how to split a sum of money, say £10. In the first stage, one person (the proposer) is free to make an offer as to how the money should be divided. So the proposer might suggest a 70:30 split in favour of the proposer, a 50:50 split that benefits both players equally, or indeed any other split imaginable. In the second stage, the other person (the responder) is free only to accept or reject the offer. If the responder accepts, then the money is carved up in the proportions suggested by the proposer. If the responder rebuffs

---

* I know, I know. Only kidding. *Some* door-to-door salespeople may be morally upstanding people.

the offer, neither player gets anything. The money gets taken away from both of them. In either case, the game is over.

To be clear: this is a one-off game. The game is not played again with the proposer and the responder switching roles. Neither is there any discussion or bargaining over how the money could be split: it's called the *ultimatum* game, a take-it-or-leave-it challenge, not the negotiation and bargaining game. What's more, the proposer and the responder are not even in the same room, so the responder can't make eye contact and try to shame the proposer into offering a fairer deal. They remain in separate rooms and deal with each other only through an intercom or by pushing buttons on a computer console. If the responder turns down the offer, both individuals walk away with nothing and they never have anything to do with each other again.

Ready to play? So let's say a researcher puts you and me in separate rooms and tells us that I get to be the proposer and you will be the responder. And the stake will be £20.

Now, if I were to offer you a 50:50 split, you'd probably accept, right? We each get £10. Free money and everybody's happy. A true win-win situation.

But consider a different scenario. What if I were to offer a split of 90:10 so I get £18 and you get a measly £2 – would you still take it?

Now the rational decision would be to accept. After all, you still get £2. If you reject the offer, you get nothing. Remember that this is a one-time game. We don't play again. Whether you take the deal or reject it, the game is over and we'll never cross paths again. From a financial perspective, taking *something* away is better than walking off empty-handed.

But at the same time you probably feel unhappy about my offer. There's a bubble of annoyance welling up inside you at my unfairness, at my greed. So you may be tempted to throw the offer back in my face.

That's precisely what many responders do. They reject offers that favour the proposer too much. When explaining their thinking, they realise that they should accept *any* offer because it's economically advantageous. But responders are not rational. In study after study, researchers typically find that around half of responders reject offers that would leave them with less than 30 per cent of the cash prize.[132]

Responders who don't feel that they're being treated fairly decide to punish their proposers for their selfishness. Yes, the responders lose out by rejecting a deal, but at least they have the satisfaction of knowing that the proposers are losing out more.

Based on the results of such studies, experts contend that most people have an innate desire for justice.[133] People don't like being treated unfairly and, when they do encounter inequity, are willing to put up with a little hardship if they can punish a transgressor. They are more than willing to bear grudges and seek retribution.

Further evidence comes from elsewhere in the animal kingdom. The brown capuchin monkey is a cute monkey about as tall as your knee. Animal behaviourists Sarah Brosnan and Frans de Waal gave their capuchin monkeys either tasty or bland treats to eat and observed their behaviour. When monkeys were given a bland treat but saw that one of their companions was being given a tasty treat, the monkeys often rejected the gifts of food to signal their displeasure at having been treated unfairly. The fact that even our primate cousins have an aversion to inequity suggests that the human desire for fairness is deeply ingrained in our behaviour.[134]

Bringing us back to the domain of influence and persuasion then, it suggests that we may wish to be mindful of how we wield the techniques at our disposal. Yes, we could use the wisdom of crowds and the principle of social influence to manipulate others into behaving as we'd like them to. We could lie about what we have in common with others and use the power of similarity to get people to like us. We could use all sorts of underhand tactics and trickery to get them to buy from us, support us, and give us their time and money and friendship. But because of the collateral damage, that only works once.

Make no mistake: the moment people realise that they were tricked, they're gone. Even if you have a further offer or opportunity that might be genuinely beneficial to them, you won't be able to persuade them to trust you again. The ultimatum game teaches us that they not only signal their disapproval and disdain for you by ignoring you; they may go out of their way to seek retribution, even if it hurts them a little too. These days, it may only take someone a handful of clicks to leave an online legacy on a blog, Twitter or other forum that permanently sullies your name.[135] Your reputation may be ruined so far and wide that your only future job options may involve asking customers, 'Would you like fries with that?' Hopefully that's an overly dramatic scenario, but it's not a total impossibility either.

Hang on then. Does that mean that we can't use *any* of the techniques that we've covered in this book? Not exactly.

The psychology of mind-reading

To explain how we *can* use these techniques in smart but not scheming, ethical but never evil ways, let's consider one final experiment. But first, may I ask you to mull over the following 10 statements?[136] Use a 5-point scale to rate the extent to which you agree with each statement on the next page, from 0 = 'does not describe me well' to 4 = 'describes me very well'. Try to answer as honestly as you can – I'm not going to check up on you – and I'll explain what to do with your scores in a few moments.

1. Before criticising somebody, I try to imagine how I would have behaved if I were in their place.
2. When I see someone being taken advantage of, I feel kind of protective towards them.
3. I sometimes try to understand my friends better by imagining how things look from their perspective.
4. I often have tender, concerned feelings for people less fortunate than me.
5. I believe that there are two sides to every question and I try to look at them both.
6. I would describe myself as a pretty soft-hearted person.
7. I try to look at everybody's side of a disagreement before I make a decision.
8. I am often quite touched by things that I see happen.
9. I usually find it very easy to see things from the other person's point of view.
10. Other people's misfortunes often disturb me a great deal.

Add up the scores for all of the odd-numbered statements, which gives you a number between 0 and 20. That is your perspective-taking score. Then add up your scores for all of the even-numbered statements (again, totalling between 0 and 20). That's your empathy score. To explain what those scores mean, let me talk you through one final study.

In 2008, a team of researchers from French, American, and Canadian business schools and universities (including from INSEAD and the Kellogg School of Management, both widely acknowledged as amongst the top 10 business schools in the world) published a paper in the influential journal *Psychological Science* discussing ways of improving people's ability to negotiate in business situations. In a simple yet ingenious experiment, the researchers asked 76 pairs of business school students to negotiate over the sale of a hypothetical piece of property, a service station. One of the MBA students was assigned the role of the owner of the station who wanted to sell; the other student was told to take the part of a property developer who wanted to buy the property – but only at the right price.

To help both parties prepare for the negotiation, each individual was given a folder of confidential information about the service station. The sellers were given facts and figures about the financial performance of the service station as well as background about their motivations, what they were hoping to achieve as the seller. The buyers were given slightly different information including a briefing on what they could afford and the concessions they might be willing to offer.

The buyers and sellers had a week to work out their plans of attack. But mere minutes before the negotiation began, the researchers split the buyers into three groups. One group was given a set of special instructions focusing on empathy; these buyers were told to empathise with the sellers of the service station as follows:

Try to understand what they are feeling, what emotions they may be experiencing in selling the station. Try to imagine what you would be feeling in the role.

A second group of buyers was assigned to a perspective-taking group. These buyers were asked to consider what the sellers were thinking:

Try to understand what they are thinking, what their interests and purposes are in selling the station. Try to imagine what you would be thinking in the role.

The third group of buyers was given no further instructions so that their performance could be used to look at how the two experimental sets of conditions might affect the negotiation outcomes. After 50 minutes of negotiating, the researchers totalled up the number of pairs in each of the three conditions that managed to reach an agreement.

Any bets as to which group was the most successful?

Only 39 per cent of the control group buyers managed to negotiate a successful agreement; 54 per cent of the empathy buyers who empathised with the feelings and emotions of the sellers reached a successful agreement. But 76 per cent of the perspective-taking group who were instructed to consider the thinking, interests, and purposes of the sellers managed to secure a successful agreement.[137]

The result suggests that we would be smart to consider at all times the thoughts, interests, and purposes of other people when we want to succeed in our interactions with them. This skill of perspective-taking is a rational, cool-headed ability that allows us to anticipate the likely behaviour and reactions of other people.

However, an additional piece of data throws a different slant on the experiment. Immediately after the negotiation ended, all of the sellers were asked to indicate how satisfied they were on a 7-point scale (where 1 = 'not at all satisfied' to 7 = 'extremely satisfied') with the way they were treated during the interaction. Yes, the perspective-taking buyers who considered the thoughts of the sellers were most successful in manoeuvring the sellers into accepting an agreement. And sellers in the perspective-taking group were significantly happier about the way they had been treated during the discussion than sellers in the control group. But it was sellers in the empathy group who were the most *satisfied* with the way they'd been treated.

Taking the results together then, perspective-taking – considering the thoughts, purposes, and interests of another person – may benefit us the most when we want to win. It's a good 'best for me' strategy that helps us to get whatever we can from a situation and trounce an opponent. But winning means creating losers. The people we beat may not be entirely happy with the outcomes that come out of such discussions, such adversarial matches.

On the other hand, empathising with people – considering the feelings and emotions that may be running through their heads – enables us to create more mutually beneficial outcomes. True, it may not confer such significant benefits for us in terms of squeezing everything we can out of an opponent. However, we may be happier with the outcomes. Empathy may be more of a long-term 'good for both of us' tactic to use.

Influencing with integrity

Going back to the 10 questions at the start of this section, consider which of the two skills you are naturally stronger at. Which score was higher – perspective-taking or empathy? Are you someone who effortlessly *thinks* about the thoughts and viewpoints of others from a more cool-headed standpoint? Or are you the kind of person who naturally *feels* what others are feeling, who connects on an emotional level to feel their ups and downs even when you may not want to?

When it comes to the realms of influence and persuasion, neither is inherently better. Perspective-taking may help us to discover the best technique for changing people's minds or altering their behaviour; it may allow us to outsmart opponents and achieve as much as we can in one-off situations. But that cold-hearted analysis of what works may not do us any favours in the long-term. People may bristle at being out manoeuvred or manipulated against their will.

Empathy may leave people feeling happier in our wake. Sometimes labelled sympathy or compassion, it may confer more modest benefits than perspective-taking in terms of influencing and persuading others. But perhaps it's a compromise that many people may find more acceptable.

Whether you're stronger in empathy or in perspective-taking ultimately doesn't matter. In the negotiation experiment with the pairs of MBA students, participants were able to engage in either perspective-taking or empathy depending on the instructions they were given. You too could hone your prowess in either skill depending on the set of mental instructions you give yourself. But the really good news is that it's only in psychological experiments that participants get told to consider only the thoughts *or* feelings of others. We don't have to choose between either perspective-taking *or* empathy. In the real world we can do *both*.

Practising principled persuasion

As a psychologist, I'm very privileged that I get to travel the world giving talks at business conferences; I also run training seminars and workshops on the psychology of the workplace. As you might imagine, I get quite a few invitations to speak to audiences of salespeople who are keen to soak up new schemes and stratagems that will allow them to sell more to their clients and customers. But whatever the audience, I always end my talks by emphasising the importance of practising principled persuasion. Remember the research about the ultimatum game: disgruntled people may *go out of their way* to punish others who've wronged them.

Suppose you want to persuade someone to buy your product. Taking their perspective and weighing up their thoughts and interests may help you to discover the most effective way of getting what you want. But is it really the right thing to do? Will the customer get enough benefit or pleasure from the product or is it only you who gains? Empathising with the other person to consider their feelings may help to guard against ripping people off, coercing them in ways they are sure to regret later.

Taking my inspiration from the different sets of instructions issued to the MBA students in the negotiation experiment, here's my attempt to blend the benefits of both perspective-taking and empathy together. The next time you want to change someone's mind or get your way, spend a couple of minutes pondering the following:

In trying to influence and persuade the people in your life, try to understand not only what they are thinking but also what they are feeling. Try to understand their interests and purposes, what they hope to achieve, their ambitions and goals. At the same time though, try to imagine the emotions and feelings that they may be experiencing too. How would you feel in that situation?

Onwards and upwards

I promised in the introduction to this book that the psychology of influence and persuasion is fascinating. As we reach the end of our journey together I hope you will feel that I've delivered on my pledge. The human mind has evolved over the course of tens of thousands of years to rely on various shortcuts: the power of social influence, non-verbal cues, the norm of reciprocity, and others. And by understanding how the mind works, we can change people's minds and guide their behaviour.

I believe that influence and persuasion are amongst the most important skills we can possess as human beings. Whatever our goals in life – to make friends, get rich, save the planet, raise a happy family – we can only benefit from being able to win people's trust and persuade them to respond favourably to our suggestions and requests. Influence and persuasion are at the core of building relationships, parenting our children, motivating colleagues, teaching new skills to family members, and dealing successfully with the myriad people we encounter every day.

I hope you've enjoyed reading about the experiments and learning the principles of persuasion. And for many readers, that may be enough. If you're motivated to incorporate the techniques into your life, consider that understanding the principles isn't the same as putting them into practice. Reading a book about how to speak French doesn't mean you'll be fluent in the language; listening to an audio book about how to play tennis won't necessarily help you to serve aces. So perhaps pick a handful of your favourite tactics to put into play. Mimic the body language of an interviewer the next time you go for a promotion or a new job. Tell cautionary tales and inspiring stories when you want to instruct your family and friends. Collect testimonials from your customers and clients. Point out the commonalities and similarities you share with the people you meet to help the relationship along.

Many persuasive people – community leaders, business people, charity workers, teachers, parents, and perhaps many of your friends – are already practitioners of the techniques we've covered in this book. They may not consciously realise they're drawing upon the psychology of influence and persuasion, but that's often how the most compelling individuals manage to achieve so much in life.

To end, I'd like to mention that I always enjoy receiving messages from readers. Let me know if you have an example of an influence and persuasion technique that works for you (or one that has perhaps worked *on* you). You can reach me at: rob@robyeung.com. Who knows? I may put your story into a future edition of this very book.

Dr Rob Yeung
www.robyeung.com
www.twitter.com/robyeung

THE INFLUENCE
TOOLKIT

I hope you've enjoyed reading about the often surprising science of influence and persuasion. Some readers will be happy to stop here. But if you're a reader who wants more specific guidance on how to apply the science in your own attempts to influence and persuade people, then read on.

In this part of the book I will summarise the key themes contained within the eight main chapters of this book. I'll also include some further advice and activities for you to try if you should wish to integrate the tools and techniques more deeply into either your personal or professional life.

This part of the book is all about doing, taking action, having a go. So have fun, be successful, but remember to influence with integrity.

Following the crowd

No matter how independent and free-spirited we each believe ourselves to be, the truth is that we're actually very much influenced by what the people around us are doing and saying. We tend to dress like the people around us. We enjoy music and food more when we know that others like the same song or the same dish too. We're even more likely to engage in activities that are illegal when we see others doing it or simply believe that they are – such as driving way over the speed limit or fiddling our taxes. While most people will deny being influenced by knowledge about what other people are doing, the research is irrefutable: even our brains are actually wired to enjoy, prefer, and follow what others seem to be doing.

But the good news is that we can consciously harness this tendency to follow the crowd too. Suppose you're trying to get a child to eat more vegetables, a friend to take her medication, or an elderly relative to do more exercise. Hectoring and badgering them with commands isn't really going to work. So avoid issuing instructions such as, 'I'm not letting you leave the table until you've eaten your greens,' 'You need to take your pill every day,' or 'You should do more exercise.'

Instead, tell the people in your life what most other people are doing. If you know that your child's friends Paul, Jasper, and Sophia and cousin Nina are all eating their vegetables then tell your child exactly that: 'Did you know that Paul, Jasper, and Sophia and your cousin Nina all eat spinach too?'

Here are some other phrases you could try to exercise social influence over the people in your life:

Phrase	Explanation and examples
'Most' or 'Many' or 'The vast majority of …'	If you're trying to get either an individual or a group of people to do more of an activity, then tell them that most people are already doing it, e.g. 'Most people at this party are getting taxis home rather than trying to drive after the amount of alcohol they've had to drink,' or 'The vast majority of university students these days seem to be juggling part-time jobs with studying. Do you think it might be sensible for you to look for one too?'

'Did you know that the average person ...?'	Similarly, use this phrase if you know that the average person tends to do more of a certain desirable activity (or less of an undesirable activity) than the person or group you're targeting, e.g. 'Did you know that the average person in the UK reads six books a year?' Or if you know that students are drinking far too much alcohol at the weekend, you could use a real statistic such as: 'Contrary to popular opinion, did you know that the average student only drinks six units of alcohol on a Saturday night?'
'87 per cent of people ...' or 'Six out of seven people ...'	This is another way to emphasise that the majority of people are already engaging in a desirable activity more than the person or group you're trying to influence, e.g. 'I read the other day that 76 per cent of people aged 50 and over have had a cholesterol test. Have you thought about having one too?' However, make sure that it is a large percentage that you are quoting (see the box 'Understanding that social influence can work in *either* direction' on page 33 of Chapter One). For example, I saw a well-intentioned but ineffective advert for an online dating service recently. It said something along the lines of: '3 per cent of couples who got married last year in the US met using our dating website.' Of course the person reading the advert is supposed to think that the US is a huge country so 3 per cent implies many thousands of people. But instead, the advert probably backfired and made people think: 'Uh-oh, only 3 per cent? It can't be a very good website then!' A better approach would have been to talk about the numbers of people who met using the website, for example, '26,452 couples who got married last year in the US met using our dating website. That's 72 couples every day getting married who met using our website. Could you be next?'

'Best-selling' or 'top seller'	Consumer goods companies do it all the time, telling the world that their brand of toothpaste, mascara, running shoe, or whatever else is the best-seller. And for good reason: it works. People like to know what other people are buying or using. So if your product or service is a 'top 10 best-seller' then let the world know. Even if you need to make a more specific claim in order to stay on the right side of the truth, it still can be quite powerful to say that you were the number one best-seller but then to mention in small print that it was only for a certain month or that you were in the 'top five best-sellers' at a particular retailer rather than across the whole country.
'Very few ...'	If you're trying to discourage people from engaging in an undesirable activity (e.g. eating too much saturated fat, sunbathing without wearing sunscreen, having unprotected sex) then emphasising that the undesirable behaviour is definitely done only by the minority can be a good trick of reverse psychology, e.g. 'I heard on the radio that very few people are eating red meat more than three times a week these days. Do you think it might be a good idea for us to cut down too?'

Of course, another way to show what people are thinking or doing is to use testimonials. That's easy enough if you run a business or organisation and want to promote your products or services. Just get satisfied customers to go on the record about what they love about what you offer.

You might want to return to the box 'Getting other people to say nice things about you' on page 43 of Chapter One. Here are a few further pointers on getting testimonials:

1. **Ask for them!** Few customers will spontaneously offer up praise for what you do. But many of them would probably say yes if you were only to ask them. So give them a ring, send them an email, or put together a simple comments card or questionnaire that will encourage people to tell you what they think of your products or services. Then you can pick the most favourable ones.

2. **Get at least three testimonials.** Remember the study by Solomon Asch in Chapter One in which he asked experimental subjects to estimate which of three lines matched a single line in length? He discovered that three was the magic number of people required to exert group influence on experimental subjects. Two isn't enough and more than a half-dozen is probably overkill.

3. **Try to match testimonials to your target customers.** In Chapter Six, I explained that we're more swayed by people who are similar to us. If you can, then, try to gather testimonials from people who are like the people you want to influence. For example, say you run a company and are trying to win over the managing director of a technology business, then digging out testimonials from other tech firms would be a smart idea. Or if you discover that 65 per cent of your customers are women under the age of 40, then it might be a good idea to mention the names and ages of the people who have given you testimonials.

Testimonials can be powerful in almost any situation in which you want to convince people that your products, your services – or even you – are worthwhile. For example, if you're a job hunter, how about adding some testimonials or comments about yourself to your

CV? A dwindling number of people include the traditional phrase 'References on request' at the bottom of their CVs. Remember though that your CV is essentially a piece of marketing literature, designed to promote you. So why not take advantage of the power of collective influence? Get a handful of glowing quotes from ex-colleagues, perhaps an ex-boss, major clients, or other individuals who might impress whoever is reading your CV.

Exercising command through body language

In Chapter Two, we came across the computer scientist Alex Pentland at the Human Dynamics Lab at MIT. In his research, he discovered that up to 90 per cent of the impact that executives had when giving a business presentation had nothing to do with the words they used. Wow. To me, that's already pretty staggering.

Even more unbelievably though, Harvard University psychologist Nalini Ambady found that people could judge the personality traits of other people by watching video clips (with the sound turned off) that lasted a mere six seconds. Together, these studies clearly indicate that first impressions matter. More importantly, that our body language has a major influence on how we're perceived.

So what can we do about it?

In descending order of importance, here are my top three tips:

Become a social chameleon

There's a lot of research looking at different, specific body language tricks that can help us to be more influential. But it can all get a bit confusing, having to think about our eye contact, the tone of our voices, smiling, our posture, and so on. So one of the most powerful tips we can learn is to consciously adopt the mannerisms of the people we're trying to influence. Rather than having to think of lots of different behaviours, we can instead focus on one set of instructions.

If you desire to be more influential and persuasive, perhaps you should return to this next paragraph (which is based on the research by William Maddux and his colleagues) before embarking on a crucial discussion – of any sort – with another person:

> *Experts recommend that you may wish to mimic the mannerisms of the person you're dealing with to get a better deal. For example, when the other person rubs his/her face, you could too. If he/she leans back or leans forward in the chair, you could too. However, they say it is extremely important that you mimic subtly enough that the other person does not notice what you are doing, otherwise this technique completely backfires. Also, avoid directing so much of your attention to the mimicking that you lose focus on the outcome of your discussion. Thus, you should find a happy medium of consistent but subtle mimicking that does not disrupt your focus.*

Remember the power of touch

Yes, your handshake matters and that's easy enough to fix (see the section 'The humble handshake' on page 70 of Chapter Two.) But remember also the research showing that touching people on the arm at some point during a discussion with them can make them more amenable to our requests.

Obviously, this has to be done delicately. I'm not suggesting that you lunge at strangers to grab them by the shoulders. No, this is about simply resting your hand or even just the tips of your fingers on their upper arm for just a few seconds *at some point during a discussion with them*. Empathetic people tend to touch other people more. Persuasive people also tend to reach out to touch the people around them more. So how about trying it for yourself?

Think about your appearance

Bear in mind the disproportionately powerful effects that grooming, clothing, personal hygiene, and appearance can have. That may sound obvious, but the message here is really about the so-called above-average effect. Most people (wrongly) believe that they are above average when it comes to many positive traits (see the box 'Beauty or beast?' on page 61 of Chapter Two). And the same is true of people's beliefs about their appearance, clothing, and personal hygiene. People who dress shabbily often don't know that they are perceived as wearing unfashionable or inappropriate clothing. People who have inappropriate haircuts or visible tattoos or piercings often think that they're edgy and cool even though others might think them slightly odd or downright weird. What one person thinks is conveying frugality and seriousness may in fact be communicating to most people frumpiness and lack of attention to detail. I'm sure you get the picture.

The point is that we can't know how other people perceive us until we ask them. So ask the people around you for candid feedback on how you come across. If you're after a promotion, it can't hurt to ask your colleagues for their honest opinions as to how you're perceived. If you're dating and want to make the right first impression, why not ask friends for advice on what you might need to tone down or do a little more?

Choosing just the right words

Research tells us that people's expectations have a huge influence on the experiences they go on to have. In one experiment, when students expected that they were going to be taught by a warm professor, they found him sociable, funny and likeable; when other students expected to meet a cold professor, they found him ruthless, humourless, and bad-tempered. Of course, all of the students had met the same professor – the only difference had been in their expectations about him.

During job interviews too, employers may – quite unwittingly – ask tougher questions of candidates whom they believe to be less qualified or from less prestigious educational backgrounds. Conversely, they may ask easier questions of candidates whom they already expect can do the job.

Psychologists often call this a self-fulfilling prophecy. When people have a certain belief about what is going to happen in an upcoming situation, they may subconsciously change their attitude and even behaviour, which means they end up getting the experience they were expecting.

Say you're at a party with your friend Amelia. You tell her you're having a great time and that there are some great people at the party. From that moment on, she may actually make more effort in her conversations with the people she meets. She may smile more, ask more questions of people, laugh a little more – all of which helps her to make a better impression on the other partygoers. In turn, they respond more warmly back to her, which of course helps her to have a better time at the party.

But the reverse could so easily happen too. Tell Amelia that you've had a couple of odd conversations at the party and that the room is packed with unfriendly people and she may again change her demeanour. She may become more guarded, more sceptical, less easily amused. Naturally, her defensiveness might make the partygoers she meets bristle in return, which simply confirms her opinions that they were unfriendly in the first place.

So how could you use this in practice?

With a few carefully chosen words, you have the potential to improve the experiences of just about everyone in your life. Consider the words you use to launch new projects or initiatives at work to your colleagues and customers. Tell them that an endeavour will be 'painful and difficult' and you create one set of expectations. Tell them that the same assignment could be 'challenging and worthwhile' and you may nudge them into a slightly more positive attitude, which may encourage them to put a bit more effort into the assignment.

When you're introducing friends to other friends, you may wish to choose your words with care too. Long before they meet, you could be saying positive words about them. Do you want someone to come across as 'determined' or 'funny' or 'intelligent'? Or someone else to come across as 'supportive', 'charming', or 'easy-going'?

Remember that the effect of words on people's expectations is a subtle one. You can't tell people that having their teeth extracted at the dentist is going to be a 'wonderful' experience and expect them to enjoy the event. The effect of our words on the people around us is more of a nudge, a gentle bump in the right direction than an outright shove. But how might *you* use it?

If you want to integrate this technique into your repertoire, how about investing a few minutes now to think about three situations, each with a specific individual, in which you could commit to choosing your words more carefully? Here you go, why not scribble them down in the table below so you won't forget to do it?

The situation and person I want to influence	What I will try to say

Labelling with language

Related research tells us that the words we use to describe people can change their behaviour. When we tell people that they are 'helpful', they may actually respond by *becoming* more helpful. When we confront others by telling them that they are 'angry', we may exacerbate situations by *encouraging* them to express more of their anger and irritation. Again, it's a form of self-fulfilling prophecy. If we tell people that they are something, they may subconsciously change their behaviour to be more like the label we've attached to them.

Psychologists call this the principle of consistency. When people hear themselves being described in a certain way, they unconsciously seek ways to behave (at least in some small way) in a fashion consistent with that description.

I've put into a table some examples of how we could use words to invoke the principle of consistency and encourage people to behave in desirable ways.

Situation	Applying the principle of consistency to be more persuasive
Someone you live with isn't contributing to tidying up the house	Avoid saying, 'You're so messy,' or 'You're so lazy.' Both statements would simply encourage *further* messiness or laziness. Instead, try saying something like: 'There are times when you are so clean and tidy and I really appreciate it when you do tidy up. Could you tidy up a little more often please?'

| A colleague is unwilling to help you with a request | Encourage cooperative behaviour by reminding your colleague of times when he or she has been helpful in the past: 'I really appreciated it back in the summer when you went out of the way to help me out. I get the impression you're someone who always wants to do a good job. Could you help me out again please?' |
| You're trying to solicit donations for a charity | Rather than just smiling and saying, 'Hello,' to passers-by, try smiling and saying, 'Hello, kind and generous people!' |

Why don't you have a go now? Fill in the table below with the situations in which *you* would like to influence people. Think about the words you might choose to invoke consistency too.

Situation	What will you say to be more persuasive?

Winning commitment one step at a time

The saying 'to break the ice' is perhaps derived from earlier times when polar explorers used special ice-breaking ships with reinforced hulls and mighty engines to crack the ice in order to allow other ships to follow in their wake. In social settings, we established in

Chapter Four that a variety of ice-breakers seem to pay dividends in a similar fashion. For example, initiating a conversation with a stranger by asking just about any question is likely to boost the chances that the stranger will say 'yes' to the request. Here are two of the most powerful ice-breaking techniques for you to try.

Slipping your foot in the door

One of the most tried and trusted ways to win commitment from someone seems to be Jonathan Freedman and Scott Fraser's foot-in-the-door technique. Remember the central premise? That asking people to agree to a small request will significantly increase the chances that they will also agree to a subsequent and much larger request.

For example, consider that two people are trying to raise funds for the same charity, say for an animal shelter. Danielle goes from door to door asking people if they would be willing to donate a one-off payment of £50 to the charity. That's a not insignificant amount of money so we can understand why only a small percentage of people would say yes to her.

But her fellow fund-raiser Midori takes a different approach and goes to other houses asking if they would be willing to pin a small badge with the charity's logo on it to their jacket lapels. That's not such a big ask and it is for a great cause – that animal shelter, remember – so we can presume that Midori might get quite a high proportion of people to agree to her request.

If Midori were then to return to those households, say a week later, to ask them if they'd be willing to donate £50 to the animal shelter, she would almost certainly find that her success rate would be many times what Danielle had achieved.

We can't say exactly what that success rate might be, but experiments in different countries and using different requests have shown that an initial, small foot-in-the-door request can open that door to people saying 'yes' to much larger requests.

There are probably dozens of situations in which you could give this request a go. To help you to think about how you'd apply the foot-in-the-door technique, have a look at the following conundrums. Given the situations below, what might your initial request be for each? To help you out, I've completed the first example.

Situation	In order to harness the foot-in-the-door effect, what might you initially ask for?
You want your boss to let you work from home every Friday	'I've got a lot of reports that I think I could complete much more quickly if I were to work from home. Could I work from home on Friday afternoon next week, please?'
Your friend wants to go away to celebrate a big birthday by having a week-long party in Amsterdam	
You want to ask your teacher or lecturer for a two-week extension on a written assignment	
You want your boss to give you a pay rise of 15 per cent	

Getting people intellectually invested

A related discovery is that people are much more likely to change their behaviour when they come up with good reasons to do so. After all, no one likes to be lectured.

When it comes to helping the people you know to change their habits – say to stop smoking or start exercising, stop drinking so much alcohol, or to do more of the household chores – avoid telling them why they need to change. Instead, ask questions to get them thinking about the benefits of changing and the disadvantages of not changing.

Again, to help you think about the practical appliance of the science, have a go at completing the table below. I've completed the first example here too.

Situation	Example questions you could ask to start them investing in the process of change
You want a loved one to get physically fitter	'Have you ever thought what the benefits might be of getting fitter?' or 'What do you think you'd be able to achieve if you could lose a bit of weight?'
You want a teenager to think about applying for a place at university	
You'd like your partner to install solar panels on the roof of your house	

Situation	Example questions you could ask to start them investing in the process of change
You need for a colleague to hand in her expenses on time every week	

Harnessing the power of stories

In Chapter Five I mentioned that humans are the only species capable of imagining things we've never seen. And it turns out that imagining being in a particular situation or behaving in a certain way increases the likelihood that people will actually put themselves in that situation or engage in a behaviour. So here's a reminder of the two main techniques you can use to tap into people's imaginations for the purposes of persuasion.

Asking people to imagine themselves in a situation

A substantial body of research suggests that we can improve our attempts to win people over by asking them simply to imagine behaving in a certain way. Remember the study (see the section 'From a foot in the door to a toehold in the mind' on page 130 of Chapter Five) in which homeowners were asked to subscribe to cable TV? They were more than twice as likely to take out a subscription when they were asked to *imagine* themselves having it as when they were simply told about its benefits.

If you want to change someone's behaviour then, the major lesson here is to avoid simply listing the benefits or telling them what to expect. Instead, tell people to 'Imagine ...' Here are just three examples.

Situation	Words to harness the power of the imagination
A toothpaste manufacturer wants to boost sales of its new whitening toothpaste	'Imagine yourself having a smile you can be proud of. Imagine being at a party and laughing and smiling and showing off your dazzling smile. Imagine all of your friends wondering how you got that Hollywood smile!'
You want a loved one to cook healthy meals at home rather than ordering in pizzas so often	'Imagine standing at the stove and stirring a delicious casserole made with your favourite meat with leeks and carrots and potatoes in a thick sauce. Then you're serving it up at the table and everyone is enjoying the food and saying how wonderful it is. Can you see that?'
You'd like your colleagues to work harder on a project	'Imagine our team not only getting nominated for this year's team prize but actually winning it. Imagine how it would feel to have everyone in the building slapping our backs and congratulating us on our achievement.'

So how might *you* use people's imaginations to persuade them to your way of thinking?

Using stories to supercharge the imagination

Asking people to 'Imagine ...' themselves in a situation is certainly a powerful way to increase the likelihood that they might put themselves into that situation. But psychologists also know that telling people stories can have a very similar effect. After all, when we hear stories, we can't help but attach mental images to the words that we're hearing or reading about.

In order to be most effective though, research tells us that the stories we tell should include vivid, concrete details. Often, these details may seem trivial or irrelevant. In a presentation we're preparing to give at work, for example, these are probably the little factoids that our bosses would urge us to edit out.

To illustrate, let me first give you some statistics on rates of skin cancer. In 2008, around 2,500 people in the UK died of skin cancer and there were over 10,000 new cases of malignant melanoma, the most common form of skin cancer.[138]

To me, those statistics are hard to compute. After all, there are tens of millions of people living in the UK, so that doesn't seem that big a deal to me. On the other hand, I know someone who had skin cancer.

I don't know her personally, but Lucy is the twin sister of a good friend of mine. Lucy apparently loved sunbathing in her twenties – I've seen lots of photos of her on various beaches all over the world in various tiny bikinis – but a couple of years ago her husband discovered some irregular moles on her skin. Her doctors told her that she had melanoma. She had the lesions cut out by a surgeon, but she has to have a scan every few years now to check that the melanoma hasn't returned. And even though she hasn't had a reoccurrence of the skin cancer so far, she has to apply a thick sun-blocking lotion the consistency of porridge every time she goes out in even moderately sunny weather.

I don't know about you, but statistics on skin cancer do little to scare me away from being out in the sun. But just thinking about sun-loving Lucy's operation really brings the risks of skin cancer to life for me.

Charities already know the power of even the shortest stories. So how could you use stories in your life? You can remind yourself about creating persuasive stories by flicking back to the box 'Telling stories to win people over' on page 149 of Chapter Five. Here are just a few further ideas for applications of the technique:

- **Prepare short stories to share during job interviews**. Say an interviewer asks you: 'Are you a good team player?' Anyone can say, 'Yes, I'm an extremely good team player.' But will the interviewer believe you? It's always better to give an example of a time you made a significant contribution to a team, because the research suggests that the concrete details will be both more memorable and persuasive: 'Yes, I'm a good team player. For example about six months ago my colleague Weiwei fell ill very suddenly despite a looming deadline. We didn't have the time to bring someone new into the team and train them up so instead I just put in much longer hours. To cover for her absence, I was getting into the office at 8 a.m. and staying till around 10 p.m. most nights and coming in on Saturdays for at least a few hours too. This lasted for about six weeks until we delivered the project on time and to budget.' That's much more demonstrative and memorable, right?

- **Include stories when you're giving presentations**. Too many people giving presentations simply click through their PowerPoint slides. But if you're trying to influence your audience and persuade them to change their behaviour in some way, a better bet would be to include at least a story or two in your presentation. If you're selling a product, don't just list its benefits. Perhaps tell the story of the first time you encountered the product and how you reacted to it. If you're trying to encourage colleagues to follow a new rule, perhaps find a genuine story of the disastrous consequences that befell someone who didn't follow the rule. I'm not suggesting that you should make stories up, simply that you could dig around in your brain to see if you can find any illustrative stories that help to bring the rest of your presentation to life.

- **Use stories as part of sales pitches**. Whether you're selling luxury cars to customers or skincare products over the counter at a department store, think about integrating stories into your sales spiels. If you've got any testimonials or positive feedback from previous customers, then share these with prospective customers. Tell them about the gentleman who bought the car and can't believe how smooth the ride is even down those country roads on the way to his second home in rural Norfolk; tell them about how that lady customer in her thirties got asked for ID to prove her age when she was trying to buy drinks in a bar. So long as they are true stories, you're almost bound to be much more compelling.

Just remember though: be sure to include those vivid, concrete details.

From commonalities and concessions to cooperation

In Chapter Six, I told the story of how having the same birth date may have drawn my parents closer together. I might never have been born if Stephen and Judy had had different birth dates! A solid body of evidence tells us that all sorts of commonalities may draw people together. For example, a further study (that I didn't cover) reports that people with similar first names to each other may also find each other more persuasive. So Nicholas is more likely to be persuaded by Nicola than Sandra; Mr Kerry is more likely to be persuaded by Mr Cory than Mr Featherington.[139]

Whenever we wish to persuade people, we would therefore do well to start by finding out a little more about them (see the box 'Harnessing the effects of similarity' on page 160 of Chapter Six). Here are a few practical pointers for making the most of what we have in common with others in order to boost our chances of getting them to cooperate with us:

- **Dress like the people you want to influence**. Research shows that people are more amenable to requests when they encounter people who dress like themselves. When I go to meet the client team at an über-hip advertising firm based in the West End of central London, I always dress down. I put away the suit and slide into my Diesel jeans; I exchange the polished black leather shoes for a pair of trainers. I even put away the black leather attaché case and throw my laptop into a distressed-leather shoulder bag. How might you modify your look to match your clients and colleagues or even the in-laws?

- **Ask lots of open-ended questions of the people you meet**. Many people enjoy talking about themselves, so give people the opportunity to tell you about their interests, their hopes and dreams, their backgrounds and life stories by asking them plenty of questions. Once you've established what you've got in common, *that's* the time to bring up how you love the same food/grew up in the same part of the country/hate the same TV show, etc.

- **Take notes after you've met new people**. If you (like many people) are prone to forgetting details about people's lives, then it makes good sense to jot down some notes on the people you've met. After all, say you've put in the hard work to find out that you and a client both have children aged six and seven years of age and that one of them is learning the violin just like your son. Oh, and both your client's best man at his wedding and your closest friend worked for the same advertising firm. Once you've discovered all of those similarities, it would be a shame to forget them. So how about capturing what you've found, perhaps in your email address book or a good old-fashioned paper notebook?

Using the door-in-the-face technique

The foot-in-the-door technique tells us that we should first ask for a small favour, which then eases the metaphorical door open to the subsequent, larger favours we may wish to ask. The door-in-the-face technique does the opposite: by asking for an overly large favour and getting that door slammed in our faces, we help to ensure that people will be more amenable to the seemingly smaller favour that follows it (see the section 'Doing favours without doing favours' starting on page 170 of Chapter Six).

The idea is to ask for a large request, but not one that is so stupidly, absurdly enormous that no one could possibly say 'yes' to it. For example, say you've been offered a job and you'd like the employer to give you a 10 per cent annual cash bonus contingent on good performance. Begin by asking perhaps for a 20 or 25 per cent bonus, but not a 250 per cent bonus!

Once your initial door-in-the-face request has been refused, your next step is to scale down your request. But *make it clear that you are making a concession*. Perhaps say something like: 'I am disappointed, but I'm willing to be reasonable, so how about giving me …?' or 'If you can't do that for me then, I could compromise by asking just for …'

To inspire your own requests, take a look at the table opposite. I've included a handful of examples of situations and the initial requests that might go alongside them. I've completed the first two, but if you want to help yourself to put the technique into practice, how about scribbling answers to the remaining two?

Situation	In order to harness the door-in-the-face effect, what might you initially ask for?
You'd like your boss to spend £300 to send you on a design course	'I was thinking it would be a great idea to do some professional development. I've been looking at options and there's an MBA course I could do. Do you think the department would be willing to invest the £3,000 per year for the two-year programme?'
You look after the children most weekends but you want this Saturday morning off to go shopping	'I'm really tired and I don't feel like I get any time to myself. A friend and I were thinking of going away for a long weekend – maybe four nights, Thursday to Monday – to recuperate. How would you feel about that?'
You need your company's IT department to buy a mid-priced computer for you to use at home	
You want to ask a bank manager to give you a business start-up loan of £5,000	

Boosting motivation by emphasising free choice

In Chapter Seven, I presented evidence that many types of prizes and incentives may actually have the opposite effect to that intended. Rather than boosting motivation, cash bonuses, awards, medals, and honours that are promised for good performance may actually reduce people's intrinsic motivation, their natural inclination to want to do well.

I realise that may sound fairly heretical. After all, employees are incentivised to perform well at work by offering them share options and cash rewards. School children are promised accolades for coming top of the class. Athletes compete for big cash prizes. Unfortunately though, the research clearly points to the fact that most organisations get it wrong. Yes, cash and awards may promote short-term performance, but the moment you stop giving people those rewards, their underlying motivation will almost certainly fall away.

Thankfully, the work of pioneering researchers such as Maarten Vansteenkiste has shown us how we can lift people's motivation not through prizes, but simply with the words we choose. There are two key recommendations that stem from the research (and for a reminder of the science, you might want to look at the boxes 'Setting goals that motivate, not discourage (part I)' on page 193 and 'Setting goals that motivate, not discourage (part II)' on page 197 of Chapter Seven):

- **Emphasise the intrinsic qualities of whatever task they're doing**. Rather than drawing people's attention to the external rewards or consequences that people could get out of a task (such as money, tangible prizes, or fame), remember that people can find many tasks inherently interesting, challenging or rewarding. For example, people often feel proud of themselves when they've learned something new. They may feel good about themselves when they feel they've helped others or contributed to the greater good.

- **Use language that highlights people's control over their lives.** Research tells us that people hate to feel coerced, that they're doing something because they *have* to do it. If we want to elevate people's intrinsic motivation further, we could use language that reinforces their feelings of being in control. So phrases such as 'you can', 'you could', 'you might', and 'we suggest that you' should boost people's motivation and persistence, compared with phrases such as 'you should' and 'you will'.

Situation	Advice
You would like to help a loved one to eat more vegetables	Steer clear of issuing a command such as: 'More vegetables will reduce your risk of certain cancers later in life and you should lose weight too.' Instead, try the indirect approach by emphasising the intrinsic pleasure to be had from them: 'Perhaps you could steam some asparagus and cover them in butter or roast some butternut squash with chopped garlic. Yum!'
You're trying to persuade a child to study hard for school exams	Avoid saying anything like: 'You have to do it. Doing it will help you to get a good job which will allow you to buy a nice house.' Instead, emphasise the intrinsic nature of the task by saying something like: 'I don't know about you, but studying physics sounds pretty cool and interesting to me. I wish I'd had the chance to learn about the building blocks of the universe when I was a kid.'

A friend is thinking about going to the gym to lose weight	Even if their motivation is primarily to shed weight and look more attractive, the science suggests we can help to enhance their motivation more by focusing on other benefits: 'You'll feel fit and full of energy and ready to tackle anything. And apparently people get these endorphin highs from exercise so you might feel really great if you get into it too.'

I'm sure you get the idea. So how about giving it a go? Who could you encourage and inspire with the right words?

Setting the scene for persuasion

In Chapter Eight, we saw that people don't always make rational decisions based purely on facts. People can be swayed by all sorts of circumstances that we might rationally expect to be irrelevant. For example, people tend to find ideas both more interesting and more persuasive when they read them on old-fashioned paper rather than on a high-tech computer screen. And people can be persuaded to part with money more readily when they are sent letters that contain photos of smiling faces. Thinking about it rationally, we would all probably agree that a smiling face *shouldn't* make a difference in our decision-making – but the science tells us that it does.

Creating encouraging environments

One of the scientific findings in researching this book that most amazed me was that children rated food as being more enjoyable when it was wrapped in McDonald's packaging than when it was wrapped in unbranded but otherwise identical packaging (see the

box 'Bringing the background to the fore' on page 221 of Chapter
Eight for a reminder). When we think about it though, that shouldn't
really surprise us. After all, companies spend billions of pounds,
dollars, and yen every year trying to advertise their brands, to make
customers and consumers believe that their goods and services really
are different. High-end clothing designers such as Gucci and Prada
can sell their plain white T-shirts for many times what a nearly identical plain white T-shirt might sell for in a high-street chain such as
Gap or Zara. Car manufacturers likewise try to persuade motorists
that their cars are special, that their engineering is more precise, their
cars more roadworthy and desirable. Restaurants, banks, supermarkets – just about any business that is trying to sell anything – think
carefully about their logos, how they lay out their floor space, how
they display their products, and so on.

Many of the features and circumstances that shouldn't factor
into our decision-making actually do. They all matter. Perception
can trump reality when it comes to people's choices. We can influence people's decisions by thinking about branding, packaging,
ambience, price, and the settings in which we present the products,
services, and even ideas that we may wish to sell.

It would be impossible to list all of the details that you might
want to think about, but here are some ideas that may help to use the
power of contexts and circumstances to help you to become more
persuasive:

- **Study businesses or products that you admire**. Why
  start from scratch when you can learn from other
  people? Visit places that you like and try to identify the
  features that you like about them. Visit car showrooms,
  bank branches, restaurants, supermarkets, hair salons,
  health spas, clothing shops, department stores, and

whatever else takes your fancy. Maybe use a camera to take snaps of features you like. Then try to analyse what it is you like about them and – most importantly – how you can either copy it or adapt it to suit your organisation, your shop, or whatever else you do.

- **Play around with your pricing**. Remember that people can be fairly irrational in their decision-making. People can sometimes believe advice that is free is less worthwhile than advice that they paid for. A bottle of wine that costs £20 is automatically assumed to taste better than one that cost only £7. People sometimes buy expensive goods not in spite of a high price but *because* of it. So think twice before offering a product or service at the lowest price possible.

- **Remember that smiling faces can be very compelling**. In 2010, economists spotted that mailshot letters that included a photo of a smiling woman's face made customers more likely to sign up for a bank loan. Humans have specially evolved centres within the brain that respond to both faces and smiles so that makes good sense. So consider incorporating photos into whatever you offer. If you have a website or company brochure, that would be an obvious location for a few smiling faces. If you have physical premises such as a shop or showroom, then posters or billboards with smiling faces might go down well too.

Restricting choice to clinch the deal

A solid body of research tells us that people can often get confused by too much choice. When visiting a stall that sold jams, customers who were presented with 24 varieties of jam were actually *less* likely to buy one than when they were offered a mere six varieties. And in another study, students who were given lots of essay choices were not only less likely to complete the assignment than students who were given fewer choices; the students with more choice also made more spelling and grammatical errors *and* wrote generally poorer essays too.

Even though we might have predicted that more choice should make people happier, it seems that the opposite is true. Too many options can cause confusion, stalling, and the failure to make a decision at all. Less choice seems to make people feel more comfortable; people find it easier to handle the cognitive load of making a choice from fewer options.

I've already mentioned some of the implications of this finding (see the box 'Turning less into more' on page 237 of Chapter Eight), but here are some additional pointers:

- **Provide lists of recommended products and services**. My favourite Cantonese Chinese restaurant in London has a menu containing nearly 300 dishes. That's fine for customers who know their Chinese cuisine inside and out but possibly rather daunting for someone who is eating there for the first time. Fortunately, the restaurant also recommends a mere four set menus. I know the manager of the restaurant pretty well and he estimated that nearly half of all customers simply choose from one of the set menus. Could you offer a short list of recommendations to help customers and consumers navigate the products and services you provide too?
- **Consider providing advice about what other customers have enjoyed**. In Chapter One, I presented evidence that we are swayed by knowledge of how other people have behaved. If you run a museum or art gallery

with thousands of works of art, perhaps highlight in a pamphlet the top 20 most viewed pieces. If you make bespoke suits, consider telling customers about your best-selling fabrics. Or if you run a bookshop with hundreds of books in the thrillers section alone, perhaps have stickers on books that say 'staff recommendation' to let customers know that someone has already enjoyed certain books.

- **Give friends specific choices rather than unlimited choice**. If you've ever asked friends, 'Where would you like to go for something to eat?' you've probably received the reply, 'I don't mind, what would you like to eat?' People often can't decide when they have too many choices on offer. So try reducing the number of options by asking something like: 'Where would you like to go for something to eat – how about the Italian, that new Thai place or the new tapas restaurant? Which would you prefer?' You'll save time and people may thank you for cutting down the number of options.

I hope you will be able to apply at least some of these techniques. Enjoy using them and remember to influence with integrity!

NOTES

Introduction

1   The declassified CIA report 'The Operational Potential of Subliminal Perception' is available from the CIA's own website: https://www.cia.gov/library/center-for-the-study-of-intelligence/kent-csi/vol2no2/html/v02i2a07p_0001.htm

2   Weir, W. (1984). 'Another Look at Subliminal "Facts"'. *Advertising Age*, October 15, 46.

3   Kassarjian, H. H., & Cohen, J. B. (1965). 'Cognitive Dissonance and Consumer Behavior: Reactions to the Surgeon General's Report on Smoking and Health'. *California Management Review*, 8, 55–64.

Chapter One: The Wisdom of Crowds

4   Asch, S. E. (1951). *Social Psychology*. Englewood Cliffs: Prentice Hall.

5   Salganik, M. J., Dodds, P. S., & Watts, D. J. (2006). 'Experimental Study of Inequality and Unpredictability in an Artificial Cultural Market'. *Science*, 311, 854–856.

6   Cai, H., Chen, Y., & Fang, H. (2009). 'Observational Learning: Evidence from a Randomized Natural Field Experiment'. *American Economic Review*, 99, 864–882.

7   Sorenson, A. T. (2006). 'Social Learning and Health Plan Choice'. *RAND Journal of Economics*, 37, 929–945.

8   Duflo, E., & Saez, E. (2002). 'Participation and Investment Decisions in a Retirement Plan: The Influence of Colleagues' Choices'. *Journal of Public Economics*, 85, 121–148.

9   Shive, S. (2010). 'An Epidemic Model of Investor Behavior'. *Journal of Financial and Quantitative Analysis*, 45, 169–198.

10 Mitchell, H. L., & Hurley, M. V. (2008). 'Management of Chronic Knee Pain: A Survey of Patient Preferences and Treatment Received'. *BMC Musculoskeletal Disorders*, 9, 123.

11 Michael Treacy and Fred Wiersema deny having manipulated the *New York Times* best-seller list. However, investigative journalist Willy Stern at *Businessweek* magazine puts together a compelling argument that something underhand did happen. You can read his full exposé at the magazine's online archives: http://www.businessweek.com/archives/1995/b343648.arc.htm.

12 Nolan, J. M., Schultz, P. W., Cialdini, R. B., Goldstein, N. J., & Griskevicius, V.

(2008). 'Normative Social Influence is Underdetected'. *Personality and Social Psychology Bulletin*, 34, 913–923.

13   Cialdini, R. (2003). 'Crafting Normative Messages to Protect the Environment'. *Current Directions in Psychological Science*, 12, 105–109.

14   The pair of objects in the first diagram is identical; the pair of objects in the second diagram is different (they are, in fact, mirror images of each other).

15   Berns, G. S., Chappelow, J., Zink, C. F., Pagnoni, G., Martin-Skurski, M. E., & Richards, J. (2005). 'Neurobiological Correlates of Social Conformity and Independence During Mental Rotation'. *Biological Psychiatry*, 58, 245–253.

16   Banerjee, A. V. (1992). 'A Simple Model of Herd Behavior'. *Quarterly Journal of Economics*. 107, 797–817.

17   For an in-depth (but very technical) review of the brain's workings and energy needs, see: Gusnard, D. A., & Raichle, M. E. (2001). 'Searching for a Baseline: Functional Imaging and the Resting Human Brain'. *Nature Reviews Neuroscience*, 2, 685–694.

18   For a more detailed discussion about the role of social learning in infant development, see: Csibra, G., & Gergely, G. (2006). 'Social Learning and Social Cognition: The Case for Pedagogy' in: Munakata, Y, & Johnson, M. H. (eds.), *Processes of Change in Brain and Cognitive Development, Attention and Performance, XXI* (pp. 249–274). Oxford: Oxford University Press.

19   Hill, S. E., & Buss, D. M. (2008). 'The Mere Presence of Opposite-Sex Others on Judgements of Sexual and Romantic Desirability: Opposite Effects for Men and Women'. *Personality and Social Psychology Bulletin*, 34, 635–647.

20   Jones, B. C., DeBruine, L. M., Little, A. C., Burriss, R. P., & Feinberg, D. R. (2007). 'Social Transmission of Face Preferences Among Humans'. *Proceedings of the Royal Society B*, 274, 899–903.

21   Pfeffer, J., Fong, C. T., Cialdini, R. B., & Portnoy, R. R. (2006). 'Overcoming the Self-Promotion Dilemma: Interpersonal Attraction and Extra Help as a Consequence of Who Sings One's Praises'. *Personality and Social Psychology Bulletin*, 32, 1–13.

Chapter Two: Secret Signals

22   Pentland, A. (2008). *Honest Signals: How They Shape Our World*. Cambridge, Massachusetts: MIT Press.

23   Ambady, N., & Rosenthal, R. (1993). 'Half a Minute: Predicting Teacher Evaluations From Thin Slices of Nonverbal Behavior and Physical Attractiveness'. *Journal of Personality and Social Psychology*, 64, 431–441.

24   You can watch the debate between Nixon and Kennedy and judge for yourself how the two candidates came across. The debate is split into two clips, both of which are available for free on the non-profit website of the Internet Archive: http://www.archive.org/details/1960_kennedy-nixon_1 and http://www.archive.org/details/1960_kennedy-nixon_2

25   A pair of studies in 1967 by psychologist Albert Mehrabian and his colleagues did indeed examine the roles that facial expressions, tone of voice, and words play in human communication. But the two studies have not only been misunderstood but also widely misquoted. Think about it: if it were true that 55 per cent of a person's impact is down to body language, 38 per cent due to the voice, and only 7 per cent from the words themselves, then we should really have little trouble understanding people from other countries, whether they're speaking Mandarin Chinese, Portuguese, or Swahili. But that's clearly not the case. For a deeper explanation as to why so many people have misunderstood Mehrabian's original findings, see: Lapakko, D. (1997). 'Three Cheers for Language: A Closer Examination of a Widely Cited Study of Nonverbal Communication'. *Communication Education*, 46, 63–67. Whenever I see self-proclaimed body language experts mention the alleged 55-38-7 rule, I know that they're likely to be quacks and frauds rather than reputable scientists!

26   Burnett, J. R., & Motowidlo, S. J. (1998). 'Relations Between Different Sources of Information in the Structured Selection Interview'. *Personnel Psychology*, 51, 963–983.

27   Hemsley, G. D., & Doob, A. N. (1978). 'The Effect of Looking Behavior on Perceptions of a Communicator's Credibility'. *Journal of Applied Social Psychology*, 8, 136–144.

28   Farroni, T., Csibra, G., Simion, F., & Johnson, M. H. (2002). 'Eye Contact Detection in Humans from Birth'. *Proceedings of the National Academy of Sciences of the United States of America*, 99, 9602–9605.

29   Chaiken, S. (1979). 'Communicator Physical Attractiveness and Persuasion'. *Journal of Personality and Social Psychology*, 37, 1387–1397.

30   Riniolo, T. C., Johnson, K. C., Sherman, T. R., & Misso, J. A. (2006). 'Hot or Not: Do Professors Perceived as Physically Attractive Receive Higher Student Evaluations?' *Journal of General Psychology*, 133, 19–35.

31   There are hundreds of studies demonstrating that more positive characteristics are generally ascribed to physically attractive people. Here are just a couple of overviews of the research: Jackson, L. A., Hunter, J. E., & Hodge, C. N. (1995). 'Physical Attractiveness and Intellectual Competence: A Meta-Analytic Review'. *Social Psychology Quarterly*, 58, 108–122. Also: Langlois, J. H., Kalakanis, L., Rubenstein, A. J., Larson, A., Hallam, M., & Snoot, M. (2000). 'Maxims of Myths of Beauty? A Meta-Analytic and Theoretical Review'. *Psychological Bulletin*, 126, 390–423.

32   Hamermesh, D. S., & Biddle, J. E. (1994). 'Beauty and the Labor Market'. *American Economic Review*, 84, 1174–1194.

33   Reinhard, M.-A., Messner, M., & Sporer S. L. (2006). 'Explicit Persuasive Intent and Its Impact on Success at Persuasion: The Determining Roles of Attractiveness and Likeableness'. *Journal of Consumer Psychology*, 16, 249–259.

34 If you want to peruse photos of some of the sales associates that Abercrombie & Fitch has working in various stores, you can visit the 'Casting' section of the retailer's website: http://www.abercrombie.co.uk.

35 Lynn, M. (2009). 'Determinants and Consequences of Female Attractiveness and Sexiness: Realistic Tests with Restaurant Waitresses'. *Archives of Sexual Behavior*, 38, 737–745.

36 Muscarella, F., & Cunningham, M. R. (1996). 'The Evolutionary Significance and Social Perception of Male Pattern Baldness and Facial Hair'. *Ethology and Sociobiology*, 17, 99–117.

37 For further, sometimes frightening examples of the disconnect between self-assessments and actual performance or behaviour, see: Dunning, D., Heath, C., & Suls, J. M. (2004). 'Flawed Self-Assessment: Implications for Health, Education, and the Workplace'. *Psychological Science in the Public Interest*, 5, 69–106.

38 Davis, D. A., Mazmanian, P. E., Fordis, M., Van Harrison, R., Thorpe, K. E., & Perrier, L. (2006). 'Accuracy of Physician Self-Assessment Compared with Observed Measures of Competence: A Systematic Review'. *Journal of the American Medical Association*, 296, 1094–1102.

39 Reis, H. T., Wilson, I., Monestere, C., Bernstein, S., Clark, K., Seidl, E., Franco, M., Gioioso, E., Freeman, L., & Radoane, K. (1990). 'What is Smiling is Beautiful and Good'. *European Journal of Social Psychology*, 20, 259–267.

40 Krumhuber, E., Manstead, A. S. R., & Kappas, A. (2007). 'Temporal Aspects of Facial Displays in Person and Expression Perception: The Effects of Smile Dynamics, Head-tilt, and Gender'. *Journal of Nonverbal Behavior*, 31, 39–56.

41 Barger, P. B., & Grandey, A. A. (2006). 'Service with a Smile and Encounter Satisfaction: Emotional Contagion and Appraisal Mechanisms'. *Academy of Management Journal*, 49, 1229–1238.

42 LaFrance, M., & Hecht, M. A. (1995). 'Why Smiles Generate Leniency'. *Personality and Social Psychology Bulletin*, 21, 207–214.

43 Schmidt, K. L., & Cohn, J. F. (2001). 'Human Facial Expressions as Adaptations: Evolutionary Questions in Facial Expression Research'. *Yearbook of Physical Anthropology*, 44, 3–24.

44 Guéguen, N. (2002). 'Touch, Awareness of Touch, and Compliance with a Request'. *Perceptual and Motor Skills*, 95, 355–360.

45 Nannberg, J. C., & Hansen, C. H. (1994). 'Post-Compliance Touch: An Incentive for Task Performance'. *Journal of Social Psychology*, 134, 301–307.

46 Guéguen, N., Jacob, C., & Boulbry, G. (2007). 'The Effect of Touch on Compliance with a Restaurant's Employee Suggestion'. *International Journal of Hospitality Management*, 26, 1019–1023.

47 Erceau, D., & Guéguen, N. (2007). 'Tactile Contact and Evaluation of the Toucher'. *Journal of Social Psychology*, 147, 441–444.

48 For a review of the evidence for both the mood and status explanations for the effectiveness of touch in securing agreement for requests, take a look at the discussion in: 'Guéguen, N. (2003). Nonverbal Encouragement of Participation in a Course: The Effect of Touching'. *Social Psychology of Education*, 13, 1–10.

49 If you're interested in research into the best ways to interview and select candidates for job vacancies, you could take a look at a paper that a colleague and I wrote: Brittain, S., & Yeung, R. (2005). 'Assessment Centres: Getting More Bang for your Buck' in: P. Grant (ed.) *Business Psychology in Practice* (pp. 113–132). London: Whurr.

50 Stewart, G. L., Dustin, S. L., Barrick, M. R., & Darnold, T. C. (2008). 'Exploring the Handshake in Employment Interviews'. *Journal of Applied Psychology*, 93, 1139–1146.

51 Ambady, N., LaPlante, D., Nguyen, T., Rosenthal, R., Chaumeton, N., & Levinson, W. (2002). 'Surgeons' Tone of Voice: A Clue to Malpractice History'. *Surgery*, 132, 5–9.

52 Oksenberg, L., Coleman, L., & Cannell, C. F. (1986). 'Interviewers' Voices and Refusal Rates in Telephone Surveys'. *Public Opinion Quarterly*, 50, 97–111.

53 Van Baaren, R. B., Holland, R. W., Steenaert, B., & van Knippenberg, A. (2003). 'Mimicry for Money: Behavioral Consequences of Imitation'. *Journal of Experimental Social Psychology*, 39, 393–398.

54 Lakin, J. L., & Chartrand, T. L. (2003). 'Using Nonconscious Behavioral Mimicry to Create Affiliation and Rapport'. *Psychological Science*, 14, 334–339.

55 For a review of evidence in support of the chameleon effect as social glue, see: Lakin, J. L., Jefferis, V. E., Cheng, C. M., & Chartrand, T. L. (2003). 'The Chameleon Effect as Social Glue: Evidence for the Evolutionary Significance of Nonconscious Mimicry'. *Journal of Nonverbal Behavior*, 27, 145–162.

56 Maddux, W. W., Mullen, E., & Galinsky, A. D. (2008). 'Chameleons Bake Bigger Pies and Take Bigger Pieces: Strategic Behavioral Mimicry Facilitates Negotiation Outcomes'. *Journal of Experimental Social Psychology*, 44, 461–468.

Chapter Three: The Power of Words and Labels

57 Kelley, H. H. (1950). 'The Warm-Cold Variable in First Impressions of Persons'. *Journal of Personality*, 18, 431–439.

58 Darley, J. M., & Gross, P. H. (1983). 'A Hypothesis-Confirming Bias in Labeling Effects'. *Journal of Personality and Social Psychology*, 44, 20–33.

59 Bargh, J. A., Gollwitzer, P. M., Lee-Chai, A., Barndollar, K., & Trötschel, R. (2001). 'The Automated Will: Nonconscious Activation and Pursuit of Behavioral Goals'. *Journal of Personality and Social Psychology*, 81, 1014–1027.

60 For the full list of the top hundred psychologists, see: Haggbloom, S. J., Warnick, R., Warnick, J. E., Jones, V. K., Yarbrough, G. L., Russell, T. M., Borecky, C. M., McGahhey, R., Powell III, J. L., Beavers, J., & Monte, E. (2002). 'The 100 Most Eminent Psychologists of the 20th Century'. *Review of General Psychology*, 6, 139–152.

61 Loftus, E. F., & Palmer, J. C. (1974). 'Reconstruction of Automobile Destruction: An Example of the Interaction Between Language and Memory'. *Journal of Verbal Learning and Verbal Behavior*, 13, 585–589.

62 Fointiat, V. (2006). '"You're Helpful" Versus "That's Clear". Social Versus Functional Label in the Foot-in-the-Door Paradigm'. *Social Behavior and Personality*, 34, 461–466.

63 Allgeier, A. R., Byrne, D., Brooks, B., & Revnes, D. (1979). 'The Waffle Phenomenon: Negative Evaluations of Those Who Shift Attitudinally'. *Journal of Applied Social Psychology*, 9, 170–182.

64 The Dutch researchers took the questions from the Trivial Pursuit game. The answers are: C: Picasso, A: Dhaka, and D: Italy. How did you do?

65 Dijksterhuis, A., & van Knippenberg, A. (1998). 'The Relation Between Perception and Behavior, or How to Win a Game of Trivial Pursuit'. *Journal of Personality and Social Psychology*, 74, 865–877.

66 http://investor.google.com/corporate/code-of-conduct.html

67 4.81 + 5.19 = 10

68 Mazar, N., Amir, O., & Ariely, D. (2008). 'The Dishonesty of Honest People: A Theory of Self-Concept Maintenance'. *Journal of Marketing Research*, 45, 633–644.

69 For a review of studies on cheating amongst university students, see: McCabe, D. L., Treviño, L. K., & Butterfield, K. D. (2001). 'Cheating in Academic Institutions: A Decade of Research'. *Ethics & Behavior*, 11, 219–232.

70 You can read the entire oath online at: http://mbaoath.org/take-the-oath/.

71 Moriarty, T. (1975). 'Crime, Commitment, and the Responsive Bystander: Two Field Experiments'. *Journal of Personality and Social Psychology*, 31, 370–376.

72 Cioffi, D., & Garner, R. (1996). 'On Doing the Decision: Effects of Active versus Passive Choice on Commitment and Self-Perception'. *Personality and Social Psychology Bulletin*, 22, 133–147.

Chapter Four: From Small Steps to Big Effects

73 Guéguen, N., Marchand, M., Pascual, A., & Lourel, M. (2008). 'Foot-in-the-Door Technique Using a Courtship Request: A Field Experiment'. *Psychological Reports*, 103, 529–534.

74 Freedman, J. L., & Fraser, S. C. (1966). 'Compliance Without Pressure: The Foot-in-the-Door Technique'. *Journal of Personality and Social Psychology*, 4, 195–202.

75 Pandelaere, M., Briers, B., Dewitte, S., & Warlop, L. (2010). 'Better Think Before Agreeing Twice: Mere Agreement: A Similarity-Based Persuasion Mechanism'. *International Journal of Research in Marketing*, 27, 133–141.

76 Müller, B. C. N., van Baaren, R. B., Ritter, S. M., Woud, M. L., Bergmann, H., Harakeh, Z., Engels, R. C. M. E., & Dijksterhuis, A. (2009). 'Tell Me Why … The Influence of Self-Involvement on Short Term Smoking Behaviour'. *Addictive Behaviors*, 34, 427–431.

Chapter Five: Invoking the Imagination and Telling Tales

77 Gregory, W. L., Cialdini, R. B., & Carpenter, K. M. (1982). 'Self-Relevant Scenarios as Mediators of Likelihood Estimates and Compliance: Does Imagining Make It So?' *Journal of Personality and Social Psychology*, 43, 89–99.

78 Michelon, P., Vettel, J. M., & Zacks, J. M. (2006). 'Lateral Somatotopic Organization During Imagined and Prepared Movements'. *Journal of Neurophysiology*, 95, 811–822.

79 Libby, L. K., Shaeffer, E. M., Eibach, R. P., & Slemmer, J. A. (2007). 'Picture Yourself at the Polls: Visual Perspective in Mental Imagery Affects Self-Perception and Behavior'. *Psychological Science*, 18, 199–203.

80 The study comparing the effectiveness of stories versus factual information was based on an unpublished piece of research, written up in: Wilson, T. D., & Brekke, N. (1994). 'Mental Contamination and Mental Correction: Unwanted Influences on Judgments and Evaluations'. *Psychological Bulletin*, 116, 117–142.

81 Small, D. A., Loewenstein, G., & Slovic, P. (2007). 'Sympathy and Callousness: The Impact of Deliberative Thought on Donations to Identifiable and Statistical Victims'. *Organization Behavior and Human Decision Processes*, 102, 143–153.

82 Speer, N. K., Reynolds, J. R., Swallow, K. M., & Zacks, J. M. (2009). Reading Stories Activates Neural Representations of Visual and Motor Experiences. *Psychological Science*, 20, 989–999.

83 Sadoski, M., Goetz, E. T., & Rodriguez, M. (2000). 'Engaging Texts: Effects of Concreteness on Comprehensibility, Interest, and Recall in Four Text Types'. *Journal of Educational Psychology*, 92, 85–95.

84 Shedler, J., & Manis, M. (1986). 'Can the Availability Heuristic Explain Vividness Effects?' *Journal of Personality and Social Psychology*, 51, 26–36.

Chapter Six: Friendship and Favours

85 See Study 1 of: Burger, J. M., Messian, N., Patel, S., del Prado, A., & Anderson, C. (2004). 'What a Coincidence! The Effects of Incidental Similarity on Compliance'. *Personality and Social Psychology Bulletin*, 30, 35–43.

86   This experiment is written up as Study 2 in the same 2004 paper by Burger and his colleagues in *Personality and Social Psychology Bulletin*.

87   Another study showed that people even prefer people who have surnames that share some of the same letters more than people who have surnames that don't share any letters. In addition to this study on surname similarity, John Jones and his colleagues provide still more evidence of the similarity effect in six other studies contained within the following paper: Jones, J. T., Pelham, B. W., Carvallo, M., & Mirenberg, M. C. (2004). 'How Do I Love Thee? Let Me Count the Js: Implicit Egotism and Interpersonal Attraction'. *Journal of Personality and Social Psychology*, 87, 665–683.

88   A classic study in the early 1970s had experimenters dressed either as 'Hippies' or 'Straights' asking to borrow a dime from students on campus who were either categorised as Hippies or Straights. As expected, Hippies were more likely to give Hippies the dime while Straights were more likely to help out fellow Straights: Emswiller, T., Deaux, K., & Willits, J. E. (1971). 'Similarity, Sex, and Requests for Small Favors'. *Journal of Applied Social Psychology*, 1, 284–291.

89   Regan, D. (1971). 'Effects of Favour and Liking on Compliance'. *Journal of Experimental Social Psychology*, 7, 627–639.

90   For an in-depth review of the sociological argument that reciprocity is a universal norm, see: Gouldner, A. W. (1960). 'The Norm of Reciprocity: A Preliminary Statement'. *American Sociological Review*, 25, 161–178.

91   Rilling, J. K., Gutman, D. A., Zeh., T. R., Pagnoni, G., Berns, G. S., & Kilts, C. D. (2002). 'A Neural Basis for Social Cooperation'. *Neuron*, 35, 395–405.

92   Singer, E., Van Hoewyk, J., & Maher, M. P. (2000). 'Experiments with Incentives in Telephone Surveys'. *Public Opinion Quarterly*, 64, 171–188.

93   James, J. M., & Bolstein, R. (1992). 'Large Monetary Incentives and Their Effect on Mail Survey Response Rates'. *Public Opinion Quarterly*, 56, 442–453.

94   Miller, R. L., Seligman, C., Clark, N. T., & Bush, M. (1976). 'Perceptual Contrast versus Reciprocal Concession as Mediators of Induced Compliance'. *Canadian Journal of Behavioural Science*, 8, 401–409.

95   The phrase 'door-in-the-face' was first coined by Robert Cialdini and his colleagues at Arizona State University: Cialdini, R. B., Vincent, J. E., Lewis, S. K., Catalan, J., Wheeler, D., & Darby, B L. (1975). 'Reciprocal Concessions Procedure for Inducing Compliance: The Door-in-the-Face Technique'. *Journal of Personality and Social Psychology*, 31, 206–215.

96   Ebster, C., & Neumayr, B. (2008). 'Applying the Door-in-the-Face Compliance Technique to Retailing'. *International Review of Retail, Distribution and Consumer Research*, 18, 121–128.

97   Strohmetz, D. B., Rind, B., Fisher, R., & Lynn, M. (2002). 'Sweetening the Till: The Use of Candy to Increase Restaurant Tipping'. *Journal of Applied Social Psychology*, 32, 300–309.

98   Seiter, J. S., & Dutson, E. (2007). 'The Effect of Compliments on Tipping Behavior in Hairstyling Salons'. *Journal of Applied Social Psychology*, 37, 1999–2007.

99   Seiter, J. S., & Weger, H. (2010). 'The Effect of Generalized Compliments, Sex of Server, and Size of Dining Party on Tipping Behavior in Restaurants'. *Journal of Applied Social Psychology*, 40, 1–12.

100 Chan, E., & Sengupta, J. (2010). 'Insincere Flattery Actually Works: A Dual Attitudes Perspective'. *Journal of Marketing Research*, 47, 122–133.

Chapter Seven: The Perils of Prizes

101 Lepper, M. R., Greene, D., & Nisbett, R. E. (1973). 'Undermining Children's Intrinsic Interest with Extrinsic Reward: A Test of the "Overjustification" Hypothesis'. *Journal of Personality and Social Psychology*, 28, 129–137.

102 For a review of the research on the unanticipated consequences of rewards on motivation, see: Deci, E. L., & Ryan, R. M. (2008). 'Facilitating Optimal Motivation and Psychological Well-Being Across Life's Domains'. *Canadian Psychology*, 49, 14–23.

103 Vansteenkiste, M., Simons, J., Lens, W., Sheldon, K. M., & Deci, E. L. (2004). 'Motivating Learning, Performance, and Persistence: The Synergistic Effects of Intrinsic Goal Contents and Autonomy-Supportive Contexts'. *Journal of Personality and Social Psychology*, 87, 246–260.

104 Kasser, T., & Ryan, R. M. (1996). 'Further Examining the American Dream: Differential Correlates of Intrinsic and Extrinsic Goals'. *Personality and Social Psychology Bulletin*, 22, 280–287.

105 Kube, S., Maréchal, M. A., & Puppe, C. (2010). 'The Currency of Reciprocity – Gift-Exchange in the Workplace'. *Institute for Empirical Research in Economics Working Paper 1424–0459*.

106 Heyman, J., & Ariely, D. (2004). 'Effort for Payment: A Tale of Two Markets'. *Psychological Science*, 15, 787–793.

107 Add 19, 10, 40 and 31 together to make 100.

Chapter Eight: The Peculiar Power of Circumstantial Persuasion

108 McNeil, B. J., Pauker, S. G., Sox, H. C., & Tversky, A. (1982). 'On the Elicitation of Preferences for Alternative Therapies'. *New England Journal of Medicine*, 306, 1259–1262.

109 Haselton, M. G., & Nettle, D. (2006). 'The Paranoid Optimist: An Integrative Evolutionary Model of Cognitive Biases'. *Personality and Social Psychology Review*, 10, 47–66.

110 Weller, J. A., Levin, I. P., Shiv, B., & Bechara, A. (2007). 'Neural Correlates of Adaptive Decision Making for Risky Gains and Losses'. *Psychological Science*, 18, 958–964.

111 Gonzales, M. H., Aronson, E., & Costanzo, M. A. (1988). 'Using Social Cognition and Persuasion to Promote Energy Conservation: A Quasi-Experiment'. *Journal of Applied Social Psychology*, 18, 1049–1066.

112 Ganzach, Y., & Karsahi, N. (1995). 'Message Framing and Buying Behavior: A Field Experiment'. *Journal of Business Research*, 32, 11–17.

113 Goldstein, R., Almenberg, J., Dreber, A., Emerson, J. W., Herschkowitsch, A., & Katz, J. (2008). 'Do More Expensive Wines Taste Better? Evidence from a Large Sample of Blind Tastings'. *Journal of Wine Economics*, 3, 1–9.

114 Plassmann, H., O'Doherty, J., Shiv, B., & Rangel, A. (2008). 'Marketing Actions Can Modulate Neural Representations of Experienced Pleasantness'. *Proceedings of the National Academy of Sciences*, 105, 1050–1054.

115 Bertini, M., Ofek, E., & Ariely, D. (2009). 'The Impact of Add-On Features on Consumer Product Evaluations'. *Journal of Consumer Research*, 36, 17–28.

116 Gino, F. (2008). 'Do We Listen to Advice Just Because We Paid For It? The Impact of Advice Cost on Its Use'. *Organizational Behavior and Human Decision Processes*, 107, 234–245.

117 Robinson, T. N., Borzekowski, D. L. G., Matheson, D. M., & Kraemer, H. C. (2007). 'Effects of Fast Food Branding on Young Children's Taste Preferences'. *Archives of Pediatrics & Adolescent Medicine*, 161, 792–797.

118 You can read both of the original articles online. 'First and Last, Do No Harm' can be accessed at: http://www.time.com/time/magazine/article/0,9171,984390,00.html while 'Dividing Line: Why We Need to Raise Hell' can be read at: http://www.time.com/time/magazine/article/0,9171,984468,00.html.

119 Murphy, P. K., Long, J. F., Holleran, T. A., & Esterly, E. (2003). 'Persuasion Online or on Paper: A New Take on an Old Issue'. *Learning and Instruction*, 13, 511–532.

120 Song, H., & Schwarz, N. (2008). 'If It's Hard to Read, It's Hard to Do: Processing Fluency Affects Effort Prediction and Motivation'. *Psychological Science*, 19, 986–988.

121 Diemand-Yauman, C., Oppenheimer, D. M., & Vaughan, E. B. (2011). Fortune favors the Bold (and the Italicized): Effects of Disfluency on Educational Outcomes. *Cognition*, 111–115.

122 Bertrand, M., Karlan, D., Mullainathan, S., Shafir, E., & Zinman, J. (2010). What's Advertising Content Worth? Evidence from a Consumer Credit Marketing Field Experiment. *Quarterly Journal of Economics*, 125, 263–305.

123 Iyengar, S. S., & Lepper, M. R. (2000). 'When Choice is Demotivating: Can One Desire Too Much of a Good Thing?' *Journal of Personality and Social Psychology*, 79, 995–1006.

Chapter Nine: Instant Influence: Speedy Techniques for Persuasion in a Hurry

124 Burger, J. M. (1986). 'Increasing Compliance by Improving the Deal: The That's-Not-All Technique'. *Journal of Personality and Social Psychology*, 51, 277–283.

125 Langer, E., Blank, A., & Chanowitz, B. (1978). 'The Mindlessness of Ostensibly Thoughtful Action: The Role of "Placebic" Information in Interpersonal Interaction'. *Journal of Personality and Social Psychology*, 36, 635–642.

126 Burger, J. M., Hornisher, J., Martin, V. E., Newman, G., & Pringle, S. (2007). 'The Pique Technique: Overcoming Mindlessness or Shifting Heuristics?' *Journal of Applied Social Psychology*, 37, 2086–2096.

127 Fennis, B. M., Das, E. H. H. J., & Pruyn, A. Th. H. (2004). '"If You Can't Dazzle Them with Brilliance, Baffle Them with Nonsense": Extending the Impact of the Disrupt-Then-Reframe Technique of Social Influence'. *Journal of Consumer Psychology*, 14, 280–290.

128 Razran, G. H. S. (1940). 'Conditioned Response Changes in Rating and Appraising Sociopolitical Slogans'. *Psychological Bulletin*, 37, 481.

129 Dabbs, J. M., & Janis, I. L. (1965). 'Why Does Eating While Reading Facilitate Opinion Change? An Experimental Inquiry'. *Journal of Experimental Social Psychology*, 1, 133–144.

130 Research shows that prohibiting an activity may often backfire: it may make it *more* alluring. In a now-classic experiment, psychologists Sharon Brehm and Marsha Weinraub found that preventing children from playing with a toy actually made the toy more attractive later on. So rather than putting activities out of bounds from people, you might be wiser to explain why it wouldn't be a good idea for them to do it, but then to state that the choice is ultimately down to them. Brehm, S. S., & Weinraub, M. (1977). 'Physical Barriers and Psychological Reactance: 2-Year-Olds' Responses to Threats to Freedom'. *Journal of Personality and Social Psychology*, 35, 830–836.

131 Another study, for example, sent emails out to participants encouraging them to click a link taking them through to the website of a children's charity. Emails that included 'but you are free to accept or refuse' resulted in a higher click-through rate: Guéguen, N., Pascual, A., Jacob, C., & Morineau, T. (2002). 'Request Solicitation and Semantic Evocation of Freedom: An Evaluation in a Computer-Mediated Communication Context'. *Perceptual and Motor Skills*, 95, 208–212.

Conclusions: Practising Principled Persuasion

132 For a short but well-written overview of studies on the ultimatum game in the influential publication *Science*, see: Nowak, M. A., Page, K. M., & Sigmund, K. (2000). 'Fairness Versus Reason in the Ultimatum Game', *Science*, 289, 1773–1775.

133 Studies show that people in *nearly* all countries around the world have the same aversion to economic injustice and a desire to punish transgressors. There is evidence that people in some hunter-gatherer tribes (for example the Machiguenga of the Peruvian Amazon) may not trade by the same rules. But given that you're reading a book, I think it's safe to assume that you live in a market economy as opposed to a tribe that survives only through hunting and gathering. To read more about how the Machiguenga not only live but also play the ultimatum game, see: Henrich, J. (2000). 'Does Culture Matter in Economic Behavior? Ultimatum Game Bargaining Among the Machiguenga of the Peruvian Amazon'. *American Economic Review*, 90, 973–979.

134 Brosnan, S. F., & de Waal, F. B. M. (2003). 'Monkeys Reject Unequal Pay'. *Nature*, 425, 297–299.

135 Research psychologists have found that good reputations are difficult to acquire and can be lost quite quickly. In contrast, bad reputations are much easier to acquire and difficult to lose. See: Baumeister, R. F., Bratslavsky, E., Finkenauer, C., & Vohs, K. D. (2001). 'Bad Is Stronger Than Good'. *Review of General Psychology*, 5, 323–370.

136 The questions are adapted from: Davis, M. H. (1980). 'A Multidimensional Approach to Individual Differences in Empathy'. *JSAS Catalog of Selected Documents in Psychology*, 10, 85.

137 Galinsky, A. D., Maddux, W. M., Gilin, D., & White, J. B. (2008). 'Why It Pays to Get Inside the Head of Your Opponent: The Differential Effects of Perspective Taking and Empathy in Strategic Interactions'. *Psychological Science*, 19, 378–384.

The Influence Toolkit

138 Statistics from the Cancer Research UK website: http://info.cancerresearchuk.org/cancerstats/.

139 Garner, R. (2005). 'What's in a Name? Persuasion Perhaps'. *Journal of Consumer Psychology*, 15, 108–116.